THE COLLEGE VEGETARIAN COOKBOOK

The College Vegetarian COOKBOOK

150 EASY, BUDGET-FRIENDLY RECIPES

STEPHANIE McKERCHER, MS, RDN

PHOTOGRAPHY BY EMULSION STUDIO

ROCKRIDGE
PRESS

Interior and Cover Designer: Julie Gueraseva
Art Producer: Sue Bischofberger
Editor: David Lytle
Production Manager: Riley Hoffman
Production Editor: Sigi Nacson

Photography © 2020 Emulsion Studio
Front cover: Vegan Banh Mi Sandwiches, page 74

ISBN: Print 978-1-64611-919-6 | Ebook 978-1-64611-920-2
R1

This cookbook is dedicated to students everywhere who are looking for feel-good food made from plants. May these recipes fuel the pursuit of your biggest dreams in and out of the classroom.

Contents

Introduction ix

CHAPTER ONE: **How to Be the Vegetarian You Want to Be** 1

CHAPTER TWO: **Breakfasts** 17

CHAPTER THREE: **Super Soups and Stews** 39

CHAPTER FOUR: **Wraps and Sandos** 61

CHAPTER FIVE: **Simple Salads** 89

CHAPTER SIX: **Oodles of Noodles** 107

CHAPTER SEVEN: **Other Entrées** 143

CHAPTER EIGHT: **Snacks and Sides** 169

CHAPTER NINE: **Desserts** 193

CHAPTER TEN: **Staples, Sauces, and Dressings** 209

Measurement Conversions 231

Resources 232

References 234

Index 236

Introduction

You're all moved in, your laptop is fully charged, and your textbooks are ready for highlighting. You made it to college. Congratulations! Now that you're on your own, there's just one more thing left to consider. What are you going to eat?

With limited time, space, budget, and kitchen experience, cooking healthy meals at home is a significant challenge for most college students. Nourishing yourself gets more complicated when you're a new vegetarian who's still unfamiliar with common plant-based ingredients and cooking techniques.

How will you get enough protein? Is it even possible to cook satisfying meals without meat? How do you make tofu taste good? These are just a few of the questions I had while transitioning from a standard Midwestern diet to a plant-based lifestyle during my college years. I was driven to eat more plants for my health, for animal welfare, and to lessen my impact on the environment. My motivations for going vegetarian were clear, but still, the shift itself wasn't always easy. Many of the staple dishes I'd grown up eating felt like they were no longer available to me, and I wasn't sure how to compose a meal that would make me feel full and energized.

I started following vegan bloggers for recipe inspiration, but most of their dishes called for exotic ingredients, advanced cooking techniques, or hours of prep time from start to finish. As a full-time student with a part-time job, plant-based cooking was starting to feel overwhelming and unattainable to me.

With more time and experimentation, though, I gradually figured things out. By the time I finished graduate school, I was able to transform vegetarian staples—including fruits, veggies, whole grains, and legumes—into crave-worthy soups, sandwiches, and pasta dishes. I learned how to make satisfying meals with just a few basic ingredients and less than an hour of prep and cook time, so making food at home was more realistic. I didn't need expensive, bulky appliances to cook these nourishing vegetarian meals, either. I found tons of healthy and great-tasting dishes that can be made in the microwave or toaster oven.

I created the vegetarian recipes in this book with all of these college-friendly principles in mind. I use simple, feel-good ingredients that provide long-lasting energy and satisfaction. A fully decked-out kitchen isn't a prerequisite to plant-based cooking, so even if you live in a dorm room or share kitchen space, you can make most of the recipes in this book.

You'll find breakfast, lunch, and dinner recipes with a balanced mix of carbohydrates, protein, and fat. Beyond fueling your active lifestyle, these meals will help you stay alert through 90-minute lectures and study effectively enough to ace your finals at the end of each semester. I don't believe in deprivation or dieting, so there are also plenty of savory snacks and desserts to satisfy even the most intense late-night cravings. With 150 vegetarian recipes to try, you'll never feel bored or undernourished.

As a food-loving dietitian, I'm excited to share everything I wish I had known about vegetarian eating during college. Ready to start cooking?

Chapter One

How to Be the Vegetarian You Want to Be

Whether motivated by potential wellness benefits, animal rights, or environmental sustainability, many individuals are transitioning to a plant-based diet. But what does it actually mean to be a vegetarian?

The truth is, there's no single definition of a vegetarian lifestyle. Vegans typically eat exclusively plant foods, while ovo-lacto vegetarians also include eggs and dairy products. Flexible vegetarians, or flexitarians, emphasize plants but also occasionally include meat, poultry, and seafood. All of these lifestyles are plant-based in their own way. There's no right or wrong approach to being a vegetarian.

Because there are some nutrients of concern for all plant-based eaters, transitioning to a vegetarian diet may take a little extra planning in the beginning. With experience, you'll soon find it's not too difficult to get enough protein or iron. One trick is to stock your pantry or dorm room with a variety of simple and nourishing plant-based ingredients. Fruits, vegetables, whole grains, nuts, beans, and lentils are budget-friendly and rich in the nutrients that support a healthy vegetarian lifestyle during college.

Getting the Right Nutrients as a Vegetarian

It's possible to get all the nutrients you need from plants, but variety matters. Choose a mix of vegetarian foods, with an emphasis on whole, minimally processed ingredients to meet your needs. Vegetables, fruits, whole grains, beans, nuts, and seeds are all great choices. Eggs and dairy products are additional sources of essential nutrients for those who want to include them.

SPECIFIC NUTRIENTS TO CONSIDER AS A VEGETARIAN

Calcium: Calcium is essential for bone health and muscle, nerve, and vascular function. Vegetarians usually don't find it challenging to get their 800 milligrams of required calcium when they include dairy products regularly. This can be more difficult for vegans, but still is possible with plant-derived sources of calcium, such as kale, fortified plant milk, and tofu made with calcium sulfate.

Iron: Iron is a mineral that is essential for transporting oxygen throughout your body. It also aids in cellular growth. Vegetarians need to consume 1.8 times as much iron as non-vegetarians because the plant-derived form can be more difficult to absorb. Even considering this increased requirement, most vegetarians don't have trouble getting enough iron. Include more beans, lentils, and grains if you think you might not be getting enough.

Omega-3 Fatty Acids: Eicosapentaenoic acid (EPA) and docosahexaenoic acid (DHA) are omega-3 fats that are involved with the inflammatory response, and they help form the structures of cell membranes. Although omega-3s are commonly found in certain types of fish and seafood, the body can also convert plant-derived alpha-linolenic acid (ALA) into EPA and DHA when necessary. Vegetarians and vegans should include plant-based sources of ALA daily, including hemp seeds, flaxseed, walnuts, chia seeds, and seaweed, to meet their needs.

Protein: Protein is a macronutrient essential for maintaining muscle and bone mass. It's also necessary for hormones, digestion, and immune function. Contrary to popular belief, most plant-based eaters actually meet or exceed their protein needs as long as they're eating enough calories. To ensure you're getting adequate protein, seek out plant-based sources of protein throughout the day, including beans, lentils, tofu, tempeh, chickpeas, and edamame. There's no need to combine different amino acids to form a "complete protein" at every meal. Eating a variety of protein-containing foods throughout the day is enough.

Vitamin B$_{12}$: A 20-year-old adult needs about 2 micrograms of vitamin B$_{12}$ daily for optimal metabolism, formation of new red blood cells and DNA, and maintenance of the central nervous system. Ovo-lacto vegetarians get some vitamin B$_{12}$ from dairy and eggs, but most vegans have to rely on fortification and supplementation. Fortified sources of vitamin B$_{12}$ include nutritional yeast, breakfast cereals, and meat alternatives.

Vitamin D: Vitamin D plays a vital role in bone health and is also essential for nerve, muscle, and immune function. Researchers suggest about 30 minutes of sun exposure daily to meet your vitamin D needs, which for a 20-year-old adult is 400 International Units (IUs) daily. You can also get vitamin D from foods, including cheese, egg yolks, and mushrooms that have been exposed to light (check the label). Vitamin D is also sometimes fortified in milk, cereal, juice, and yogurt.

HOW FOOD IMPACTS YOUR HEALTH AND MOOD

The food-and-mood connection is real, and prioritizing balanced meals and snacks is one of the surest ways to give your body and mind long-lasting energy, so you don't fall into a funk. The importance of balance is related to the way your body processes nutrients.

When you eat a lot of carbohydrate-containing foods (such as fruits or sugary desserts), your body processes those nutrients by releasing more sugar into your blood. This extra influx of sugar leads to a quick spike in energy, but as soon as it's gone, you're more likely to feel hungry, moody, and sluggish. The same symptoms come up when you skip a meal or go too long without eating.

You can get around the blood sugar trap by eating balanced meals and snacks with complex carbohydrates (such as beans and whole grains), protein, and healthy fats throughout the day. Balanced meals give your body different types of fuel to work with, so it releases sugar into your system more gradually. The result is long-lasting energy that supports an active lifestyle and maintains a positive mood throughout even the most stressful college moments.

None of this is to say eating sugar is bad. Sometimes when you go for the "healthier" sugar-free cookies, you just eat more because it's not satisfying. Mindfully indulging in the foods you're craving staves off deprivation and helps prevent binging later on. Sometimes the healthiest thing you can eat is a sugary cookie. Life is all about balance.

Great Ingredients for Exam Time

Your brain thrives on energy and nutrients from the food you eat. Here are the best ingredients to include when you need to cram for your final exams.

FLAX, HEMP, AND CHIA SEEDS: A diet rich in omega-3 fatty acids supports optimal brain function in humans. If you're not getting omega-3s from fish, include plenty of flax, hemp, and chia seeds in your diet. These brain-boosting seeds have alpha-linolenic acid (ALA), which your body can convert to omega-3s.

WALNUTS: Walnuts are an additional source of plant-based ALA that can help you reach your omega-3 needs without eating fish. They're also energy-dense and packable, making them an ideal snack for studying.

MATCHA GREEN TEA: Green tea contains an amino acid called l-theanine, which can help you stay more focused and energized. Matcha also has high levels of antioxidants and a moderate amount of caffeine to support brain alertness without the jitters that sometimes come with too much coffee.

FRUITS AND VEGETABLES: Eating fruits and vegetables throughout the day is one of the most efficient ways to fuel your brain for learning. Your brain thrives on carbohydrate-containing foods like berries and dark leafy greens. Fresh, canned, and frozen produce is also packed with the antioxidants and phytonutrients that keep your brain running smoothly.

DARK CHOCOLATE: We all know chocolate is the ideal study snack for satisfying a sweet tooth, but antioxidants in cacao beans could also be beneficial for your brain. Look for bars that have a high percentage of cacao (85% or more) to limit added sugars.

The Many Benefits of Vegetarianism

There are a lot of benefits linked to eating more plants. Many individuals believe vegetarian eating could be beneficial for your health, budget, and the environment, but the advantages don't stop there.

Most significant for me personally, the shift toward a plant-based lifestyle forced me to learn more about cooking. I no longer wanted to eat many of the foods I was used to, so I was forced to step outside my comfort zone to try something new. I gained a lot of new favorite foods from this experience and learned vegetarian cooking can be brimming with color, flavor, and texture. Shifting toward a plant-based diet helped me fall in love with food.

The perks of going vegetarian are so far-reaching that making the switch is worth exploring. To give you a better idea of what you can gain from eating more plants, let's discuss three of the most commonly cited benefits of vegetarianism: better health, lower food costs, and less damage to the environment.

YOUR HEALTH

A well-planned vegetarian diet is nutritionally adequate during college and beyond. It's the position of the Academy of Nutrition and Dietetics that, when properly planned, vegan and vegetarian diets are healthy and appropriate at all stages of life, even if you're pregnant or breastfeeding.

In addition to providing all the essential nutrients the human body needs, plant-based foods are packed with wellness-promoting antioxidants, phytonutrients, fiber, and gut-boosting prebiotics. Because of these compounds, vegans and vegetarians are not only surviving without meat, they're also thriving. Plant-based eaters have a lower risk for many of the chronic health conditions that are common in the United States, such as diabetes and cancer.

Over the past couple of decades, many observational studies have concluded that people who follow a plant-based eating pattern rich in legumes, whole grains, vegetables, fruits, and nuts have a lower risk for diabetes. This may be because fiber-rich foods, such as beans and lentils, are especially beneficial for blood-sugar management. In contrast, eating a lot of red meat and processed meat is associated with a higher risk of diabetes.

Vegetarians also have a lower overall risk of cancer, with additional studies indicating non-vegetarians are more likely to be diagnosed with gastrointestinal and prostate carcinomas. While more studies are needed, the proposed mechanism may be the fiber and phytonutrients in plant-based foods, which seem to help protect against cancer development. You don't have to eliminate all animal products to be healthy, but scientific evidence strongly supports including more plant-based foods in your diet.

YOUR BUDGET

Price is one of the most common barriers I hear from people who are trying to switch to a vegetarian diet. While it's true that food costs can add up quickly when you're eating out at trendy cafés or buying packaged meals at the market, plant-based eating doesn't have to hurt your budget. You don't need fancy restaurants or exotic ingredients to nourish yourself.

Here's the truth: eating more vegetarian meals could actually save you money in the long run. Really! One study found that a plant-based diet costs about $750 less per year. That means you could save up enough cash to travel over spring break just by nixing your meat habit.

Since meat is one of the most expensive foods to purchase at the market, you can save big by swapping in beans or tofu for meat or poultry. Dried pasta, brown rice, lentils, and canned tomatoes are also economical and nutrient-dense choices for vegetarians. Keep these pantry items on hand and you'll always have plenty of options for nourishment.

Buying staple ingredients in bulk is another easy way to slash your grocery bill. Dried pantry goods, such as grains, beans, and lentils, are available in the bulk section of most grocery stores and have a long shelf life. If space is a concern, try splitting bulk groceries with roommates or fellow vegetarian friends. This way, you can take advantage of bulk pricing without the burden of storing large quantities of food without a full kitchen or pantry.

THE ENVIRONMENT

While you don't need to eat plants exclusively to reduce your impact, many scientists believe plant-based eating is friendlier to the environment. This is because animal-based diets require more natural resources and cause more severe damage to the environment during production.

Greenhouse gases, such as carbon, methane, and nitrous oxide, are being released into the atmosphere at higher rates than ever before. These gases absorb heat and disperse it throughout the planet, causing global warming.

Great Ingredients for Recovery

Moderation is essential, but you may still overindulge on occasion. When you do, try adding these vegetarian foods to help you feel better the next morning.

GINGER: Many studies show ginger can help with nausea. Steep fresh ginger in hot water to make a simple tea or grate it into Asian-inspired dishes to help calm your symptoms.

EGGS: Eggs are an affordable source of protein that are packed with essential vitamins and minerals. They also contain an amino acid called cysteine, which helps break down acetaldehyde, the primary mediator of hangover-derived headaches and nausea.

SWEET POTATOES: Baked, roasted, or mashed, sweet potatoes are a nutrient-dense vegetable to opt for the morning after a party. They have more potassium than a banana, which helps replenish electrolytes that are often lost after drinking alcohol.

BEANS: Beans are a nutrient-dense source of plant-based protein to help manage a hangover. They provide potassium (an electrolyte), iron, and B vitamins. Try black, kidney, or cannellini beans in a batch of vegetable soup.

EDAMAME: Also rich in plant-based protein, edamame soybeans can be steamed in the microwave for a quick, nutrient-packed snack. Try them with a sprinkle of salt to replenish electrolytes and get more folate, vitamin K, and magnesium.

AVOCADO: Creamy avocado is easy to incorporate into smoothies or as a toast topping the morning after overindulging. Avocado has more potassium than a banana and is rich in vitamin C, which works as an antioxidant to help clear cellular damage.

One scientific calculation found that greenhouse gas emissions from vegetarian diets are 29 percent lower than non-vegetarian eating patterns. This could be because producing meat leads to higher carbon emissions and produces more methane and nitrous oxide than plant alternatives. Carbon, methane, and nitrous oxide are all greenhouse gases that are damaging the environment. Animal agriculture is also associated with increases in air pollution and land degradation.

Vegetarian diets, on the other hand, generally require fewer natural resources and cause less environmental damage than animal-based eating patterns. It takes less water, fossil fuels, pesticides, and fertilizers to grow plant-based foods, which means vegetarian lifestyles are associated with lower greenhouse gas emissions.

For these reasons, many scientists are calling for a reduction in livestock production in the United States and other developed nations, where overall meat consumption is the highest. If you're shifting toward a vegetarian diet because you want to lessen your carbon footprint, the meatless recipes in this book will help you do it.

Taking Stock

In this section, you'll learn how to efficiently and affordably set up and stock your cooking space during college.

Even if you don't have access to a full kitchen, you can make use of the suggested items in a dorm room or a shared kitchenette. To save space, look for products that combine multiple items into one, such as spice blends or canned tomatoes with added basil. If budget is a concern, invest in bulk storage systems for dried goods like beans and rice, which are more affordable than purchasing smaller packages over and over again.

One nice thing about eating vegetarian is that most of the proteins, such as beans, lentils, and other members of the pulse family, are actually cheaper than buying meat. Try black beans or pinto beans for Mexican-style dishes and use chickpeas for Mediterranean-inspired food. Cannellini beans taste delicious pureed into a creamy bean dip. Canned beans are conveniently ready to eat in seconds. You can also buy dried beans, which take longer to prepare but are usually more economical than canned.

If you find you have a little extra room in your grocery budget, splurge on a few fun extras. High-quality spices, matcha green tea powder, fermented miso, and nutritional yeast may cost a little bit more upfront, but the flavor and nutritional value of these foods make them worth every penny. Plus, they have a relatively long shelf life, so you only have to invest in them once in a while.

HOW TO STOCK A COLLEGE "PANTRY"

Here are the most important ingredients to keep stocked during college.

Must-Have Vegetarian Staples

Beans and pulses: Include a variety of canned or dried black beans, pinto beans, chickpeas, or kidney beans. Lentils and dried split peas are also protein-packed options.

Canned tomatoes: Use canned tomatoes as the base for bean chili or pasta sauce. You can buy tomatoes whole, diced, crushed, or pressed into tomato paste.

Cooking oil: Grapeseed oil has a neutral flavor and high smoke point, which makes it perfect for cooking. Canola oil is another budget-friendly option. Try olive oil for salad dressings and low-heat applications.

Dried grains and pasta: Whole grains, including barley and farro, add plant-based nutrients and satisfying texture to soups, salads, and bowls. Dried pasta is a budget-friendly staple to always keep on hand.

Frozen fruits and vegetables: Use frozen fruit for smoothies. Pre-chopped vegetables are ideal for stir-fries and soup.

Spices: Salt, pepper, oregano, rosemary, and cumin are versatile spices to have in your arsenal. Spice blends, such as curry powder or chili powder, help save space since multiple spices are mixed into one small bottle. Spices lose aroma and flavor with time, so try not to buy too much.

Plant-Based Add-Ons

Matcha: This finely ground green tea powder can be whisked with water to make a traditional tea, or combined with frothed milk to make it a latte. Matcha is packed with antioxidants and may also help with focus and learning.

Miso: A traditional Japanese ingredient, miso is usually made with soybeans, salt, and rice. Look for miso in the refrigerated section to take advantage of its gut-boosting benefits derived from the fermentation process.

Nutritional yeast: Long-time vegans know the best way to get cheesy flavor without any cheese is to use nutritional yeast. Look for this yellow seasoning in the bulk or natural foods aisle at your grocery store.

HOW TO STOCK A COLLEGE "KITCHEN"

Knife and cutting board: A high-quality knife and cutting board is essential for healthy cooking. Preparing fruits and vegetables is a lot more enjoyable when you have quality equipment.

Mixing bowls: You'll need at least a couple of large mixing bowls to combine ingredients. Look for bowls that nest or stack to save more space.

Pot with a lid: You'll need a pot with a lid to make soups and sauces. Opt for a 12-quart stockpot if you can only choose one. A small saucepan can also be useful for heating up smaller portions.

Skillet: The skillet I use most is a 12-inch skillet with a lid. Cast-iron skillets are durable and affordable (you can often find them at thrift stores), but they require some maintenance and can be heavy to handle. Stainless-steel frying pans are durable and nonstick, but they're usually more expensive than cast iron.

Baking sheet and muffin tin: Baking sheets are necessary for roasting vegetables and proteins in the oven. Beyond muffins, you can use a muffin tin for baking single-serve egg dishes and casseroles.

Oven mitts: Use oven mitts to safely handle hot dishes going in and out of the oven.

Baking dish: Use an 8-by-11-inch glass baking dish to make tofu or shareable casseroles. Some come with a lid so you can use the same dish to store leftovers.

Blender: Though not necessary, a blender helps make smoothies, salsa, plant milk, and quick sauces. Small models and fruits are the most affordable and don't take up as much space as full-size versions.

Food processor: A food processor isn't essential, but you can use one to make homemade hummus, bean dip, or nut butter. Look for small models that are more budget-friendly and space-conscious.

How to Make a Shopping List

Making a shopping list is one of the best ways to stay on budget while reducing food waste. You can buy what you need and restock pantry staples, so you always have healthy options on hand.

I like to break down my grocery list into categories according to how my local supermarket is set up. This makes it easier to get through all my shopping efficiently. The fresh produce is located near the entrance, so I add fresh fruits and vegetables to my list first. The bakery is right behind the produce, so I add those items next. Then I move into the center aisles to pick up bulk foods and canned and packaged products. Finally, I list anything I need from the refrigerated and frozen sections.

Have you ever heard that you should only shop the outside perimeter? It's a myth. There are so many nutritious foods in the center aisles of the grocery store. This is where I buy canned beans and tomatoes, whole grains, and nuts and seeds. There's no need to skip this section of the supermarket.

Grocery List Template

This template is organized according to the sections of most standard grocery stores, designed to make your shopping experience more efficient.

FRESH PRODUCE: 3 to 5 types of vegetables and fruit

BAKERY: bread, buns, flatbreads, pizza dough

BULK OR PACKAGED FOODS: grains, dried or canned beans, lentils, canned tomatoes, crackers, coffee, tea

REFRIGERATED FOODS: yogurt, cheese, miso, dairy or plant milk

VEGETARIAN PROTEINS: tofu, tempeh, dairy alternatives

FROZEN FOODS: frozen vegetables, edamame, cooked grains

Common Cooking Terms

It's okay if you're a cooking newbie. Here are the common cooking terms and techniques you'll need to understand how to make the recipes in this book.

Bake: to cook using dry heat, usually in an oven.

Blend: to combine ingredients in a blender, often to make smoothies and sauces.

Boil: a form of cooking where food is submerged in bubbling liquid, usually water or broth.

Chill: allowing food to cool in the refrigerator or freezer, often used to set and thicken ingredients.

Dice: chopping ingredients into small pieces of a uniform size.

Froth: vigorously stirring milk or another liquid until it begins to bubble; it can be done with an automatic frother or by hand with a whisk or a fork.

Pulse: while using a blender or food processor, blending food in short, repetitive bursts until the desired consistency is reached.

Puree: (n) a smooth, creamy food usually made from fruits or vegetables; (v) to blend, grind, or mash food until is a smooth consistency.

Roast: a form of cooking that uses dry heat and high temperatures (usually over 375°F), typically done in the oven.

Simmer: a form of cooking where food is submerged in a liquid that is heated to just below its boiling point.

Steam: a form of cooking that uses steam to heat food. Usually done in a steaming pot or microwave.

Steep: soaking food or tea in a liquid to extract its flavor.

Thaw: the act of defrosting or heating frozen food or liquid.

Toast: a form of cooking that browns food, such as bread or nuts, from exposure to heat, usually done in a toaster or under the broiler in the oven.

Whisk: using a fork or whisk to beat or stir ingredients with a light and rapid movement. Common for preparing eggs, salad dressings, or whipped cream.

Where to Store It All

As a college student, you probably have limited space to store your food. Here are the most affordable food storage options for tight spaces.

Glass Jars

The cheapest and most environmentally friendly packaging solution is to clean out and reuse jars from packaged foods such as nut butters and pasta sauces. You can also buy new glass jars to store homemade sauces, dressings, and salads. Glass jars come in all sizes, and you can swap in reusable lids to replace the metal ones, which are prone to rust.

Reusable storage bags

You may pay a little more up front when you buy reusable storage bags, but you'll save money over time since you don't have to replace them as often as disposable versions. Look for reusable silicone bags that are microwave-safe and dishwasher-friendly. You can also use these to store leftovers and chopped fruits and vegetables in the freezer.

Aluminum foil

Aluminum foil is an easy way to wrap up sandwiches and burritos when you want to grab something to go. It is perfect for packing meals when you know you're going to be away from home.

Bulk storage bins

Use large plastic storage bins with lids for bulk items, such as rice, flour, and dried beans. Look for bins that come with an airtight lid to keep food fresh. Store dried pantry items in a cool, dark place. If you don't have a dedicated pantry, a closet or hallway also works.

About the Recipes

Now that you understand the basics of a vegetarian diet, it's time to get cooking! There are 150 vegetarian recipes here to choose from, with everything from breakfast to dinner and dessert included.

Following the recipes in this cookbook will teach you the basics of healthy, vegetarian cooking. All the ingredients are listed according to the order in which they're used in the recipes. The ingredients are followed by a list of uncomplicated instructions that are also arranged in the order in which they should be done.

What makes this cookbook different? These recipes are easy, affordable, and college-friendly. It's the only genuinely beginner-friendly cookbook for vegetarian college students.

EASY

The recipes in this book are made to be simple and accessible for vegetarians who are short on time and space and utterly new to grocery shopping and cooking.

Between lectures and studying for exams, you probably feel like there's not a lot of extra time to cook healthy food at home. Luckily, there are plenty of vegetarian meals you can make in an hour or less. The recipes that follow are all beginner-friendly, and many require only a few minutes of active work in the kitchen. There are also plenty of meals you can batch-cook ahead of time for busy days on the horizon.

As a college student, you won't have time to run to multiple stores to search for exotic ingredients, so these recipes are made with staple foods that are available at most supermarkets. Stock up on vegetables, fruits, whole grains, beans, and nuts, and you'll be able to make many of these dishes without even taking an extra trip to the store.

You don't need a lot of space to make the recipes in this book, either. Most recipes call for fewer than 10 ingredients, so it's okay if you don't have a large, dedicated pantry to store food. Even if you live in a dorm room or share an apartment with roommates, you can still prepare simple and nourishing meals at home.

AFFORDABLE

All the recipes in this book are made to fit into a college-student budget, so you'll find plenty of recipes that utilize affordable ingredients, such as beans, rice, and dried pasta. Canned tomatoes also make an appearance since they're budget-friendly and have a long shelf life.

Food waste is another budget-related consideration, since tossing out food is kind of like throwing your grocery funds straight into the trash. Try to plan ahead and purchase only as many fresh ingredients as you know you can use. When you accidentally buy too much, chop and freeze the produce or use it to make a large batch of soup or chili. When you don't purchase enough, turn to your stock of frozen and canned ingredients to make up the difference. Many of the ingredients called for are used repeatedly throughout the book, so there's less chance of not using up fresh produce.

Almost all of the ingredients are affordable, but there are a few exceptions. Matcha is a little pricey, for example, but it's full of antioxidants and brain-boosting compounds that will help you focus before finals. A homemade matcha latte is also much less expensive than the one you'd buy at the local coffee shop. When you notice an ingredient that costs a little bit more than you're used to, it's because the additional cost is entirely worth it.

COLLEGE-FRIENDLY

Most college days are packed with long hours attending lectures, writing papers, and studying for exams, but there are also plenty of date nights, tailgating parties, and group dinners. Whether you're looking for a great-tasting breakfast you can prepare in advance, a packable plant-based lunch that holds up in your school bag, or a romantic pasta dinner to share on a Friday night, you'll find it here.

For convenient everyday eating, there are grab-and-go breakfasts, packable snacks, and make-ahead meals that don't require a lot of time or effort. Think toast and overnight oats for breakfast, wraps and sandwiches for lunch, chips and dip for an afternoon snack, and grain bowls or stir-fries for dinner.

Most recipes serve two people, so you won't be bombarded with leftovers, but there are also shareable options for those times when you're not eating alone. Try black bean quesadillas for a tailgating party or bring cheesy vegan popcorn to your next study group. Soups and stews are easy to batch-cook for a crowd, and baked egg casseroles are ideal for weekend brunching. Even the omnivores in your life will want a taste. I guarantee it.

Dessert doesn't have to be off-limits, and you don't need to be an expert baker to enjoy them. Quick mug cakes and homemade chocolate peanut butter cups are ideal treats for one. When you want to celebrate the end of the semester, share a no-bake blueberry cheesecake that's sure to wow your friends. There's a recipe here for every college occasion and type of vegetarian.

Freezer
Friendly
Breakfast
Burritos,
page 33

Chapter Two

Breakfasts

Is breakfast the most important meal of the day? Not necessarily. Lunch and dinner are essential, too! There is something powerful about what you choose to eat after you wake up, though. Properly fueling your body and mind can help you feel energized and ready to take on the challenges of the day. Skipping breakfast can have the opposite effect, leaving you with a severe case of brain fog or moodiness and lethargy. So, whether it's sweet or savory, hot or cold, at home or on the run, these meals will fill you up and help you get moving each morning.

Cinnamon Oat Milk Latte 18

Rejuvenating Citrus Smoothie 19

No-Bake Green Tea Energy Bars 20

Spicy Chickpea-Avocado Toast 22

Apple Pie Granola 23

Peanut Butter and Banana Overnight Oats 24

Tropical Chia Pudding Parfait 25

Spinach and Mushroom Baked Egg Cups 26

Whole-Grain Carrot Cake Muffins 27

Lemon-Blueberry Yogurt Bowls 29

Triple-Berry Flax Oatmeal 30

Sweet Potato Pancakes 31

Freezer-Friendly Breakfast Burritos 33

Ultimate Vegan Breakfast Sandwiches 35

Broccoli Cheddar Strata 37

Cinnamon Oat Milk Latte

MAKES 1 SERVING · PREP TIME: 3 MINUTES · COOK TIME: 1 MINUTE 30 SECONDS

DORM-FRIENDLY | MICROWAVABLE

**1 cup unsweetened
Creamy Oat Milk
(page 210)**

**1 teaspoon maple syrup
(optional for sweetness;
omit if oat milk is
already sweetened)**

**½ teaspoon ground
cinnamon, plus
additional for topping**

**½ cup hot brewed espresso
coffee or strong brewed
dark coffee**

Oat milk is a creamy, dairy-free alternative to animal milk. Its neutral flavor tastes delicious with coffee and a bit of cinnamon. This quick and easy latte is warm and comforting, and it also provides a boost in energy for early classes and long study sessions. If you don't have an espresso machine, use regular brewed coffee instead. This recipe is easy to make in a dorm room with a microwave, but you can also heat the ingredients on the stovetop, if you prefer.

1. Stir together the oat milk, maple syrup, and cinnamon in a large, microwave-safe mug or bowl. (It's okay if the cinnamon doesn't fully incorporate into the oat milk before it's heated.)

2. Cover with a paper towel and microwave on high for 1 minute 30 seconds or until hot.

3. Whisk vigorously with a small whisk or fork to froth the milk and fully incorporate the cinnamon into the oat milk.

4. Add the brewed espresso coffee.

5. Sprinkle with additional cinnamon, if desired.

Substitute: You can use any type of milk for this recipe. If you're looking for a latte with plant-based protein, try soy milk. It's one of the only dairy-free milk alternatives that has as much protein as cow's milk.

PER SERVING (1 CUP): Calories: 80; Total fat: 3g; Carbohydrates: 11g; Fiber: 1g; Protein: 2g; Calcium: 460mg; Vitamin D: 4mcg; Vitamin B$_{12}$: 0µg; Iron: 1mg; Zinc: 0mg

Rejuvenating Citrus Smoothie

MAKES 2 SERVINGS • PREP TIME: 10 MINUTES

3 cups frozen
mango chunks

1 cup unsweetened soy
milk (or milk of choice)

4 teaspoons grated
orange zest

Juice of 2 large oranges

4 tablespoons ground
flaxseed

½ teaspoon ground ginger
(optional)

Rejuvenating citrus and mango make this smoothie the ideal pick-me-up the morning after a night out. This refreshing beverage is balanced with nutrients and contains ginger to ease digestion and ground flaxseed for omega-3s. Oranges and mangos are both excellent sources of vitamin C, which is an antioxidant that helps repair cellular damage in the body. If you like your smoothies on the sweeter side, add a teaspoon of sugar or maple syrup.

1. Place the mango, soy milk, orange zest, orange juice, ground flaxseed, and ginger (if using) in a blender.

2. Cover and blend on high for 30 seconds, or until smooth and creamy.

3. If the consistency is too thick, add more soy milk or orange juice, cover, and blend again. If the consistency is too thin, add more ground flaxseed or frozen mango chunks, cover, and blend again.

Tip: If you want to cut out some of the preparation steps to make this recipe quicker and easier, omit the grated orange zest and use bottled orange juice instead of fresh oranges.

PER SERVING: Calories: 348; Total fat: 11g; Carbohydrates: 58g; Fiber: 10g; Protein: 11g; Calcium: 242mg; Vitamin D: 2mcg; Vitamin B_{12}: 1μg; Iron: 2mg; Zinc: 2mg

No-Bake Green Tea Energy Bars

MAKES 8 BARS • PREP TIME: 15 MINUTES, PLUS 1 HOUR TO FREEZE

GREAT FOR SHARING | MAKES LEFTOVERS | NO COOKING REQUIRED

1¼ cups chopped
   pitted dates
¾ cup walnut halves
   and pieces
½ cup whole almonds
2 tablespoons ground
   flaxseed
1 tablespoon matcha
1 tablespoon
   vanilla extract
¼ teaspoon kosher salt

Matcha is a finely ground green tea powder that's originally from Japan. Besides caffeine, green tea also contains l-theanine, an amino acid that helps promote calm focus and energy without the jitters associated with too much coffee. With energy-promoting ingredients, these bars are the perfect snack for studying. If you don't have a food processor, you could also make these energy bars by hand. Use a knife and cutting board to chop the nuts, and use your hands to mix the ingredients and form the dough.

1. Combine the dates, walnuts, almonds, ground flaxseed, matcha, vanilla, and salt in a food processor.

2. Pulse 10 times, scraping down the sides with a spatula as needed, or until the mixture sticks together when pressed between your fingers.

3. Transfer the dough to an 8-inch square baking dish (or similarly sized pan) lined with parchment paper or aluminum foil. (This makes the bars easier to remove later on.)

4. Cover with plastic wrap and freeze overnight or for at least 1 hour.

5. Remove the baking dish from the freezer and carefully lift out the parchment paper or aluminum foil to remove the nut mixture.

6. Slide the nut mixture onto a cutting board and slice into 8 rectangular pieces. Serve.

Storage: Cover or wrap each bar separately and refrigerate for up to 2 weeks or freeze for up to 3 months.

Mix it up: You can use this basic recipe to make all sorts of energy bar flavors. Instead of matcha, try mixing in a tablespoon of cinnamon, pumpkin pie spice, or cocoa powder.

PER SERVING (1 BAR): Calories: 202; Total fat: 12g; Carbohydrates: 21g; Fiber: 4g; Protein: 4g; Calcium: 48mg; Vitamin D: 0mcg; Vitamin B_{12}: 0µg; Iron: 1mg; Zinc: 1mg

Spicy Chickpea-Avocado Toast

MAKES 2 SERVINGS · PREP TIME: 10 MINUTES · COOK TIME: 2 MINUTES

DORM-FRIENDLY

2 slices whole-grain bread

1 avocado, peeled and pitted

1 (15-ounce) can chickpeas, drained and rinsed

2 tablespoons fresh lemon juice

¼ teaspoon cayenne

½ teaspoon nutritional yeast (optional)

Kosher salt

Toasted bread topped with nutrient-rich avocado is an easy, no-cook breakfast for a busy weekday morning. I like to add cooked chickpeas, which I mash in the same bowl as the avocado, for extra fiber and plant-based protein. This savory breakfast contains a balance of nutrients that will help you feel satisfied for hours. Make it with any type of bread, including gluten-free varieties, if desired. You can also add an egg (fried or scrambled) on top for extra protein.

1. Toast the bread in a toaster or toaster oven for 1 to 2 minutes. If you don't have a toaster, brown the bread under the broiler in the oven or in a greased skillet on a hot plate burner.

2. In a small bowl, mash the avocado and chickpeas together.

3. Add the lemon juice, cayenne, nutritional yeast (if using), and salt.

4. Spread the chickpea mixture on each piece of the toasted bread. Serve immediately.

Tip: If you don't have chickpeas, try swapping in canned cannellini beans because they have a smooth, creamy texture that makes them ideal for mashing and pureeing.

PER SERVING: Calories: 457; Total fat: 20g; Carbohydrates: 58g; Fiber: 20g; Protein: 18g; Calcium: 104mg; Vitamin D: 0mcg; Vitamin B$_{12}$: 0µg; Iron: 4mg; Zinc: 3mg

Apple Pie Granola

MAKES 12 SERVINGS · PREP TIME: 10 MINUTES · COOK TIME: 50 MINUTES

GREAT FOR SHARING | MAKES LEFTOVERS

3 cups old-fashioned
   rolled oats
1 cup walnut or pecan
   halves (or a mix of both)
2 tablespoons sugar
1 tablespoon ground
   cinnamon
1 teaspoon ground allspice
1 teaspoon ground ginger
½ teaspoon kosher salt
6 dates, pitted
   and chopped
½ cup unsweetened
   applesauce
¼ cup olive oil
¼ cup maple syrup

Storage: Store the granola in an airtight container in a cool, dry area for up to 6 months.

Tip: If you have a nut allergy or want to make this recipe more affordable, try substituting seeds for the walnuts and pecans. Pumpkin and sunflower seeds are budget-friendly and work great in homemade granola.

Granola lasts for up to 6 months, so I recommend preparing a large batch to ensure you have leftovers. Not all granulated (cane) sugar is vegan, so look for organic if that's important to you. Similarly, not all oats are gluten-free, so look for the gluten-free certification if necessary. While baking the granola, pause to stir it every 10 to 15 minutes to promote even cooking. I like to set a timer so I don't forget. Eat this granola on its own or serve it with yogurt, milk, or chia pudding.

1. Preheat the oven to 325°F.

2. In a large bowl, stir together the oats, walnuts, sugar, cinnamon, allspice, ginger, and salt until well mixed.

3. Add the dates and stir to mix.

4. Add the applesauce, olive oil, and maple syrup, stirring until everything is evenly coated.

5. Transfer the mixture to a baking sheet and bake for 50 minutes, stirring every 10 to 15 minutes, or until the edges are golden brown.

6. Cool the granola for at least 10 minutes before serving. Granola gets crispier as it cools.

PER SERVING: Calories: 297; Total fat: 14g; Carbohydrates: 38g; Fiber: 6g; Protein: 8g; Calcium: 47mg; Vitamin D: 0mcg; Vitamin B$_{12}$: 0µg; Iron: 2mg; Zinc: 2mg

Peanut Butter and Banana Overnight Oats

MAKES 2 SERVINGS • PREP TIME: 5 MINUTES, PLUS 8 HOURS TO CHILL

DORM-FRIENDLY | NO COOKING REQUIRED

1 cup old-fashioned
    rolled oats

1 cup soy milk (or milk
    of choice)

1 medium banana, sliced

2 tablespoons
    peanut butter

1 teaspoon ground
    cinnamon

¼ teaspoon kosher salt
    (omit if peanut butter
    contains salt)

OPTIONAL TOPPINGS

Maple syrup

Chopped peanuts

Cacao nibs or
    chocolate chips

Overnight oats are a simple grab-and-go breakfast to make even if you don't have access to a microwave or stovetop. Dried oats usually have to be cooked, but when you mix them with milk and refrigerate them overnight, they absorb some of the liquid and soften enough to eat. This meal takes only a few minutes to prepare, and it's balanced with nutrients to help you feel good. Feel free to scale up the recipe to make enough jars to last all week.

1. Divide the oats, soy milk, banana, peanut butter, cinnamon, and salt (if using) between 2 jars and stir to mix.

2. Top with the maple syrup, peanuts, and cacao nibs or chocolate chips, if desired.

3. Seal the jars and refrigerate overnight.

Tip: Substitute tahini (sesame seed paste) or sunflower seed butter and omit the chopped peanuts if you have a peanut allergy. Almond or cashew butter also works well if you're able to tolerate nuts in your diet.

PER SERVING: Calories: 506; Total fat: 15g; Carbohydrates: 76g; Fiber: 11g; Protein: 22g; Calcium: 219mg; Vitamin D: 2mcg; Vitamin B_{12}: 1µg; Iron: 4mg; Zinc: 4mg

Tropical Chia Pudding Parfait

MAKES 2 SERVINGS · PREP TIME: 10 MINUTES, PLUS 8 HOURS TO CHILL

1½ cups unsweetened soy milk (or milk of choice)

⅓ cup chia seeds

2 teaspoons vanilla extract

2 teaspoons maple syrup (omit if milk is sweetened)

⅛ teaspoon kosher salt

1 cup frozen mango chunks, thawed

1 cup frozen pineapple chunks, thawed

½ cup unsweetened coconut flakes

....

Storage: Seal the jars and refrigerate for up to 1 week.

....

Tip: Mix up the fruit to create different flavor profiles for the chia pudding parfaits. Instead of the tropical fruits, try substituting berries (blueberries, raspberries, blackberries, or sliced strawberries) or sliced banana.

Similar to oats, when chia seeds are soaked in milk overnight, they thicken and form a pudding-like consistency that's ideal for fruit parfaits. Mix vanilla chia pudding with tropical fruits to create an energizing breakfast you can make ahead and pack into your school bag for busy weekdays. If you don't have a freezer to store fruit, opt for fresh or canned varieties. Look for canned fruit stored in juice (instead of syrup) to avoid unnecessary sugars.

1. In a medium bowl, whisk the soy milk, chia seeds, vanilla, maple syrup, and salt together until well mixed.

2. Cover the bowl and refrigerate overnight.

3. Divide one-half of the chia mixture between 2 jars.

4. Divide one-half of the mango, pineapple, and coconut flakes between the jars.

5. Divide the remaining chia mixture between the jars.

6. Add the remaining mango, pineapple, and coconut flakes to each jar. Serve.

PER SERVING: Calories: 444; Total fat: 21g; Carbohydrates: 55g; Fiber: 17g; Protein: 12g; Calcium: 470mg; Vitamin D: 3mcg; Vitamin B_{12}: 2µg; Iron: 4mg; Zinc: 3mg

Spinach and Mushroom Baked Egg Cups

MAKES 6 SERVINGS · PREP TIME: 10 MINUTES · COOK TIME: 20 MINUTES

GREAT FOR SHARING | MAKES LEFTOVERS

Grapeseed oil or nonstick cooking spray

1 cup chopped fresh baby spinach

1 cup sliced button mushrooms

1 cup shredded mozzarella cheese

12 large eggs

2 teaspoons dried oregano

½ teaspoon red pepper flakes (optional)

¼ teaspoon kosher salt

Storage: Place the egg cups in an airtight container and refrigerate for up to 4 days or freeze for up to 6 months.

Mix it up: You can use many different fresh, frozen, and canned vegetables to make baked egg cups. Any type of cheese will also work for this recipe. For Mexican-inspired flavors, try substituting tomatoes, peppers, and cheddar jack cheese.

If you like your breakfasts to be savory, but still want a quick and easy meal you can make ahead, you'll love these egg cups. They're perfectly portioned for grab-and-go eating (1 egg per cup) and are even freezer-friendly so you can prep them weeks in advance. Serve baked egg cups with whole-grain toast, an English muffin, or a bagel to round out the meal. Skip the cheese to make this recipe dairy-free.

1. Preheat the oven to 350°F. Lightly grease 6 cups of a 12-cup muffin tin.

2. Divide the spinach, mushrooms, and mozzarella among 6 cups of the muffin tin. In a medium bowl, beat the eggs (whisk until no longer streaky), then add the oregano, red pepper flakes (if using), and salt. Divide the egg mixture among the muffin cups, leaving a ¼-inch space at the top of the cups for the eggs to rise. (If desired, pour the beaten eggs into a liquid measuring cup for easier pouring.) Bake the cups for 20 minutes, or until golden brown and puffy.

3. Allow the egg cups to cool slightly before removing with a spatula and transferring them to a plate. Serve.

PER SERVING: Calories: 205; Total fat: 14g; Carbohydrates: 2g; Fiber: g; Protein: 17g; Calcium: 161mg; Vitamin D: 4mcg; Vitamin B$_{12}$: 1µg; Iron: 2mg; Zinc: 2mg

Whole-Grain Carrot Cake Muffins

MAKES 12 MUFFINS · PREP TIME: 15 MINUTES · COOK TIME: 15 MINUTES

Grapeseed oil or nonstick cooking spray

1¾ cups whole wheat flour

2 teaspoons ground cinnamon

1½ teaspoons baking powder

½ teaspoon ground ginger

½ teaspoon baking soda

½ teaspoon kosher salt

2 cups grated carrots

½ cup walnut halves and pieces

2 large eggs

1 cup plain or vanilla Greek yogurt

⅓ cup unsweetened applesauce

⅓ cup maple syrup

Balanced with fiber from whole-wheat flour, as well as protein and fats from walnuts, eggs, and Greek yogurt, these muffins are an energizing breakfast you can take anywhere. Whole grains help stabilize blood sugar and promote longer-lasting energy, so you won't experience a crash after starting your day with this baked treat. If you're new to whole grains, bake the muffins with a blend of all-purpose and whole-wheat flour the first time. Skip the walnuts if you'd prefer to make these muffins nut-free.

1. Preheat the oven to 425°F and grease a 12-cup muffin tin.

2. In a large bowl, stir together the flour, cinnamon, baking powder, ginger, baking soda, and salt until well blended. Fold in the carrots and walnuts.

3. In a medium bowl, beat the eggs until well blended Add the yogurt, applesauce, and maple syrup.

4. Pour the liquid ingredients into the bowl of dry ingredients and stir until just combined.

5. Divide the batter among the cups of the muffin tin (about ⅓ cup batter per cup). Bake the muffins for 15 minutes, or until they are golden on top and an inserted toothpick comes out clean.

continues →

Whole-Grain Carrot Cake Muffins *continued*

6. Remove the muffins from the oven and allow them to cool in the pan for 5 minutes, then transfer to a metal rack to cool completely. If the muffins are sticking to the pan, slide a butter knife around the edges to loosen them. Serve.

....

Storage: Place the muffins in an airtight container and store at room temperature for up to 2 days, in the refrigerator for up to 4 days, or in the freezer for up to 3 months.

....

Tip: Make this recipe easier by purchasing shredded carrots at the grocery store. If you have a shredding attachment, you can also use your food processor to shred the whole carrots.

PER SERVING (1 MUFFIN): Calories: 147; Total fat: 5g; Carbohydrates: 23g; Fiber: 3g; Protein: 6g; Calcium: 82mg; Vitamin D: 0mcg; Vitamin B$_{12}$: 0μg; Iron: 1mg; Zinc: 1mg

Lemon-Blueberry Yogurt Bowls

MAKES 2 SERVINGS • PREP TIME: 5 MINUTES

DORM-FRIENDLY | NO COOKING REQUIRED

2 cups plain or vanilla Greek yogurt

2 tablespoons ground flaxseed (optional)

2 teaspoons grated lemon zest (reserve some for topping, if desired)

1 tablespoon fresh lemon juice

½ teaspoon ground cinnamon (optional)

½ teaspoon vanilla extract (optional)

1 cup (about 6 ounces) fresh blueberries (or use thawed frozen berries)

¼ cup chopped almonds, toasted if desired

2 to 4 teaspoons maple syrup or honey (depending on desired sweetness)

When you're late for class but still want to start the day with a substantial breakfast, these yogurt bowls will come to your rescue. Use any type of yogurt for this recipe, including dairy-free varieties. If you have access to an oven, try toasting the almonds to help bring out their flavor. Preheat the oven to 325°F, spread the almonds on a baking sheet, and bake for about 5 minutes. You can also toast the nuts in a skillet over low to medium heat. Just be sure to stir them often to prevent burning.

1. In a medium bowl, stir together the yogurt, flaxseed (if using), lemon zest, lemon juice, and cinnamon and vanilla (if using).

2. Divide the mixture between 2 bowls or jars and top with the blueberries and almonds.

3. Drizzle with maple syrup or honey and garnish with the remaining grated lemon zest, if desired.

Tip: Make this dish easier with store-bought lemon juice; skip the grated lemon zest if you choose this route. You can also buy sliced or chopped almonds to cut out some of the meal prep.

PER SERVING: Calories: 211; Total fat: 8g; Carbohydrates: 27g; Fiber: 0g; Protein: 9g; Calcium: 308mg; Vitamin D: 0mcg; Vitamin B$_{12}$: 1µg; Iron: 0mg; Zinc: 2mg

Triple-Berry Flax Oatmeal

MAKES 1 SERVING · PREP TIME: 5 MINUTES · COOK TIME: 2 MINUTES

1 cup unsweetened soy milk (or milk of choice)

½ cup old-fashioned rolled oats

2 tablespoons ground flaxseed

½ teaspoon ground cinnamon

⅛ teaspoon ground ginger (optional)

⅛ teaspoon kosher salt

½ cup frozen triple berry blend (strawberries, raspberries, blackberries)

It's possible to cook homemade oatmeal even if you don't have access to a stovetop or hot plate. This microwavable oatmeal bowl incorporates frozen fruit for flavor and nutrients. There's no need to thaw the frozen fruit before you add it to the oats. As the mixture warms, the fruit juices release into the oatmeal. The finished result is delicious. I like my oatmeal on the thinner side, but if you prefer thicker oats, use ¾ cup of soy milk instead of a full cup.

1. In a medium microwave-safe bowl, stir together the soy milk, oats, flaxseed, cinnamon, ginger (if using), and salt. Add the frozen triple berry blend.

2. Cover the bowl, allowing the corner to vent, and microwave on high for 1 minute and 30 seconds. Stir, replace the cover, and microwave on high for an additional 30 seconds, or until the berries are warm and the oats are softened. Stir again and allow the oatmeal to cool and thicken for a couple of minutes before serving.

Mix it up: Change the type of fruit and spices to give this microwavable oatmeal bowl a whole new taste. Try the tropical fruits from the Tropical Chia Pudding Parfait on page 25 or make this with frozen diced apples or pears.

PER SERVING: Calories: 523; Total fat: 14g; Carbohydrates: 79g; Fiber: 15g; Protein: 24g; Calcium: 414mg; Vitamin D: 3mcg; Vitamin B_{12}: 1µg; Iron: 5mg; Zinc: 5mg

Sweet Potato Pancakes

MAKES 2 SERVINGS · PREP TIME: 5 MINUTES · COOK TIME: 10 MINUTES

ONE PAN

1 small sweet potato

½ cup unsweetened soy milk (or milk of choice)

1 large egg

1 tablespoon maple syrup

1 teaspoon vanilla extract

½ cup whole wheat flour

½ teaspoon baking powder

½ teaspoon ground cinnamon

¼ teaspoon ground ginger

¼ teaspoon kosher salt

Grapeseed oil or nonstick cooking spray

OPTIONAL FOR SERVING

Maple syrup

Chopped nuts, such as pecans or walnuts

Greek yogurt or whipped cream

Are you looking for more ways to incorporate vegetables at breakfast? Sweet potatoes are a nutritious choice for both sweet and savory morning meals. I love how they add color and natural sweetness to these whole-wheat pancakes, which are also flavored with warm cinnamon and ginger. Substitute flax eggs if you're vegan or want to make this recipe egg-free. To make flax eggs, whisk 1 tablespoon ground flaxseed with 2½ tablespoons water and wait until the mixture is thickened to the consistency of a beaten egg.

1. Pierce the sweet potato with a fork, wrap it in a paper towel, and microwave on high for 5 minutes, or until softened. Allow the sweet potato to cool enough to handle. Slice it in half and use a spoon to scoop out the flesh into a large bowl, then mash with a potato masher or fork. You should have around ⅓ cup mashed sweet potato.

2. Add the soy milk, egg, maple syrup, and vanilla to the sweet potato and whisk until combined. It's okay if there are some lumps of sweet potato.

3. Gradually add the flour while stirring constantly.

4. Add the baking powder, cinnamon, ginger, and salt.

continues →

5. Heat a large greased or nonstick skillet over medium heat. Pour about ¼ cup of the batter into the skillet, cooking 2 pancakes at a time. Cook for 3 minutes, or until bubbles begin to form. Flip and cook for 2 minutes more, or until golden.

6. Transfer the cooked pancakes to a plate and keep warm. Clean and grease the skillet again as needed. Repeat with the remaining batter, cooking another batch of 2 pancakes. Turn down the heat if the bottoms turn brown before the center is cooked.

7. Serve the pancakes with maple syrup, chopped nuts, and yogurt or whipped cream, if desired.

....

Storage: Store leftover pancakes in an airtight container in the refrigerator for up to 5 days or freeze for up to 2 months.

....

Make it easier: Substitute canned pumpkin puree for the sweet potato in this recipe. You can skip the first step and add the pumpkin right to the bowl and start mixing with the other ingredients.

PER SERVING (2 PANCAKES): Calories: 255; Total fat: 4g; Carbohydrates: 46g; Fiber: 6g; Protein: 10g; Calcium: 192mg; Vitamin D: 2 mcg; Vitamin B_{12}: 1mcg; Iron: 2mg; Zinc: 2mg

Freezer-Friendly Breakfast Burritos

MAKES 6 SERVINGS · PREP TIME: 25 MINUTES · COOK TIME: 20 MINUTES

MAKES LEFTOVERS

2 tablespoons grapeseed oil, or more as needed

1 small onion, diced

1 bell pepper (any color), seeded, cored, and diced

3 jalapeño peppers, sliced (optional; remove ribs and seeds for mild flavor)

2 cups cooked black beans

1 tablespoon chili powder

1 tablespoon ground cumin

Kosher salt

10 large eggs, lightly beaten

6 large flour tortillas

1 cup shredded cheddar cheese (optional)

¾ cup chopped scallions, both white and green parts (1 bunch; optional)

Your future self will thank you for preparing a batch of freezer-friendly breakfast burritos for the week ahead. Keep them on hand to reheat on days when you have an early lecture. Plate up these burritos with avocado or guacamole, salsa, Mexican-style hot sauce, and sour cream or plain yogurt. I also like to sprinkle the burritos with fresh cilantro and scallions for color. Leave out the cheese to make them dairy-free.

1. Heat the oil in a large skillet over medium heat. Once the oil is shiny, add the onion and cook for 4 minutes, or until translucent.

2. Add the bell pepper, jalapeños (if using), black beans, chili powder, cumin, and salt. Cook for 5 minutes, or until the peppers are softened, stirring occasionally. Transfer the mixture to a bowl or plate.

3. Reduce the heat to medium-low and add more oil to the skillet if needed. Pour in the beaten eggs and cook for 8 minutes, stirring occasionally, or until no liquid remains and the eggs are cooked all the way through. Remove the skillet from the heat.

continues →

4. To assemble the burritos, warm the tortillas for 20 seconds in the microwave (in batches of 2 to 3), then lay a tortilla on a flat surface.

5. Spread one-sixth of the bean and vegetable mixture in the center of the tortilla.

6. Spoon one-sixth of the cooked eggs on top.

7. Sprinkle some of the cheese and scallions (if using) on top.

8. Roll the tortilla up and wrap it with parchment paper or aluminum foil.

9. Repeat with the remaining tortillas until all the ingredients are used. Once you have finished, place the wrapped burritos in a freezer-safe bag and freeze.

10. To reheat, unwrap one of the burritos, place it on a damp paper towel–lined plate, and microwave on high for 3 minutes.

Tip: Omit the eggs and cheese to make these breakfast burritos vegan. You can also use scrambled tofu instead of the eggs and nutritional yeast instead of the cheese if you want to keep the protein content similar to the original recipe.

PER SERVING: Calories: 345; Total fat: 15g; Carbohydrates: 34g; Fiber: 7g; Protein: 19g; Calcium: 121mg; Vitamin D: 2mcg; Vitamin B_{12}: 1µg; Iron: 4mg; Zinc: 2mg

Ultimate Vegan Breakfast Sandwiches

MAKES 2 SANDWICHES · PREP TIME: 30 MINUTES · COOK TIME: 8 MINUTES

ONE PAN

2 tablespoons grapeseed oil

½ teaspoon garlic powder

½ teaspoon onion powder

½ teaspoon ground turmeric

Kosher salt

Freshly ground black pepper

1 (14-ounce) block extra-firm tofu, drained, pressed (see Tip, page 50), and cut into rectangles

4 slices whole-grain bread (or 2 sliced bagels or English muffins), toasted if desired

½ cup fresh baby spinach (or lettuce of choice)

½ red bell pepper, sliced into strips

1 avocado, peeled, pitted, and sliced

Protein-packed tofu makes this breakfast sandwich filling and energizing. Coated with garlic and onion powder for flavor and ground turmeric for color, tofu acts as an egg substitute in this recipe. Break the tofu into bite-size pieces with your hands if you want it to look like scrambled eggs. I prefer rectangular slices to make the tofu more sandwich-friendly. You can serve these sandwiches with any of your favorite sandwich condiments, including mayonnaise and mustard.

1. In a medium bowl, whisk together the oil, garlic powder, onion powder, and turmeric, and season with salt and pepper.

2. Place a large skillet over medium heat.

3. Dip the tofu pieces in the oil mixture to coat them and then spread the tofu in the skillet. Cook for 5 minutes, or until the tofu separates easily from the pan.

4. Flip and cook for an additional 3 minutes, or until the other side of the tofu separates easily from the pan.

5. Lay 2 slices of bread (or one half of 2 bagels or English muffins) on a flat surface.

continues →

Ultimate Vegan Breakfast Sandwiches *continued*

6. Divide the spinach, red bell pepper slices, avocado, and cooked tofu between the bread slices. Place the remaining pieces of bread (or other half of the bagel or English muffin) on top of each.

7. Cut the sandwiches in half if desired and serve.

. . . .

Protein swaps: Substitute scrambled or fried eggs if you include them in your diet. If you're looking for another plant-based alternative, try mashed chickpeas or cannellini beans.

PER SERVING (1 SANDWICH): Calories: 670; Total fat: 45g; Carbohydrates: 44g; Fiber: 14g; Protein: 34g; Calcium: 478mg; Vitamin D: 0mcg; Vitamin B$_{12}$: 0µg; Iron: 7mg; Zinc: 4mg

Broccoli Cheddar Strata

MAKES 6 SERVINGS · PREP TIME: 10 MINUTES · COOK TIME: 55 MINUTES

Grapeseed oil or nonstick cooking spray

6 large eggs

2 cups milk

½ teaspoon garlic powder (or 4 garlic cloves)

½ teaspoon kosher salt

¼ teaspoon freshly ground black pepper

2½ cups chopped broccoli florets

2½ cups torn leftover bread (from about ½ loaf)

1 cup (8 ounces) shredded cheddar cheese

....

Mix it up: You can change the vegetables and type of cheese to create endless flavor combinations for the strata. Try butternut squash with goat cheese or spinach and mushrooms with mozzarella.

Looking for a weekend brunch that's easy to share? A strata is a crowd-pleasing casserole made with eggs, bread, and cheese. What's not to love? This is also the best way to use up leftover bread. The strata will turn out even better when the loaf is a little bit stale because it adds texture. It's also common to include vegetables in a strata. This version has broccoli to bump up the color, flavor, and nutritional value of the dish.

1. Preheat the oven to 350°F and grease an 8-by-11-inch glass baking dish.

2. In a large bowl, whisk the eggs, milk, garlic powder, salt, and pepper until no longer streaky.

3. Add the broccoli, bread, and cheese.

4. Pour the mixture into the baking dish, spreading it out evenly, and bake uncovered for 55 minutes or until the center is set and the top is golden.

5. Cool the strata for at least 5 minutes before slicing it into 6 pieces.

....

Storage: Store leftover strata pieces in an airtight container in the refrigerator for up to 4 days.

PER SERVING: Calories: 254; Total fat: 14g; Carbohydrates: 17g; Fiber: 2g; Protein: 17g; Calcium: 297mg; Vitamin D: 2mcg; Vitamin B$_{12}$: 1µg; Iron: 2mg; Zinc: 2mg

10-Minute Miso Soup,
page 42

Chapter Three

Super Soups and Stews

Is there anything cozier than a warm bowl of soup? Hearty and convenient, these soups and stews are the epitome of plant-based comfort food. I like to make a large batch of soup every Sunday because it's easy to reheat and eat for lunch or dinner all week. Hot meals are ideal for the colder months, but you don't have to miss out on the nutritional benefits of produce-packed soups during summer break, either. Try cold soups, such as gazpacho, for a refreshing warm-weather twist.

Cooling Cucumber-Basil Soup 40

Watermelon Gazpacho 41

10-Minute Miso Soup 42

Vegan Tomato Bisque 43

Creamy Carrot-Ginger Soup 45

Pinto Bean and Tortilla Soup 47

No-Chicken Tofu Noodle Soup 49

Mushroom French Onion Soup 51

Vegan Corn Chowder 52

High-Protein Lentil Soup 53

Broccoli Cheese Soup with Croutons 54

Irish-Inspired Potato Stew 56

Vegan Gumbo 57

Pumpkin and Black Bean Chili 58

Peanut Stew 59

Cooling Cucumber-Basil Soup

MAKES 2 SERVINGS · PREP TIME: 5 MINUTES

DORM-FRIENDLY | NO COOKING REQUIRED

1 large English cucumber,
   peeled and chopped
½ cup plain Greek yogurt
⅓ cup fresh basil, plus
   extra for serving
2 tablespoons fresh
   lemon juice
1 garlic clove, chopped
2 tablespoons olive
   oil, plus additional
   for serving
Kosher salt
Freshly ground
   black pepper

Tip: Greek yogurt is a type of strained yogurt that's thicker and higher in protein than other common yogurt varieties. You can substitute Icelandic skyr for a similar result. Regular and nondairy yogurts also work, especially if you're looking for a lighter, more drinkable soup.

Refreshing and cooling on a hot day, cucumber basil soup is a must-try during the warm months of summer break. This simple soup is easy to make in a small blender and is balanced with carbohydrates, protein, and fat to help you feel energized. Serve it with fresh basil leaves and finely diced cucumber and red onion. Like many soups, this one gets thicker in the refrigerator, so add a little water before serving if you make it ahead.

1. Place the cucumber, Greek yogurt, basil, lemon juice, garlic, and olive oil in a blender and pulse 10 times, or until the soup is creamy.

2. Taste and season with salt and pepper, if needed.

3. Divide the soup between 2 bowls and drizzle with olive oil and fresh basil leaves, if desired.

Storage: Store leftover soup in an airtight container in the refrigerator for up to 2 days.

PER SERVING: Calories: 180; Total fat: 16g; Carbohydrates: 8g; Fiber: 1g; Protein: 3g; Calcium: 104mg; Vitamin D: 0mcg; Vitamin B$_{12}$: 0µg; Iron: 1mg; Zinc: 1mg

Watermelon Gazpacho

MAKES 4 SERVINGS • PREP TIME: 10 MINUTES

4 cups chopped seedless watermelon

1¼ cups chopped English cucumber (½ medium)

1 red bell pepper, seeded, cored, and chopped

¼ cup fresh parsley leaves

1 garlic clove, minced

1 teaspoon grated lemon zest (from 1 medium)

2 tablespoons fresh lemon juice (from 1 medium)

Kosher salt

Freshly ground black pepper

Gazpacho is a cold soup that originated in Spain. It's often made with tomato, but this version incorporates watermelon for a fruity twist. It's quick and easy to make if you have a blender, but you can also prep by hand in a pinch. Finely dice the ingredients with a knife and cutting board, add them to a bowl, and then use a masher (or the back of a spoon) to crush and muddle everything together. Don't forget to pack up the leftovers! Gazpacho is even better the next day since the flavors have more time to meld.

1. Put the watermelon, cucumber, bell pepper, parsley, garlic, lemon zest, and lemon juice in a blender and pulse 5 times, or until the soup is liquid-like, but not totally pureed.

2. Season to taste with salt and pepper. Serve.

Storage: Store leftover soup in an airtight container in the refrigerator for up to 1 week.

Substitute: Try making this gazpacho with fresh tomatoes if watermelon isn't available in your area. You can also try making it with other fresh fruits, such as strawberries.

PER SERVING: Calories: 60; Total fat: 0g; Carbohydrates: 14g; Fiber: 1g; Protein: 2g; Calcium: 25mg; Vitamin D: 0mcg; Vitamin B$_{12}$: 0µg; Iron: 1mg; Zinc: 0mg

10-Minute Miso Soup

MAKES 1 SERVING · PREP TIME: 5 MINUTES · COOK TIME: 5 MINUTES

¼ **cup frozen shelled edamame (massage the bag to help separate the beans)**

¼ **cup diced fresh shiitake or cremini mushrooms**

1 small scallion, both white and green parts, chopped

1½ cups water

1½ tablespoons miso paste

Sesame seeds (optional)

Substitute: If you don't have mushrooms, try substituting broccoli or baby bok choy for the vegetables in this soup. Frozen (blanched and chopped) vegetables are also convenient options because you can add them to the soup without thawing.

Typically made with fermented soybeans, salt, and rice, miso is a flavorful seasoning paste that originated in Japan. Use it to add savory flavor to this speedy microwavable soup. This meal for one doesn't require a lot of effort, but it still has flavor and plant-based protein from edamame. Look for fermented miso in the refrigerated section of your grocery store and add it at the end of the cooking process to preserve more of its heat-sensitive probiotics.

1. Stir together the edamame, mushrooms, scallion, and water in a large, microwave-safe mug or bowl. Place a paper towel on top and microwave on high for 2 minutes.

2. Carefully remove the bowl from the microwave and stir.

3. Spoon the miso paste into a small bowl.

4. Pour about ¼ cup liquid from the cooked soup into the miso and use a fork or small whisk to mix.

5. Pour the miso mixture into the soup and stir until evenly mixed.

6. Garnish with sesame seeds, if desired, and serve immediately.

PER SERVING: Calories: 181; Total fat: 4g; Carbohydrates: 31g; Fiber: 7g; Protein: 10g; Calcium: 53mg; Vitamin D: 1mcg; Vitamin B$_{12}$: 0µg; Iron: 2mg; Zinc: 3mg

Vegan Tomato Bisque

MAKES 4 SERVINGS · PREP TIME: 5 MINUTES · COOK TIME: 25 MINUTES

DORM-FRIENDLY | GREAT FOR SHARING | MAKES LEFTOVERS | ONE POT

2 tablespoons
   grapeseed oil
1 small onion, diced
   (about ¾ cup)
3 garlic cloves, smashed
2 cups vegetable broth
1 (28-ounce) can crushed
   tomatoes
1 tablespoon dried basil
1 teaspoon dried thyme
2 cups plain unsweetened
   soy milk (or plain
   dairy-free milk
   of choice)
Kosher salt
Freshly ground
   black pepper

A bisque is a rich and creamy soup that traditionally calls for cream. Bisques also often contain shellfish and other types of seafood. This plant-based version of the comforting soup is made with pantry-friendly ingredients, such as canned tomatoes and dried herbs. Soy milk adds protein and a creamy texture. Serve this 30-minute lunch with fresh herbs and Whole-Grain Croutons (page 228) or a chunk of crusty bread.

1. Heat the oil in a 12-quart stockpot over medium heat. Once the oil is shiny, add the onion and cook for 4 minutes, stirring often, or until onion is translucent.

2. Add the garlic and cook for an additional minute.

3. Add the broth, tomatoes, basil, and thyme.

4. Bring the soup to a boil, reduce the heat to low, and simmer for 10 minutes, or until the onion is softened.

5. Add the soy milk and season with salt and pepper. Warm briefly, then remove the pot from the heat.

6. Taste the soup and adjust the seasonings as desired.

continues →

SUPER SOUPS AND STEWS   43

Vegan Tomato Bisque *continued*

7. Transfer the soup in batches to a blender and pulse until the soup is smooth and creamy. Pulse only a few times if you want the soup to have a chunkier texture.

8. Transfer the pureed soup to a large bowl as you process the batches. Serve.

....

Storage: Store leftover soup in an airtight container in the refrigerator for up to 1 week or freeze for up to 3 months.

....

Substitute: If you include dairy in your lifestyle, substitute cow's milk for the soy milk in this recipe. Other plant milk varieties also work; just make sure they're unsweetened and plain (not vanilla flavored).

PER SERVING: Calories: 214; Total fat: 9g; Carbohydrates: 30g; Fiber: 5g; Protein: 7g; Calcium: 194mg; Vitamin D: 1mcg; Vitamin B$_{12}$: 1µg; Iron: 5mg; Zinc: 1mg

Creamy Carrot-Ginger Soup

MAKES 4 SERVINGS · PREP TIME: 15 MINUTES · COOK TIME: 30 MINUTES

DORM-FRIENDLY | GREAT FOR SHARING | MAKES LEFTOVERS | ONE POT

2 tablespoons grapeseed oil, or more as needed

1 small onion, diced

3 cups diced carrots

1 small sweet potato, peeled and diced

1 (1½-inch) piece of fresh ginger, peeled and grated

3 garlic cloves, chopped

1 teaspoon ground turmeric (optional)

2 cups vegetable broth

1 (13.6-ounce) can unsweetened coconut milk

Kosher salt

Freshly ground black pepper

This creamy carrot soup is a rich source of beta-carotene, which is the plant-based precursor to vitamin A. Beta-carotene is found in many orange-colored plants, including carrots and sweet potatoes. Eat this delicious soup to promote a robust immune system and healthy skin and eyes. It's light enough to serve as a side dish, but you can also add a can of chickpeas (drain and rinse them first) to make this soup into a main dish.

1. Heat the 2 tablespoons oil in a 12-quart stockpot over medium heat. Once the oil is shiny, add the onion and cook for 4 minutes, stirring often, or until the onion is translucent.

2. Add the carrots, sweet potato, ginger, garlic, and turmeric (if using), then cook for 10 minutes.

3. Add more oil or adjust the heat if the vegetables are sticking to the pan or starting to burn.

4. Add the broth and coconut milk. Bring the soup to a boil, reduce the heat to low, and cook for 10 minutes, or until the carrots and sweet potato are tender.

continues →

5. Season with salt and pepper to taste. Remove the soup from the heat.

6. Transfer the soup in batches to a blender and blend for 30 seconds or until the soup is smooth and creamy. Transfer the pureed soup to a large bowl as you process the batches. Serve.

Storage: Store leftover soup in an airtight container and refrigerate for up to 1 week or freeze for up to 3 months.

Tip: You can make the soup prep easier by swapping in frozen chopped carrots for the fresh ones in this recipe. Canned carrots are another option if you'd like to do less chopping.

PER SERVING: Calories: 337; Total fat: 28g; Carbohydrates: 23g; Fiber: 4g; Protein: 4g; Calcium: 68mg; Vitamin D: 0mcg; Vitamin B_{12}: 0µg; Iron: 4mg; Zinc: 1mg

Pinto Bean and Tortilla Soup

MAKES 6 SERVINGS · PREP TIME: 10 MINUTES · COOK TIME: 25 MINUTES

2 tablespoons grapeseed oil, or more as needed

1 small white onion, diced

2 medium carrots, diced

1 or 2 jalapeño peppers, chopped (remove seeds, if desired)

3 garlic cloves, chopped

1 tablespoon ground cumin

1 tablespoon chili powder

Kosher salt

1 (28-ounce) can crushed tomatoes

4 cups vegetable broth

6 (5-inch) corn tortillas, cut into 1-inch pieces

2 (15-ounce) cans pinto beans, drained and rinsed

This blended soup incorporates Mexican-inspired flavors and blended corn tortillas for a thick and hearty texture that's sure to leave you feeling satisfied. The recipe yield is large enough to share with friends and study buddies. Try serving this plant-based soup with an array of taco toppings to make it more party-worthy. Some of my favorite toppings for this soup are avocado slices or guacamole, salsa, cilantro, scallions, and sliced jalapeño peppers. It also tastes great topped with crunchy tortilla chips.

1. Heat the 2 tablespoons oil in a 12-quart stockpot over medium heat. Once the oil is shiny, add the onion and cook for 4 minutes, stirring often, or until the onion is translucent.

2. Add the carrots, jalapeños, garlic, cumin, and chili powder. Season to taste with salt and cook for an additional 5 minutes. Add more oil if needed to prevent sticking.

3. Add the tomatoes and broth and increase the heat to high. Bring the soup to a boil, reduce the heat to low, and add the tortillas. Simmer the soup for 10 minutes.

continues →

Pinto Bean and Tortilla Soup *continued*

4. Transfer the soup in batches to a blender and blend for 30 seconds or until the soup is smooth and creamy. Transfer the soup to a large bowl as you process the batches.

5. Add the pinto beans. Serve.

....

Storage: Store leftover soup in an airtight container in the refrigerator for up to 1 week.

....

Protein swaps: If you want to switch out the pinto beans, canned black beans make an ideal substitute. You can also use cooked tofu, tempeh, or lentils to round out this dish with a good source of plant-based protein.

PER SERVING: Calories: 304; Total fat: 7g; Carbohydrates: 54g; Fiber: 13g; Protein: 12g; Calcium: 136mg; Vitamin D: 0mcg; Vitamin B$_{12}$: 0µg; Iron: 6mg; Zinc: 2mg

No-Chicken Tofu Noodle Soup

MAKES 4 SERVINGS • PREP TIME: 10 MINUTES • COOK TIME: 20 MINUTES

GREAT FOR SHARING | ONE POT

2 tablespoons
   grapeseed oil
1 small onion, diced
1 large carrot, diced
2 celery stalks, diced
4 garlic cloves, chopped
1 tablespoon dried thyme
1 (14-ounce) block
   extra-firm tofu, drained,
   pressed (see Tip,
   page 50), and chopped
4 cups vegetable broth
2 ounces dried whole
   wheat spaghetti (or
   other pasta of choice)
1 cup water (optional)
⅓ cup chopped fresh
   parsley (optional)
Kosher salt
Freshly ground
   black pepper

This vegetarian take on chicken noodle soup is made with protein-rich tofu. If you're making this soup ahead of time, you may want to cook and store the pasta separately from the rest of the soup. This prevents the noodles from absorbing all the soup broth while sitting in the refrigerator.

1. Heat the oil in a 12-quart stockpot over medium heat. Once the oil is shiny, add the onion, carrot, and celery, and cook for 5 minutes, or until the onion is translucent.

2. Add the garlic and thyme and cook for an additional 1 minute.

3. Add the chopped tofu and vegetable broth. Increase the heat to high, cover, and bring to a boil. Add the spaghetti and cook for 8 minutes, or until al dente.

4. If there's not enough liquid, pour in the water as needed.

5. Add the parsley (if using) and season with salt and pepper to taste. Serve.

continues →

No-Chicken Tofu Noodle Soup *continued*

Storage: Store leftover soup in an airtight container in the refrigerator for up to 1 week. Add more water before reheating if there isn't enough broth.

Tip: To prepare a block of tofu, drain the liquid, wrap it in a towel, and press it by placing something heavy (such as a cast iron skillet) on top for at least 30 minutes.

Protein swaps: Substitute 2 cups cooked chickpeas or cannellini beans for the tofu, if desired. You can also substitute dried lentils for a budget-friendly option. If you use lentils, boil them for about 8 minutes before adding the pasta to the pot.

PER SERVING: Calories: 232; Total fat: 13g; Carbohydrates: 20g; Fiber: 3g; Protein: 12g; Calcium: 201mg; Vitamin D: 0mcg; Vitamin B_{12}: 0µg; Iron: 3mg; Zinc: 2mg

Mushroom French Onion Soup

MAKES 2 SERVINGS · PREP TIME: 10 MINUTES · COOK TIME: 20 MINUTES

DORM-FRIENDLY | ONE POT

1 tablespoon olive oil

1 tablespoon unsalted butter

1 cup thinly sliced onion (1 medium)

1 cup sliced fresh mushrooms

3 cups mushroom or vegetable broth

2 teaspoons dried thyme

Kosher salt

Freshly ground black pepper

2 slices provolone cheese

2 slices whole-grain bread

Substitute: If you don't have any bread, substitute with croutons or skip the bread altogether. Instead of provolone cheese, try Swiss or Gruyère. Top the bread with nut cheese or nutritional yeast to make this recipe dairy-free.

This quick and easy soup is the ideal romantic starter for your next date night. Any type of mushroom will work, including baby bella and larger portobello caps. Toasted bread topped with provolone finishes off this classic soup, but it's okay to skip this step if you don't have access to a toaster oven or broiler to melt the cheese.

1. Heat the oil and butter in an 8-quart stockpot over medium-low heat. Once the butter is melted, add the onion and cook gently, stirring occasionally, for 5 minutes, or until translucent.

2. Add the mushrooms and cook for an additional 3 minutes.

3. Add the broth and thyme, and season with salt and pepper.

4. Increase the heat to high and bring the soup to a boil. Once the soup is boiling, reduce the heat to low and simmer for 5 minutes.

5. Place a slice of provolone on top of each piece of bread and toast in a toaster oven or under the oven broiler until the cheese is melted.

6. Divide the soup between 2 bowls and place a piece of toasted bread on top of each. Serve immediately.

PER SERVING: Calories: 361; Total fat: 26g; Carbohydrates: 21g; Fiber: 3g; Protein: 12g; Calcium: 253mg; Vitamin D: 0mcg; Vitamin B$_{12}$: 0µg; Iron: 1mg; Zinc: 2mg

Vegan Corn Chowder

MAKES 4 SERVINGS · PREP TIME: 10 MINUTES · COOK TIME: 20 MINUTES

DORM-FRIENDLY | GREAT FOR SHARING | MAKES LEFTOVERS | ONE POT

2 tablespoons
    grapeseed oil
½ cup diced red onion
3 cups frozen corn kernels
1 red bell pepper, cored,
    seeded, and diced
2 jalapeño peppers, seeded
    and diced (optional)
1 tablespoon ground cumin
1 tablespoon chili powder
4 cups plain unsweetened
    soy milk (or plain
    unsweetened milk
    of choice)
2 cups cooked black beans
    (or 2 [15-ounce] cans,
    drained and rinsed)
Kosher salt

Tip: If you include dairy in your lifestyle, substitute cow's milk for the soy milk in this recipe. Other plant milk varieties also work; just make sure they're unsweetened and plain (not vanilla flavored).

Frozen corn and simple spices make this soup convenient for days when you have to create something out of pantry staples. Chowders are typically made with milk or cream, but this plant-based version uses soy milk instead. Creamy Oat Milk (page 210) would also be delicious in this recipe. Serve this hearty dish with avocado, sliced jalapeño, fresh cilantro, and/or tortilla chips, if you have them.

1. Heat the oil in a 12-quart stockpot over medium heat. Once the oil is shiny, add the onion and cook for 4 minutes, stirring often, or until the onion is translucent.

2. Add the corn, bell pepper, jalapeño (if using), cumin, and chili powder. Cook for 5 minutes, or until the corn is thawed. Add the soy milk and increase the heat to high. Once the mixture is boiling, reduce the heat to low and simmer for 10 minutes.

3. Transfer the soup in batches to a blender and blend for 30 seconds or until the soup is smooth and creamy. Transfer the blended soup to a large bowl and add the black beans. Season to taste with salt. Serve.

Storage: Store leftover soup in an airtight container in the refrigerator for up to 1 week or freeze for up to 3 months.

PER SERVING: Calories: 431; Total fat: 13g; Carbohydrates: 67g; Fiber: 13g; Protein: 19g; Calcium: 344mg; Vitamin D: 3mcg; Vitamin B$_{12}$: 2µg; Iron: 5mg; Zinc: 3mg

High-Protein Lentil Soup

MAKES 4 SERVINGS · PREP TIME: 10 MINUTES · COOK TIME: 25 MINUTES

DORM-FRIENDLY | GREAT FOR SHARING | MAKES LEFTOVERS | ONE POT

2 tablespoons grapeseed oil

1 small onion, diced (½ cup)

1 large carrot, diced (1 cup)

2 celery stalks, diced (1 cup)

½ teaspoon kosher salt

¼ teaspoon freshly ground black pepper

3 garlic cloves, chopped

1 tablespoon ground cumin

2 cups dried lentils

1 (28-ounce) can crushed tomatoes

4 cups vegetable broth

2 cups water, or more as needed

Protein swaps:
If you want to switch things up, try making this soup with green or yellow split peas. Like lentils, dried peas belong to the legume family, which is a sustainable source of plant-based protein.

Lentils are an affordable source of plant-based protein and they make soups heartier and more satisfying. This soup is loaded with the nutrient-dense pulses to provide long-lasting energy for your busiest days. The carbohydrates and protein in lentils also help your body recover after a tough workout. Keep a portioned batch in your freezer, so you always have the option to reheat a bowl after the gym.

1. Heat the oil in a 12-quart stockpot over medium heat. Once the oil is shiny, add the onion, carrot, celery, salt, and pepper and cook for 5 minutes or until the onion is translucent. Add the garlic and cumin and cook for an additional 1 minute.

2. Add the lentils, tomatoes, broth, and 2 cups water. Cover the pot and increase the heat to high. Once the mixture is boiling, reduce the heat to medium-low and simmer for 15 minutes, or until the lentils are softened. Add an additional cup of water as needed if you want the soup to be thinner.

3. Adjust the salt and pepper to taste. Serve.

Storage: Store leftover soup in an airtight container in the refrigerator for up to 1 week or freeze for up to 3 months. You may need to add more water before reheating the soup.

PER SERVING: Calories: 510; Total fat: 9g; Carbohydrates: 87g; Fiber: 15g; Protein: 28g; Calcium: 101mg; Vitamin D: 0mcg; Vitamin B_{12}: 0µg; Iron: 11mg; Zinc: 4mg

Broccoli Cheese Soup with Croutons

MAKES 4 SERVINGS · PREP TIME: 20 MINUTES · COOK TIME: 30 MINUTES

GREAT FOR SHARING | MAKES LEFTOVERS

FOR THE CROUTONS

2 cups torn leftover bread, in 2-inch pieces
1 tablespoon olive oil
1 teaspoon dried thyme
Kosher salt
Freshly ground black pepper

FOR THE SOUP

2 tablespoons unsalted butter
1 small onion, diced (½ cup)
1 large carrot, diced (1 cup)
4 garlic cloves, chopped
1 tablespoon dried thyme
¼ cup all-purpose flour
2 cups vegetable broth
2 cups milk
2 cups chopped broccoli florets
8 ounces cheddar cheese, freshly grated (about 2 cups)

Broccoli cheese soup is a comforting classic to make for lunch or as a starter for a dinner with friends. (Who doesn't love broccoli and cheddar cheese?) This rich and creamy soup is delicious all on its own, but I like it even better topped with homemade croutons. The croutons only take 15 minutes to bake, and they're a convenient way to use up old bread. Opt for a whole-grain loaf if you want to maximize the fiber content of this dish.

1. **To make the croutons:** Preheat the oven to 375°F.

2. In a medium bowl, toss together the bread, olive oil, and thyme. Season with salt and pepper to taste and spread the bread cubes on an unlined baking sheet. Bake for 15 minutes or until golden. Remove from the oven and set aside to cool.

3. **To make the soup:** Heat the butter in a 12-quart stockpot over medium heat. Once the butter is melted, add the onion and carrot and cook for 5 minutes or until the onion is translucent. Add the garlic and thyme and cook for an additional 1 minute.

4. Add the flour and cook for 3 minutes, stirring often. Add the broth, milk, and broccoli and increase the heat to high. Once the mixture is boiling, reduce the heat to low and simmer for 5 minutes or until the broccoli is softened.

5. Add the cheese and simmer until it is melted. Divide the soup among 4 bowls and top each bowl with a few croutons.

Storage: Store leftover soup in an airtight container in the refrigerator for up to 1 week or freeze for up to 3 months. Leftover croutons can be stored in an airtight container at room temperature for 3 days.

Tip: Packaged shredded cheese usually contains an ingredient to prevent it from sticking together. Because of this, commercially shredded cheese may not mix into the soup as well as freshly grated. If you don't mind the texture change, use it here to make preparation easier.

PER SERVING: Calories: 513; Total fat: 33g; Carbohydrates: 32g; Fiber: 2g; Protein: 23g; Calcium: 592mg; Vitamin D: 1mcg; Vitamin B_{12}: 1μg; Iron: 2mg; Zinc: 3mg

Irish-Inspired Potato Stew

MAKES 4 SERVINGS • PREP TIME: 10 MINUTES • COOK TIME: 55 MINUTES

DORM-FRIENDLY | GREAT FOR SHARING | MAKES LEFTOVERS | ONE POT

2 tablespoons grapeseed
    oil, or more as needed

1 medium onion, diced

4 cups peeled and chopped
    potatoes

2 cups diced carrots

3 garlic cloves, chopped

1 tablespoon dried thyme

4 cups vegetable broth

1 cup dried split
    peas, rinsed

Kosher salt

Freshly ground
    black pepper

4 scallions, both white and
    green parts, chopped

Storage: Store leftover stew in an airtight container in the refrigerator for up to 1 week or freeze for up to 3 months.

Potato stew is hearty and comforting. It's a great dish to make for dinner on a cold, wintry day. Traditional Irish stew includes meat (often lamb), but this vegan version uses protein-packed split peas instead. Be sure to buy split peas, since they cook more quickly than whole dried peas.

1. Heat the 2 tablespoons oil in a 12-quart stockpot over medium heat. Once the oil is shiny, add the onion and cook for 4 minutes, stirring often, or until the onion is translucent.

2. Add the potatoes, carrots, garlic, and thyme and cook for 10 minutes, stirring occasionally, and adding more oil as needed to prevent sticking.

3. Add the broth and dried peas, cover, and increase the heat to high. Cook until the peas are softened, about 35 minutes. Season the stew to taste with salt and pepper. Transfer the stew to bowls and garnish with the scallions.

Make it easier: Swap in canned beans or canned lentils for the split peas. Since canned beans and lentils are already cooked, you can save about 30 minutes when you use them in this recipe.

PER SERVING: Calories: 404; Total fat: 8g; Carbohydrates: 70g; Fiber: 18g; Protein: 16g; Calcium: 78mg; Vitamin D: 0mcg; Vitamin B_{12}: 0µg; Iron: 4mg; Zinc: 3mg

Vegan Gumbo

MAKES 2 SERVINGS · PREP TIME: 10 MINUTES · COOK TIME: 20 MINUTES

DORM-FRIENDLY | ONE POT

2 tablespoons
grapeseed oil
½ medium onion,
diced (1 cup)
1 cup diced celery
1 green bell pepper, cored,
seeded, and diced
1 tablespoon Cajun
seasoning
3 cups vegetable broth
1 (15-ounce) can red
kidney beans, drained
and rinsed
1 cup chopped fresh
collard greens

Sautéing a mix of green pepper, onion, and celery, which is known as the "holy trinity" in Cajun cooking, is the first step in making a New Orleans–style gumbo. This hearty stew originated in Louisiana and traditionally included meat and shellfish. My vegetarian version incorporates red kidney beans as the protein. Garnish with scallions or parsley and serve it with cooked brown rice to make it even more satisfying.

1. Heat the oil in a 12-quart stockpot over medium heat. Once the oil is shiny, add the onion, celery, and green pepper and cook for 5 minutes or until the onion is translucent.

2. Add the Cajun seasoning and cook for an additional 1 minute.

3. Add the broth, kidney beans, and collard greens. Bring the soup to a simmer and cook for 10 minutes.

Storage: Store leftover soup in an airtight container in the refrigerator for up to 1 week or freeze for up to 3 months.

Protein swaps: Instead of kidney beans, substitute tofu, tempeh, or cannellini beans. You can also use sliced plant-based sausages if you happen to have them on hand.

PER SERVING: Calories: 357; Total fat: 15g; Carbohydrates: 45g; Fiber: 13g; Protein: 13g; Calcium: 111mg; Vitamin D: 0mcg; Vitamin B$_{12}$: 0µg; Iron: 5mg; Zinc: 2mg

Pumpkin and Black Bean Chili

MAKES 4 SERVINGS · PREP TIME: 10 MINUTES · COOK TIME: 20 MINUTES

DORM-FRIENDLY | GREAT FOR SHARING | MAKES LEFTOVERS | ONE POT

2 tablespoons grapeseed oil, or more as needed

1 small onion, diced

1 large carrot, diced

1 cup frozen corn kernels

2 tablespoons chili powder

1 tablespoon ground cumin

½ teaspoon kosher salt

¼ teaspoon freshly ground black pepper

1 (28-ounce) can crushed tomatoes

1 (15-ounce) can pumpkin puree

1 cup vegetable broth

2 (15-ounce) cans black beans, drained and rinsed

2½ cups chopped fresh kale (1 pound)

Having a few friends over for the game? Bean chili makes the ideal meal to serve at a tailgating party. Even if you're not usually a fan of pumpkin, give this chili a try. The canned squash puree acts as a thickener (not a flavor enhancer). This recipe is also great for meal prep since you can batch-cook chili ahead of time and store it in the freezer for up to 3 months.

1. Heat the 2 tablespoons oil in a 12-quart stockpot over medium heat. Once the oil is shiny, add the onion and cook for 4 minutes, stirring often, or until the onion is translucent.

2. Add the carrot, corn, chili powder, cumin, and salt and pepper and cook for 5 minutes. Add more oil as needed to prevent sticking.

3. Add the crushed tomatoes, pumpkin puree, vegetable broth, black beans, and chopped kale and cook for 10 minutes, or until the chili is hot and the carrot is softened. Serve.

Storage: Store leftover chili in an airtight container in the refrigerator for up to 1 week or freeze for up to 3 months.

Tip: Instead of black beans, try substituting kidney beans, pinto beans, lentils, or tempeh. If you can't find canned pumpkin, substitute 2 cups mashed sweet potatoes or pureed butternut squash.

PER SERVING: Calories: 429; Total fat: 11g; Carbohydrates: 72g; Fiber: 26g; Protein: 21g; Calcium: 337mg; Vitamin D: 0mcg; Vitamin B$_{12}$: 0µg; Iron: 9mg; Zinc: 3mg

Peanut Stew

MAKES 2 SERVINGS · PREP TIME: 10 MINUTES · COOK TIME: 25 MINUTES

ONE POT

1 tablespoon grapeseed oil

1 small onion, diced

1 medium sweet potato, peeled and chopped (1¼ cups)

1 (1-inch) piece of fresh ginger, peeled and grated

2 garlic cloves, chopped

¼ teaspoon cayenne (optional)

2 cups vegetable broth

2 tablespoons tomato paste

⅓ cup peanut butter

½ cup chopped fresh collard greens or kale

Peanut soups are a staple of West and Central African cuisines. In Ghana, peanut stew is often served with fufu, a dumpling-like food made from plantains, yams, and other starchy vegetables. This recipe is a simplified version that incorporates easy-to-find sweet potatoes for starch. Garnish this one-pot stew with cilantro and chopped peanuts, and serve it with cooked brown rice to make it a date night–worthy dinner.

1. Heat the oil in a 12-quart stockpot, Dutch oven, or deep skillet over medium heat. Add the onion, sweet potato, ginger, garlic, and cayenne (if using), and cook for 5 minutes or until the onion is translucent.

2. Add the broth, tomato paste, and peanut butter and bring to a simmer.

3. Add the collard greens or kale and simmer for 15 minutes, or until the sweet potato is softened. Serve.

Storage: Store leftover soup in an airtight container in the refrigerator for up to 1 week or freeze for up to 3 months.

Tip: If you have a peanut allergy, try making this stew with sunflower seed butter. Add canned beans or cooked tofu if you want to bump up the protein.

PER SERVING: Calories: 418; Total fat: 29g; Carbohydrates: 34g; Fiber: 6g; Protein: 12g; Calcium: 81mg; Vitamin D: 0mcg; Vitamin B$_{12}$: 0µg; Iron: 2mg; Zinc: 1mg

**Mushroom
Cheesesteaks,**
page 84

Chapter Four

Wraps and Sandos

Sandwiches and wraps are a lunchtime staple for a good reason. They're packable, easy to make in advance, and you can bite into them while you're on the move or in the middle of studying. Most traditional sandwich recipes incorporate meat, but there's a wide world of vegetarian options, too. Whether it's from Greek yogurt, beans, eggs, tofu, lentils, or tempeh, these sandos incorporate plant-based protein to help you feel nourished and satisfied.

Green Goddess Cucumber-Avocado Sandwiches 62

Cranberry and Chickpea Salad Sandwiches 63

Spicy Peanut-Tofu Lettuce Wraps 64

Curried Egg Salad Sandwiches 65

Smoky Lentil and Portobello Mushroom Wraps 66

Lemon Basil and Smashed White Bean Sandwiches 68

Loaded Carrot Dogs 69

Mediterranean Falafel Pitas 71

Roasted Sweet Potato and Hummus Sandwiches 73

Vegan Banh Mi Sandwiches 74

Chickpea and Coconut Curry Wraps 76

Crispy Eggplant BLTs 77

Vegan Sushi Burritos 78

Veggie and White Bean Pesto Melt 79

Chili-Lime Tempeh Burritos 80

Freezer-Friendly Bean Burgers 81

Lentil Sloppy Joes 83

Mushroom Cheesesteaks 84

Tempeh Reubens 85

Buffalo Tofu Sandwiches 87

Green Goddess Cucumber-Avocado Sandwiches

MAKES 2 SANDWICHES • PREP TIME: 5 MINUTES

DORM-FRIENDLY | NO COOKING REQUIRED

½ cup plain Greek yogurt

1 medium avocado, peeled, pitted, and mashed

¾ cup chopped fresh parsley

2 tablespoons fresh lemon juice

1 garlic clove, minced

¼ teaspoon kosher salt

⅛ teaspoon freshly ground black pepper

4 slices whole-grain bread

½ English cucumber, peeled and sliced

½ cup fresh baby spinach

Green goddess dressing was conceived in honor of a play by William Archer called *The Green Goddess.* The original recipe blended herbs, spinach, and egg yolks. Today, the dressing is enjoyed in a variety of forms, but almost always features fresh greens and herbs. This take on green goddess is a thick and creamy sandwich spread made with satisfying protein from Greek yogurt and healthy fats from avocado. You can also enjoy this spread as a dip with raw carrots, cucumbers, bell pepper strips, or crackers.

1. Put the yogurt, avocado, parsley, lemon juice, garlic, salt, and pepper in a food processor and process for 1 minute, or until creamy, pausing to scrape down the sides with a spatula as needed.

2. Spread the yogurt mixture on each slice of bread. Divide the cucumber slices and spinach between 2 slices of bread. Place the other slices, spread-side down, on top of the vegetables. Cut the sandwiches in half, if desired. Serve.

Mix it up: Instead of parsley, make this sandwich spread with a mix of fresh basil and spinach to change the flavors. For a South of the Border twist, use fresh cilantro and lime juice.

PER SERVING (1 SANDWICH): Calories: 373; Total fat: 20g; Carbohydrates: 41g; Fiber: 13g; Protein: 14g; Calcium: 185mg; Vitamin D: 0mcg; Vitamin B$_{12}$: 0µg; Iron: 3mg; Zinc: 2mg

Cranberry and Chickpea Salad Sandwiches

MAKES 2 SANDWICHES · PREP TIME: 10 MINUTES

DORM-FRIENDLY | MAKE AHEAD | NO COOKING REQUIRED

1 (15-ounce) can chickpeas, drained and rinsed

⅓ cup plain Greek yogurt

⅓ cup dried cranberries

¼ cup fresh basil leaves, torn (or 1 tablespoon dried)

1 tablespoon apple cider vinegar

¼ teaspoon kosher salt

⅛ teaspoon freshly ground black pepper

4 slices whole-grain bread, toasted if desired

These make-ahead chickpea salad sandwiches are a favorite I've been making for years. I love that they're made with protein-packed chickpeas instead of poultry. They're easy to prep ahead of time, and you can pack one into your bag to eat between classes. I often add lettuce, sliced tomato, onion, or microgreens to give these sandwiches even more flavor and texture. Another choice for serving is to use a large tortilla (I like the spinach flavor) instead of bread, thereby making a wrap.

1. In a small bowl, stir together the chickpeas and yogurt. Use a fork or potato masher to mash the chickpeas slightly.

2. Add the cranberries, basil, vinegar, salt, and pepper, and stir to mix thoroughly.

3. Spread the chickpea mixture on 2 slices of bread.

4. Top with the remaining bread slices. Serve.

Mix it up: Use raisins instead of cranberries and add 1 tablespoon of curry powder to give these sandwiches a new flavor profile. You can also use fresh cilantro or mint instead of basil.

PER SERVING (1 SANDWICH): Calories: 427; Total fat: 7g; Carbohydrates: 75g; Fiber: 14g; Protein: 19g; Calcium: 166mg; Vitamin D: 0mcg; Vitamin B_{12}: 0μg; Iron: 5mg; Zinc: 3mg

Spicy Peanut-Tofu Lettuce Wraps

MAKES 2 WRAPS · PREP TIME: 5 MINUTES · COOK TIME: 10 MINUTES

DORM-FRIENDLY | ONE PAN

1 tablespoon coconut oil
  (or grapeseed oil)
½ (14-ounce) block
  extra-firm tofu, drained,
  pressed (see Tip,
  page 50), and cubed
¼ teaspoon kosher salt
½ cup cooked brown rice
1½ cups Spicy Peanut
  Sauce (page 215) or
  store-bought sauce
2 large romaine
  lettuce leaves
¼ cup chopped fresh
  cilantro
Chopped peanuts
  (optional)

....

Protein swaps: If
you want to avoid cooking
the tofu, try swapping in
shelled edamame, which you
can steam in the microwave
before mixing with the brown
rice and spicy peanut sauce.
This is an excellent option if
you don't have a stovetop or
hot plate.

Inspired by Thai cuisine, these wraps are made with crispy tofu for protein and brown rice for fiber. Don't worry if it seems like the tofu is sticking to the bottom of the pan at first. This means it's not ready to be stirred or flipped just yet. Once the bottom is thoroughly cooked, the tofu will easily separate from the pan.

1. Heat the coconut oil in a large skillet over medium heat. Once melted, arrange the tofu in a single layer in the skillet, sprinkle with the salt, and cook for 5 minutes, or until the bottom of the tofu is golden brown and easily separates from the pan.

2. Flip the tofu and cook for 3 minutes more, or until the other side is golden brown and easily separates from the pan. Transfer to a large bowl.

3. Add the brown rice and spicy peanut sauce to the bowl. Then, divide the tofu mixture between the lettuce leaves. Add the cilantro and peanuts (if using). Serve immediately.

....

Tip: To cook perfect brown rice, bring 6 cups of water and a dash of kosher salt to a boil over high heat in a large saucepan and add 1 cup rinsed brown rice. Reduce to medium-low and boil, uncovered, for 30 minutes. Drain, cover, and set aside for 10 to 15 minutes. This makes about 4 cups cooked rice.

PER SERVING (1 WRAP): Calories: 532; Total fat: 35g; Carbohydrates: 30g; Fiber: 4g; Protein: 29g; Calcium: 389mg; Vitamin D: 0mcg; Vitamin B$_{12}$: 0µg; Iron: 4mg; Zinc: 4mg

Curried Egg Salad Sandwiches

MAKES 2 SANDWICHES · PREP TIME: 10 MINUTES

DORM-FRIENDLY | MAKE-AHEAD | ONE BOWL | NO COOKING REQUIRED

4 large hard-boiled eggs, chopped

½ cup plain Greek yogurt

3 scallions, both white and green parts, chopped

1 celery stalk, diced

1 tablespoon grainy mustard

2 teaspoons curry powder

¼ teaspoon kosher salt

¼ teaspoon freshly ground black pepper

4 slices whole-grain bread

Tip: To make perfect hard-boiled eggs, place a medium saucepan filled three-fourths full of lightly salted water on high heat and bring to a boil. Gently lower the eggs into it, reduce heat to keep a medium boil, and cook for 7 minutes (for a soft center) or 8 minutes (for a harder center). As soon as they're done, transfer eggs to ice water to get them to stop cooking.

Hard-boiled eggs are a convenient and budget-friendly source of B vitamins, essential minerals, and protein. You can sometimes find hard-boiled eggs in the refrigerated section of the supermarket, which can make this recipe quick and easy to prepare. For the most affordable option, boil the eggs yourself on the stovetop; the process only takes about 7 minutes (see Tip). Serve this salad on whole-grain bread with lettuce, tomato, onion, or any of your favorite sandwich toppings.

1. In a medium bowl, mix the eggs, yogurt, scallions, celery, mustard, curry powder, salt, and pepper until well combined.

2. Spread the egg salad on 2 slices of bread and top with the remaining slices of bread. Cut the sandwiches in half, if desired. Serve.

Protein swap: Use cubed tofu, chickpeas, or white beans to make this recipe egg-free. For a vegan variation, use one of these plant-based protein sources along with plain dairy-free yogurt.

PER SERVING: Calories: 338; Total fat: 14g; Carbohydrates: 30g; Fiber: 6g; Protein: 23g; Calcium: 219mg; Vitamin D: 2mcg; Vitamin B_{12}: 1µg; Iron: 4mg; Zinc: 3mg

Smoky Lentil and Portobello Mushroom Wraps

MAKES 2 WRAPS · PREP TIME: 5 MINUTES · COOK TIME: 10 MINUTES

DORM-FRIENDLY | ONE PAN

¼ cup grapeseed oil, plus
some to coat skillet

1 tablespoon tahini

1 tablespoon apple
cider vinegar

2 teaspoons
smoked paprika

1 teaspoon ground cumin

¼ teaspoon cayenne
(optional)

¼ teaspoon kosher salt

2 fresh portobello
mushroom caps, cut into
2-inch pieces

1 cup cooked lentils

2 leaves fresh kale, thick
stems cut out and leafy
parts chopped

2 large corn tortillas

The smoked paprika gives the portobello mushrooms plenty of smoky flavor, while the lentils bump up the fiber and protein in this tasty lunch. Lentils come in a few different colors, including red, brown, green, and yellow; any type works for this recipe. To save time, prep the lentils in advance or opt for canned, frozen, or microwavable packages.

1. In a large bowl, whisk together the ¼ cup oil, the tahini, vinegar, smoked paprika, cumin, cayenne (if using), and salt.

2. Add the mushrooms and toss with your hands until they're evenly coated with the sauce.

3. Pour a little oil into a large skillet and preheat it over medium heat.

4. Transfer the mushrooms to the skillet and cook for 5 minutes, stirring occasionally, or until the mushrooms soften and darken in color. Add a little more oil as needed to prevent the mushrooms from sticking.

5. Add the lentils and kale and cook for 3 minutes, or until the kale is wilted.

6. Wrap the tortillas in a paper towel or a clean cloth and microwave on high for 20 seconds. Lay the tortillas on a clean work surface and spread the mushroom mixture on them. Fold up the sides and then roll up each tortilla to form a wrap. Serve immediately.

Substitute: Tahini is a ground sesame seed paste that's often found either near the peanut butter or in the Middle Eastern section of the grocery store. If you can't find it, substitute creamy peanut butter or almond butter (see Lemon Tahini recipe, page 214).

PER SERVING: Calories: 608; Total fat: 36g; Carbohydrates: 58g; Fiber: 14g; Protein: 19g; Calcium: 232mg; Vitamin D: 0mcg; Vitamin B_{12}: 0µg; Iron: 8mg; Zinc: 3mg

Lemon Basil and Smashed White Bean Sandwiches

MAKES 2 SANDWICHES · PREP TIME: 10 MINUTES

DORM-FRIENDLY | MAKE AHEAD | NO COOKING REQUIRED

1 (15-ounce) can cannellini beans, drained and rinsed

⅓ cup fresh basil leaves

2 garlic cloves, minced

2 tablespoons fresh lemon juice

1 tablespoon olive oil, or more as needed

¼ teaspoon kosher salt

⅛ teaspoon freshly ground black pepper

4 slices whole-grain bread

½ cup fresh baby spinach or torn lettuce

½ ripe medium tomato, sliced

Cannellini beans are also known as white kidney beans. They're available canned or dried in most grocery stores. The smooth, buttery texture of cannellini beans makes them ideal for pureeing into a protein-packed sandwich spread. To save time, I like to make the bean spread in a food processor, but you can also mash the beans with the back of a fork and finely chop the basil and garlic by hand.

1. Put the cannellini beans, basil, garlic, lemon juice, 1 tablespoon olive oil, salt, and pepper in a food processor. Process until smooth, pausing to scrape down the sides with a spatula as needed. If it isn't mixing, gradually add more oil and process again.

2. Spread the bean mixture on each slice of bread. Divide the spinach or lettuce and the tomato between 2 of the bread slices. Place the other slices of bread, spread-side down, on top of the tomato. Cut the sandwiches in half, if desired. Serve.

Mix it up: There are endless opportunities for changing the flavors of these white bean sandwiches. Instead of fresh basil, try spinach, parsley, or cilantro. You can also add ground spices. Try curry powder, Cajun seasoning, za'atar, or a dash of cayenne.

PER SERVING: Calories: 377; Total fat: 10g; Carbohydrates: 55g; Fiber: 13g; Protein: 19g; Calcium: 110 mg; Vitamin D: 0mcg; Vitamin B$_{12}$: 0µg; Iron: 4mg; Zinc: 2mg

Loaded Carrot Dogs

MAKES 2 SERVINGS · PREP TIME: 10 MINUTES, PLUS 30 MINUTES TO MARINATE
COOK TIME: 20 MINUTES

MAKE AHEAD

Kosher salt

2 medium carrots, peeled and cut to match bun length

2 tablespoons soy sauce

2 tablespoons apple cider vinegar

1 teaspoon smoked paprika

1 teaspoon maple syrup

2 hot dog buns

OPTIONAL FOR SERVING

2 tablespoons ketchup

2 tablespoons mustard

¼ cup diced onion

¼ cup sliced jalapeño pepper

If you're headed to a campus cookout and want a plant-based option that isn't a veggie burger, try vegan carrot dogs. The carrots are marinated in salty soy sauce and smoky paprika to mimic the flavors of pork-based hot dogs. You can boil and marinate the carrots in advance, so you only have to reheat them on a grill or skillet when you're ready to eat them. They're microwavable, too. Wrap the marinated carrots in a damp paper towel and microwave on high for 30 seconds, or until warm.

1. Place a medium saucepan filled three-fourths full of lightly salted water on high heat and bring to a boil. Add the carrots, carefully using tongs, and boil until the vegetables are fork-tender, about 15 minutes.

2. While the carrots are boiling, place the soy sauce, vinegar, smoked paprika, and maple syrup in a sealable medium plastic bag, seal the bag, and shake it until the ingredients are mixed.

3. Add the hot boiled carrots to the bag, seal again, and let the carrots marinate for at least 30 minutes or in the refrigerator overnight.

continues →

Loaded Carrot Dogs *continued*

4. Preheat a grill pan or outdoor grill and grill the carrots until hot and lightly marked with grill marks, rotating every couple of minutes to evenly cook the vegetable.

5. Place the carrots inside the hot dog buns and top with the ketchup, mustard, onion, and jalapeño, if desired.

....

Mix it up: Load up these carrot dogs just like you would a regular hot dog. In addition to the toppings here, you can try topping them with Red Cabbage and Cilantro Slaw (page 93), Pumpkin and Black Bean Chili (page 58), sauerkraut, or relish.

PER SERVING: Calories: 165; Total fat: 2g; Carbohydrates: 31g; Fiber: 3g; Protein: 6g; Calcium: 105mg; Vitamin D: 0mcg; Vitamin B$_{12}$: 0µg; Iron: 2mg; Zinc: 1mg

Mediterranean Falafel Pitas

MAKES 2 PITAS • PREP TIME: 15 MINUTES • COOK TIME: 30 MINUTES

DORM-FRIENDLY

FOR THE FALAFEL

¼ cup grapeseed oil

1 (15-ounce) can chickpeas, drained and rinsed well

½ cup whole wheat flour

½ cup diced red onion

½ cup shredded carrot

1 tablespoon ground cumin

¼ teaspoon kosher salt

⅛ teaspoon freshly ground black pepper

FOR THE PITAS

2 pita flatbreads, 1 inch trimmed off tops of each, warmed if desired

½ cup sliced cucumber

½ cup sliced tomato

½ cup sliced red onion

¼ cup tahini

2 tablespoons fresh lemon juice

Falafel is a staple dish in the Middle East, made from ground fava beans or chickpeas (also known as garbanzo beans). It was created by the Christian Copts of Egypt, who were not allowed to eat meat during holidays. Now it's typically served in a pita with hummus, tahini dip, and fresh and pickled vegetables. Traditional falafel is deep-fried, but it can also be baked or lightly fried in less oil to reduce the fat content. The fava and chickpeas are a great source of fiber and protein to provide long-lasting energy.

1. **To make the falafel:** Preheat the oven to 375°F and pour the oil onto a rimmed baking sheet. Tilt the baking sheet until the surface is evenly coated with the oil.

2. Put the chickpeas, flour, red onion, carrot, cumin, salt, and pepper in a food processor and process for 1 minute or until a thick paste forms.

3. Use your hands to roll the mixture into balls, about 2 tablespoons for each ball, and transfer the balls to the baking sheet, arranging them in a single layer.

continues →

4. Bake the falafels for 30 minutes, carefully flipping them halfway through; be careful because the falafels and oil on the baking sheet are very hot. Let the falafels cool enough to handle, about 15 minutes.

5. **To make the pitas:** Open the pockets of the pita breads and place half the baked falafels into each. Stuff each pita bread with some cucumber, tomato, red onion, tahini, and lemon juice. Serve.

....

Tip: If you don't have access to an oven, try pan-frying the falafels in a skillet. Coat the skillet with about ¼ inch of oil and spread the falafels in a single layer in the pan. Cook until the bottoms turn golden brown and then flip and cook on the other side, about 12 minutes in total.

PER SERVING (1 PITA): Calories: 850; Total fat: 48g; Carbohydrates: 89g; Fiber: 18g; Protein: 24g; Calcium: 274mg; Vitamin D: 0mcg; Vitamin B_{12}: 0µg; Iron: 10mg; Zinc: 5mg

Roasted Sweet Potato and Hummus Sandwiches

MAKES 2 SANDWICHES · PREP TIME: 10 MINUTES · COOK TIME: 15 MINUTES

DORM-FRIENDLY | ONE PAN | TOASTER OVEN

1 small sweet potato, peeled and sliced thinly lengthwise

1 tablespoon grapeseed oil

¼ teaspoon kosher salt

⅛ teaspoon freshly ground black pepper

4 slices whole-grain bread, toasted if desired

½ cup Classic Hummus (page 222) or store-bought hummus

1 small avocado, peeled, pitted, and sliced

½ cup fresh baby spinach

¼ cup fresh basil

Mix it up: Use any type of sandwich spread for this recipe. Instead of hummus, try White Bean Sandwich Spread (page 223) or the yogurt-based Green Goddess spread (see page 62).

With a sweet flavor and starchy texture, sweet potatoes are a stellar way to add flavor, energy, and heartiness to almost any plant-based sandwich. In this sandwich, thinly sliced sweet potato is paired with protein-packed hummus and sliced avocado for a creamy texture and a dose of healthy fats. Try roasting the sweet potato in a toaster oven if you don't have a regular oven.

1. Preheat the oven or a toaster oven to 400°F. Line a baking sheet with parchment.

2. Spread the sweet potato slices in a single layer on the baking sheet, brush the slices with the oil, and sprinkle them with the salt and pepper. Roast the sweet potato for 15 minutes, or until golden and softened. Let the sweet potato slices cool enough to be able to handle, about 15 minutes.

3. Lay the bread slices on a flat surface. Spread 2 tablespoons of hummus on each piece of bread.

4. Evenly lay the sweet potato slices, the avocado, spinach, and basil on 2 of the bread slices.

5. Top with the remaining bread slices, hummus-side down. Cut the sandwiches in half, if desired. Serve.

PER SERVING (1 SANDWICH): Calories: 547; Total fat: 30g; Carbohydrates: 60g; Fiber: 17g; Protein: 15g; Calcium: 131mg; Vitamin D: 0mcg; Vitamin B$_{12}$: 0µg; Iron: 3mg; Zinc: 2mg

Vegan Banh Mi Sandwiches

**MAKES 2 SANDWICHES • PREP TIME: 10 MINUTES,
PLUS 30 MINUTES TO MARINATE • COOK TIME: 10 MINUTES**

DORM-FRIENDLY | MAKE AHEAD | ONE PAN

1 tablespoon grapeseed
oil, plus some to
grease skillet

1 tablespoon soy sauce

1 teaspoon honey or
maple syrup

1 (1-inch) piece of
fresh ginger, grated
(or 1¼ teaspoons
ground ginger)

½ (14-ounce) block
extra-firm tofu, drained,
pressed, and sliced into
4 pieces

2 (6-inch) baguettes,
cut into 4 slices (or
2 sandwich rolls, halved)

1 cup pickled vegetables
(such as pickled carrots
and jalapeños)

¼ cup mayonnaise
(regular or vegan)

¼ cup fresh cilantro

From Hoa Ma, Vietnam, *banh mi* (pronounced BON-MEE) is Vietnamese for "bread." This sandwich was originally reserved for the wealthy, but Vietnamese chefs changed the recipe and started selling it at an affordable price during the 1950s. A banh mi is typically a fusion of airy baguette, pickled vegetables, spices, herbs, and grilled meats. It can easily be made vegetarian by subbing in tofu or portobello mushrooms. Marinate and cook the tofu ahead of time to make assembly of this sandwich a breeze.

1. In a small bowl, whisk together the 1 tablespoon oil, the soy sauce, honey, and ginger and transfer the mixture to a sealable medium plastic or reusable silicone bag.

2. Add the tofu pieces to the bag, seal it, and marinate for at least 30 minutes or in the refrigerator overnight.

3. Lightly oil a skillet and preheat it over medium heat.

4. Arrange the tofu in a single layer in the skillet and cook for 4 minutes, or until the pieces easily separate from the pan. Flip them over and cook for an additional 4 minutes, or until they again easily separate from the pan.

5. Divide the tofu between 2 of the baguette slices and top with the pickled vegetables, mayonnaise, and cilantro. Place the remaining baguette slices on top. Serve.

Tip: Instead of using store-bought pickles, make your own by using a favorite recipe or try Quick Pickled Carrots and Vegetables (page 174).

PER SERVING (1 SANDWICH): Calories: 400; Total fat: 23g; Carbohydrates: 31g; Fiber: 3g; Protein: 17g; Calcium: 287mg; Vitamin D: 0mcg; Vitamin B_{12}: 0µg; Iron: 4mg; Zinc: 2mg

Chickpea and Coconut Curry Wraps

MAKES 2 WRAPS · PREP TIME: 5 MINUTES · COOK TIME: 20 MINUTES

DORM-FRIENDLY | ONE PAN

1 tablespoon grapeseed oil

½ cup diced onion

1 tablespoon curry powder

¼ teaspoon garlic powder

¼ teaspoon ground ginger

¼ teaspoon kosher salt

¼ teaspoon freshly ground
black pepper

2 cups chopped
broccoli florets

1 (15-ounce) can
chickpeas, drained
and rinsed

1 (13.5-ounce) can
unsweetened
coconut milk

2 large flour tortillas

....

Protein swaps:
Instead of chickpeas, try
simmering dried lentils
in the curry sauce for
about 15 minutes, or until
they're tender. Cubed
tofu also works well as a
plant-based protein source
for this recipe.

Coconut curry is a staple vegetarian meal, but it's usually not easy to pack up and eat on the run. This recipe takes care of that problem by wrapping a thick and creamy coconut curry in a tortilla for convenient portability. If the curry is too thin, keep cooking until it thickens.

1. Heat the oil in a large skillet over medium heat. Once the oil is shiny, add the onion and cook for 4 minutes or until translucent.

2. Add the curry powder, garlic powder, ground ginger, salt, and pepper, and cook for 1 minute more.

3. Add the broccoli and chickpeas and cook for 3 minutes, or until the broccoli turns bright green.

4. Add the coconut milk and simmer for 10 minutes or until the curry is thickened.

5. Wrap the tortillas in a paper towel or a clean cloth and microwave them for 20 seconds. Lay them on a clean work surface.

6. Divide the curry between the tortillas, fold up the sides of the tortillas, and roll them up to form the wraps. Serve immediately.

PER SERVING (1 WRAP): Calories: 780; Total fat: 53g; Carbohydrates: 64g; Fiber: 15g; Protein: 21g; Calcium: 199mg; Vitamin D: 0mcg; Vitamin B$_{12}$: 0µg; Iron: 12mg; Zinc: 4mg

Crispy Eggplant BLTs

MAKES 2 SANDWICHES · PREP TIME: 10 MINUTES, PLUS 30 MINUTES SALTING TIME
COOK TIME: 30 MINUTES

DORM-FRIENDLY | ONE PAN | TOASTER OVEN

½ small eggplant, peeled and cut into thin slices (see Tip)

1 to 2 tablespoons kosher salt

1 tablespoon grapeseed oil

1 tablespoon soy sauce

2 teaspoons smoked paprika

2 teaspoons maple syrup

½ teaspoon freshly ground black pepper

¼ cup mayonnaise (regular or vegan)

4 slices whole wheat bread

4 lettuce leaves

1 ripe medium tomato, sliced

Tip: To cut the eggplant, first slice off the stem end and peel. Then cut it in half lengthwise. Slice one of the halves again and use a knife to cut ⅛-inch-thick strips along the flat edge of the eggplant. Save the remaining half for other uses.

Traditionally, BLT sandwiches are made with bacon, lettuce, tomato, and mayonnaise. In this version, eggplant takes the place of the "B" to decrease the saturated fat, to layer on the fiber and antioxidants, and to make this classic sandwich vegetarian. Eggplant retains a lot of water, so don't skip the salting step if you want the "bacon" to be crispy.

1. Place the eggplant slices in a colander and sprinkle generously with the salt. Wait 30 minutes, rinse, and then pat dry.

2. Preheat the oven to 300°F. Line a baking sheet with parchment.

3. In a medium bowl, whisk together the oil, soy sauce, smoked paprika, maple syrup, and black pepper.

4. Add the eggplant slices and toss until evenly coated with the sauce. Arrange the eggplant on the baking sheet in a single layer and bake for 30 minutes or until dry and crispy. Remove the eggplant from the oven and allow to cool for 5 minutes before assembling the sandwiches.

5. Spread the mayonnaise on 2 slices of bread. Arrange the eggplant pieces, lettuce, and tomato on top. Place the remaining bread slices on top and cut the sandwiches in half, if desired. Serve.

PER SERVING: Calories: 385; Total fat: 19g; Carbohydrates: 43g; Fiber: 10g; Protein: 13g; Calcium: 160mg; Vitamin D: 0mcg; Vitamin B$_{12}$: 0µg; Iron: 3mg; Zinc: 2mg

Vegan Sushi Burritos

MAKES 2 BURRITOS · PREP TIME: 10 MINUTES · COOK TIME: 3 MINUTES

DORM-FRIENDLY | MICROWAVABLE | ONE BOWL

**1 cup frozen
  shelled edamame**
**½ cup cooked brown rice
  (see Tip, page 64)**
½ cup shredded carrot
1 tablespoon soy sauce
1 teaspoon ground ginger
1 teaspoon maple syrup
½ teaspoon garlic powder
2 sheets nori seaweed

Sushi burritos are similar to sushi, except the fish and rice are rolled up into a larger burrito shape and served whole, instead of being sliced into bite-size pieces. Just like traditional sushi rolls, sushi burritos can be customized in different ways. Instead of fish, for example, this recipe incorporates edamame, which has a whopping 11 grams of protein in a ½-cup serving. The wrap for this burrito is made of nori, which is a type of seaweed. Nori is purchased dry and is very brittle until it is dampened with a wet cloth or paper towel.

1. Heat the edamame in the microwave in a small bowl according to the package instructions, then transfer it to a large bowl.

2. Add the rice, carrot, soy sauce, ginger, maple syrup, and garlic powder.

3. Use a damp cloth or paper towel to wipe the nori sheets until they become soft and flexible.

4. Lay the nori sheets on a flat surface. Spoon the edamame mixture into the center of each nori sheet, then fold in the sides and roll up to form burritos. Serve immediately.

Substitute: If you can't find nori, try using rice paper (spring roll wrappers) instead. You can also skip the wrap altogether and turn this recipe into a sushi bowl.

PER SERVING (PER WRAP): Calories: 180; Total fat: 5g; Carbohydrates: 26g; Fiber: 6g; Protein: 11g; Calcium: 72mg; Vitamin D: 0mcg; Vitamin B$_{12}$: 0µg; Iron: 2mg; Zinc: 2mg

Veggie and White Bean Pesto Melt

MAKES 4 SANDWICHES · PREP TIME: 5 MINUTES · COOK TIME: 10 MINUTES

1 (15-ounce) can white beans (such as cannellini or Great Northern), drained and rinsed

1 cup Carrot-Top Pesto (page 218) or store-bought pesto

1 tablespoon unsalted butter

8 slices whole-grain bread

1 ripe medium tomato, sliced

1 cup shredded mozzarella cheese

Grapeseed oil or nonstick cooking spray

Mix it up: Don't have any mozzarella? Try these sandwiches with cheddar, pepper jack, or goat cheese instead—any type of cheese that melts when heated. You can also look for plant-based butter and cheese alternatives to make this recipe vegan.

Next time you have friends over for a study session, whip up these cheesy pesto melts for a quick and energizing meal. The sandwiches are prepared the same way as for grilled cheese, but they have the added benefit of herbaceous pesto flavor, plus fiber and protein from the white beans.

1. In a medium bowl, mash the beans with a potato masher or a fork until they form a lumpy paste.

2. Add the pesto and stir to combine.

3. Spread a little butter on each piece of bread. Turn 4 of the pieces over so they are butter-side down and spread the bean mixture on the other side. Top the bean mixture with the tomato and mozzarella cheese. Place the remaining bread slices, butter-side up, on top of the cheese.

4. Pour a little oil into a large skillet or grill pan and heat over medium heat. When the skillet is hot, place the sandwiches in it in a single layer (cook in batches, if needed). Cook for 5 minutes, or until the bread is golden. Carefully flip the sandwiches and cook for an additional 5 minutes, or until the other side is golden and the cheese is melted. Serve.

PER SERVING (1 SANDWICH): Calories: 657; Total fat: 47g; Carbohydrates: 40g; Fiber: 9g; Protein: 25g; Calcium: 387mg; Vitamin D: 0mcg; Vitamin B_{12}: 1µg; Iron: 4mg; Zinc: 3mg

Chili-Lime Tempeh Burritos

MAKES 2 WRAPS · PREP TIME: 10 MINUTES · COOK TIME: 10 MINUTES

DORM-FRIENDLY | ONE PAN

2 tablespoons
   grapeseed oil
¼ cup diced red onion
1 (8-ounce) block firm
   tempeh, crumbled
1 cup frozen corn kernels
1 tablespoon fresh
   lime juice
2 teaspoons chili powder
2 teaspoons ground cumin
½ cup chopped fresh
   cilantro
2 large flour
   tortillas, warmed
½ cup Spicy Blender
   Salsa (page 219) or
   store-bought salsa
½ cup Chunky Guacamole
   (page 220) or store-
   bought guacamole

....

Protein swaps: If
you have an allergy to soy
or just can't find tempeh in
your area, swap in a can of
black beans or pinto beans.
Drain and rinse the canned
beans before adding them
to the skillet with the
other ingredients.

Burritos are a classic lunchtime meal since they're energizing and easy to eat on the go. It's simple to heat up the burrito filling in a skillet, but you could also cook the tempeh mixture in the microwave. Just add everything to a microwave-safe dish along with a couple tablespoons of water. Microwave until hot and then drain any excess liquid before scooping the filling into warmed tortillas.

1. Heat the oil in a medium skillet over medium heat.

2. Once the oil is shiny, add the onion and cook for 4 minutes or until translucent.

3. Add the tempeh, corn, lime juice, chili powder, and cumin, and cook for 3 minutes, stirring occasionally, or until tempeh is warmed.

4. Add the cilantro and turn off the heat.

5. Lay a tortilla on a flat surface and spoon half the tempeh mixture into the center. Top with some salsa and guacamole. Fold over each side and then roll up the tortilla to form the burrito. Repeat with the remaining tortilla.

6. Serve immediately, or place them in an airtight container and refrigerate for up to 1 week or freeze for up to 3 months.

PER SERVING (1 WRAP): Calories: 642; Total fat: 38g; Carbohydrates: 59g; Fiber: 10g; Protein: 29g; Calcium: 229mg; Vitamin D: 0mcg; Vitamin B$_{12}$: 0µg; Iron: 7mg; Zinc: 3mg

Freezer-Friendly Bean Burgers

MAKES 4 SERVINGS · PREP TIME: 10 MINUTES · COOK TIME: 10 MINUTES

DORM-FRIENDLY | GREAT FOR SHARING | MAKES LEFTOVERS | ONE PAN

2 (15-ounce) cans
 black beans, drained
 and rinsed
1 cup cooked brown rice
 (see Tip, page 64)
1 large carrot, shredded
 and squeezed dry
¼ cup diced onion
¼ cup chopped fresh
 cilantro
1 large egg, lightly beaten
1 tablespoon tomato paste
1 tablespoon chili powder
½ teaspoon kosher salt
¼ teaspoon freshly ground
 black pepper
Grapeseed oil or nonstick
 cooking spray
4 hamburger buns

Bean burgers are a classic vegetarian alternative to ground beef patties for a tailgating party. This recipe uses beaten eggs, which act as a binder to hold the burgers together. For a vegan alternative, try flax eggs (whisk 1 tablespoon ground flaxseed with 2½ tablespoons water and allow the mixture to sit for 5 minutes, or until it thickens to the consistency of a beaten egg). These plant-based burgers are freezer-friendly, so they're ideal for meal prep, but you can also serve them right out of the skillet, if preferred.

1. In a large bowl, mash the black beans with a fork or a potato masher.

2. Add the rice, carrot, onion, cilantro, egg, tomato paste, chili powder, salt, and pepper and stir until combined.

3. Use your hands to form 4 patties. Press until the patties stick together. (If patties aren't as firm as you'd like, chill them on a plate in the refrigerator for 30 minutes.)

continues →

Freezer-Friendly Bean Burgers *continued*

4. Pour a little oil into a large skillet and heat over medium-high heat. When the skillet is hot, arrange the patties in it in a single layer (cook in batches, if needed) and cook for 5 minutes, or until the bottom turns golden brown. Flip the patties and cook for an additional 5 minutes, or until both sides are golden and the patties are cooked through. Serve on hamburger buns.

5. To freeze, wrap each patty in aluminum foil or parchment paper and store in a freezer-safe bag. To reheat, unwrap a burger patty and microwave on a plate for 3 minutes, or until hot. You can also reheat patties in a greased skillet.

....

Mix it up: Use this recipe as a basic formula to make all types of bean burgers. Swap in chickpeas for the black beans and add 1 tablespoon of curry powder to give these patties some Indian flare.

PER SERVING: Calories: 375; Total fat: 4g; Carbohydrates: 67g; Fiber: 15g; Protein: 18g; Calcium: 134mg; Vitamin D: 0mcg; Vitamin B$_{12}$: 0µg; Iron: 5mg; Zinc: 2mg

Lentil Sloppy Joes

MAKES 4 SERVINGS · PREP TIME: 5 MINUTES · COOK TIME: 15 MINUTES

GREAT FOR SHARING

1 tablespoon grapeseed oil

¼ cup diced onion

3 garlic cloves, minced

2 cups cooked lentils

1 (15-ounce) can
tomato sauce

1 tablespoon soy sauce

1 teaspoon chili powder

1 teaspoon ground cumin

¼ teaspoon cayenne
(optional)

4 rolls or hamburger buns

Storage: Store leftover sloppy joe filling in an airtight container in the refrigerator for up to 1 week.

Sloppy joes are an American classic traditionally made with ground beef, onions, and tomato sauce or ketchup. Most credit for the creation goes to a cook named Joe at Floyd Angell's Café in Sioux City, Iowa. Legend has it that Joe added tomato sauce to his "loose meat" sandwich, and the iconic "sloppy joe" sandwich was born. Whether you decide to choose meat or go plant-based with lentils (as in this recipe), you're getting a healthy serving of protein.

1. Heat the oil in a large skillet over medium heat.

2. Once the oil is shiny, add the onion and cook for 4 minutes or until translucent.

3. Add the garlic and cook for 1 additional minute.

4. Add the lentils, tomato sauce, soy sauce, chili powder, cumin, and cayenne (if using). Simmer the mixture for 10 minutes, or until it is warmed through and thickened.

5. Divide the lentil mixture among the rolls or hamburger buns and serve.

Protein swaps: Instead of lentils, try this recipe with crumbled tempeh or canned beans. Just make sure you drain and rinse the beans before stirring them into the skillet with the other ingredients.

PER SERVING: Calories: 308; Total fat: 6g; Carbohydrates: 51g; Fiber: 11g; Protein: 15g; Calcium: 142mg; Vitamin D: 0mcg; Vitamin B$_{12}$: 0μg; Iron: 7mg; Zinc: 2mg

Mushroom Cheesesteaks

MAKES 2 SANDWICHES · PREP TIME: 5 MINUTES · COOK TIME: 15 MINUTES

TOASTER OVEN

1 tablespoon grapeseed oil

½ sweet onion, thinly sliced

2 fresh portobello
mushroom caps, cut into
¼-inch slices

½ teaspoon crushed dried
rosemary (optional)

¼ teaspoon cayenne
(optional)

¼ teaspoon kosher salt

⅛ teaspoon freshly ground
black pepper

2 hoagie rolls, halved

2 slices provolone cheese

Substitute: If you
can't find portobello mushroom caps, swap in 2¼ cups
sliced cremini, shiitake, or
baby bella mushrooms.
Instead of provolone
cheese, use Swiss.

A cheesesteak is typically made with thin slices of sautéed ribeye steak and melted cheese, placed on a long, crusty roll. This vegetarian take on Philadelphia's classic sandwich incorporates sliced portobello mushrooms, rosemary, and cayenne instead. To boost the flavor, add a touch of acid and crunch with pickled veggies of any kind.

1. Preheat the oven or toaster oven to 400°F. Line a baking sheet with parchment.

2. Heat the grapeseed oil in a large skillet over medium heat.

3. Once the oil is shiny, add the onion and cook for 4 minutes or until translucent.

4. Add the mushrooms, rosemary (if using), cayenne (if using), salt, and pepper and cook for 2 minutes, or until the mushrooms begin to darken in color.

5. Arrange the hoagie rolls cut-side up on the baking sheet. Evenly divide the mushroom mixture between 2 of the hoagie halves and top with the provolone cheese.

6. Bake until the cheese is melted, about 5 minutes.

7. Place the hoagie halves on top of the mushroom cheese halves and serve.

PER SERVING (1 SANDWICH): Calories: 320; Total fat: 16g; Carbohydrates: 31g; Fiber: 3g; Protein: 14g; Calcium: 304mg; Vitamin D: 0mcg; Vitamin B$_{12}$: 1µg; Iron: 2mg; Zinc: 2mg

Tempeh Reubens

MAKES 2 SANDWICHES • PREP TIME: 5 MINUTES • COOK TIME: 15 MINUTES

DORM-FRIENDLY | ONE PAN

4 teaspoons unsalted butter

4 slices rye bread

1 tablespoon grapeseed oil, plus more to grease skillet

1 tablespoon soy sauce

1 teaspoon smoked paprika

2 teaspoons apple cider vinegar

1 (8-ounce) block firm tempeh, sliced into 4 pieces

¼ cup Russian dressing

½ cup sauerkraut

2 slices Swiss cheese (optional)

The Reuben sandwich is a classic combo of salty corned beef, tangy sauerkraut, and sharp Swiss cheese. This recipe calls for sliced tempeh instead of beef to create a vegetarian version. Tempeh is fermented soybeans pressed into blocks, similar to tofu, but with more of a nutty, earthy flavor that works well for this flavorful sandwich recipe. To make your own Russian dressing, whisk 2 tablespoons of mayonnaise with 1 tablespoon of ketchup and 1 teaspoon of horseradish.

1. Spread the butter on one side of each piece of bread.

2. In a small bowl, whisk together the 1 tablespoon oil, the soy sauce, smoked paprika, and vinegar.

3. Lightly grease a large skillet and place it over medium heat.

4. Brush the spiced oil onto the tempeh pieces and arrange them in the skillet in a single layer. Cook for 6 minutes, flipping halfway through, or until the tempeh is warmed through. Transfer the cooked tempeh to a plate or bowl and set aside.

5. Place the bread, butter-side down, in a single layer in the skillet (cook in batches, if needed) and cook until golden, about 3 minutes. Remove the bread from the skillet to a clean work surface, placing the slices with the golden cooked side down.

continues →

6. Spread the Russian dressing on the top of each piece of bread.

7. Divide the fried tempeh, sauerkraut, and Swiss cheese (if using) between 2 of the slices. Place the remaining pieces of bread, dressing-side down, on top of the tempeh mixture. Serve immediately.

....

Tip: To make this recipe vegan, use vegan butter or coconut oil instead of butter and omit the Swiss cheese. If you don't have Swiss cheese but still want the melty texture it provides, try a couple slices of provolone instead.

PER SERVING (1 SANDWICH): Calories: 600; Total fat: 36g; Carbohydrates: 47g; Fiber: 5g; Protein: 27g; Calcium: 185mg; Vitamin D: 0mcg; Vitamin B$_{12}$: 0µg; Iron: 6mg; Zinc: 2mg

Buffalo Tofu Sandwiches

MAKES 2 SANDWICHES · PREP TIME: 5 MINUTES, PLUS 30 MINUTES TO MARINATE
COOK TIME: 10 MINUTES

DORM-FRIENDLY | ONE PAN

½ (14-ounce) block firm tofu, drained, pressed, and sliced into 4 pieces
¼ cup buffalo-style hot sauce, plus additional for serving
Grapeseed oil or nonstick cooking spray
¼ cup crumbled blue cheese (optional)
2 sandwich rolls, halved
½ cup fresh baby spinach or torn lettuce of choice
¼ cup thinly sliced onion

....

Mix it up: If you're looking for a way to make these sandwiches more portable, try turning them into wraps. Just use 2 warmed flour tortillas instead of buns for a satisfying weekday lunch.

Chicken wings coated with buffalo sauce is one of the most loved American bar snacks. This vegetarian take is made with tofu instead of chicken, but it still has all the classic flavors from the hot sauce and crumbled blue cheese. Cut the tofu into smaller pieces and serve that on slider buns for a fun appetizer to share with friends during the game.

1. Brush the tofu pieces with the hot sauce and place them on a plate or in a container, cover, and allow them to marinate for at least 30 minutes or in the refrigerator overnight.

2. Lightly oil a large skillet and preheat it over medium heat.

3. Arrange the tofu in a single layer in the skillet and cook the tofu pieces for 4 minutes, or until they easily separate from the pan. Flip them over and cook for an additional 4 minutes, or until the other side easily separates. Remove the skillet from the heat.

4. Brush the tofu with more hot sauce and sprinkle with the blue cheese (if using).

5. Divide the tofu between the sandwich rolls and top with the spinach or lettuce and onion. Serve.

PER SERVING: Calories: 209; Total fat: 8g; Carbohydrates: 25g; Fiber: 2g; Protein: 11g; Calcium: 193mg; Vitamin D: 0mcg; Vitamin B$_{12}$: 0µg; Iron: 3mg; Zinc: 1mg

**Chili–Lime
Taco Salad,**
page 105

Chapter Five

Simple Salads

Salads sometimes get a bad rap in the food world, but dark leafy greens don't have to be boring and unsatisfying. In fact, there are plenty of salad recipes that you can make without even one shred of lettuce! My favorite strategy for building a crave-worthy salad is variety. Tossing in lots of different fruits and veggies amps up the color and flavor. Nuts and seeds provide a crunchy texture and a little extra fiber and protein. Beans, lentils, and soy make any mix more filling, and you can't go wrong with a zesty vinaigrette or creamy tahini dressing. Ready to meet your new favorite lunchtime companions?

Cucumber-Mango Salad 90

Thai-Inspired Peanut Salad 91

Strawberry and Avocado Spinach Salad 92

Red Cabbage and Cilantro Slaw 93

Make-Ahead Kale Salad 94

Vegan Greek Salad with Tofu Feta 95

Caprese Pasta Salad 96

Creamy Greek Yogurt Potato Salad 97

Edamame Mason Jar Salad 98

Vegan Caesar Salad 99

Sun-Dried Tomato and Farro Salad 100

Cranberry, Walnut, and Brussels Sprouts Salad 101

Harvest Butternut Squash and Quinoa Salad 102

Sesame-Ginger Soba Noodle Salad 104

Chili-Lime Taco Salad 105

Cucumber-Mango Salad

MAKES 2 SERVINGS · PREP TIME: 10 MINUTES

1 ripe mango, pitted and cut into 1-inch-wide strips

1 cucumber, halved lengthwise, seeded, and cut into 4-inch-long and 1-inch-wide strips

⅓ cup chopped fresh cilantro

1 jalapeño pepper, sliced

1 teaspoon grated lime zest

1 tablespoon fresh lime juice

Kosher salt

This Mexican-inspired salad combines mango, spicy jalapeño peppers, zippy lime, and refreshing cucumber to make a quick side salad that's just right for a hot summer day. Try adding jicama spears to give this salad a little extra crunch. You can often find jicama—a white tuber popular in Mexican cooking—already chopped and packaged in the produce section of the supermarket. Serve this salad with tacos or black beans and rice to complete the meal.

1. In a large bowl, toss together the mango, cucumber, cilantro, jalapeño, lime zest, and lime juice until well mixed. Season to taste with salt.

2. Transfer to 2 plates and serve immediately.

Substitute: Use frozen mango chunks instead of fresh mango, if desired. Thaw them in the refrigerator or in the microwave. Canned mango also works for this recipe. Look for fruit canned in fruit juice (not syrup) and strain the fruit from the canning liquid before using.

PER SERVING: Calories: 125; Total fat: 1g; Carbohydrates: 30g; Fiber: 4g; Protein: 3g; Calcium: 40mg; Vitamin D: 0mcg; Vitamin B$_{12}$: 0µg; Iron: 1mg; Zinc: 0mg

Thai-Inspired Peanut Salad

MAKES 4 SERVINGS · PREP TIME: 15 MINUTES

DORM-FRIENDLY | GREAT FOR SHARING | MAKES LEFTOVERS | NO COOKING REQUIRED

2½ cups frozen shelled
   edamame, thawed
2 cups shredded
   red cabbage
2 cups chopped fresh
   baby spinach
1 cup shredded carrots
1 cup roasted peanuts
1½ cups Spicy Peanut
   Sauce (page 215) or
   store-bought sauce
⅓ cup chopped fresh
   cilantro

This crunchy salad is full of Thai-inspired flavor from peanuts and cilantro. It's like a salad version of Thailand's popular pad Thai noodle dish. There's enough protein from the edamame and peanuts to make this salad a satisfying meal, but it's also an excellent partner for the Creamy Carrot-Ginger Soup on page 45. Unlike many salads, this one does keep well in the refrigerator, so make it on the weekend to pack up for healthy lunches throughout the week.

1. In a large bowl, toss together the thawed edamame, red cabbage, spinach, carrots, roasted peanuts, and peanut sauce until well mixed.

2. Add the cilantro and lightly toss to mix. Serve.

Storage: Store leftover salad in an airtight container in the refrigerator for up to 1 week.

Make it easier: Look for a bag of coleslaw vegetables to use in place of the cabbage, spinach, and carrots. Doing so will cut your chopping and prep time.

PER SERVING: Calories: 415; Total fat: 23g; Carbohydrates: 33g; Fiber: 12g; Protein: 22g; Calcium: 145mg; Vitamin D: 0mcg; Vitamin B$_{12}$: 0µg; Iron: 4mg; Zinc: 3mg

Strawberry and Avocado Spinach Salad

MAKES 2 SERVINGS · PREP TIME: 10 MINUTES

DORM-FRIENDLY | NO COOKING REQUIRED

3 cups fresh baby spinach

1 cup sliced fresh strawberries

1 medium avocado, peeled, pitted, and diced

¾ cup Lemon Tahini Dressing (page 214) or store-bought dressing

¼ cup sunflower seeds, toasted if desired

¼ cup chopped fresh basil (optional)

Make this salad right around the start of summer break, when strawberries, avocado, spinach, and fresh herbs are all at their seasonal peak. Seasonal fruits and vegetables taste better, tend to have more nutrients, and usually cost less than out-of-season produce. Delicate green salads, especially those paired with avocado, are best enjoyed immediately after preparing them. Leave the dressing on the side and squeeze lemon juice over the avocado if you want it to hold up a little bit longer.

1. In a large bowl, combine the spinach, strawberries, and avocado.

2. Pour in the dressing and toss gently until the ingredients are evenly coated.

3. Add the sunflower seeds and basil (if using) and gently toss until just incorporated. Serve immediately.

Protein swaps: Use 1 can of drained and rinsed chickpeas instead of (or in addition to) sunflower seeds for more protein. You can also include chopped almonds or hemp hearts.

PER SERVING: Calories: 432; Total fat: 32g; Carbohydrates: 31g; Fiber: 15g; Protein: 13g; Calcium: 162mg; Vitamin D: 0mcg; Vitamin B_{12}: 0µg; Iron: 4mg; Zinc: 3mg

Red Cabbage and Cilantro Slaw

MAKES 4 TO 8 SERVINGS · PREP TIME: 10 MINUTES

DORM-FRIENDLY | GREAT FOR SHARING | MAKES LEFTOVERS | NO COOKING REQUIRED

**3 cups shredded
red cabbage**

1 cup shredded carrots

**1 cup chopped fresh
cilantro**

**¼ cup sunflower or
pumpkin seeds
(optional; see Tip)**

**2 scallions, both white and
green parts, chopped**

¼ cup olive oil

**2 tablespoons apple
cider vinegar**

1 teaspoon honey

Kosher salt

**Freshly ground
black pepper**

....

Storage: Store leftover salad in an airtight container in the refrigerator for up to 1 week.

Red cabbage is a smart veggie to add to your arsenal, since it's inexpensive and has a relatively long shelf life. Left whole, cabbage can stay fresh for up to 2 months in the refrigerator. Red cabbage is also packed with fiber and is a good source of B vitamins, iron, and calcium. One of my favorite ways to use this vegetable is in this cilantro-spiked slaw, which is dressed with a light and refreshing vinaigrette. This salad serves 4 as a side or 8 as a topping for tacos and sandwiches.

1. In a large bowl, mix the red cabbage, carrots, cilantro, sunflower or pumpkin seeds (if using), and scallions.

2. In a small bowl, whisk together the olive oil, vinegar, and honey. Season to taste with salt and pepper. Pour the dressing over the cabbage mixture and toss until the vegetables are evenly coated. Serve immediately.

....

Tip: To toast the sunflower or pumpkin seeds, preheat the oven (or a toaster oven) to 350°F and spread the seeds on a baking sheet. Bake for 5 minutes, or until the seeds are golden and very aromatic.

PER SERVING (AS SIDE): Calories: 162; Total fat: 14g; Carbohydrates: 10g; Fiber: 3g; Protein: 1g; Calcium: 48mg; Vitamin D: 0mcg; Vitamin B_{12}: 0µg; Iron: 1mg; Zinc: 0mg

Make-Ahead Kale Salad

MAKES 2 TO 4 SERVINGS · PREP TIME: 5 MINUTES

1 pound fresh kale, chopped

1 (15-ounce) can chickpeas, drained and rinsed

⅓ cup chopped almonds

⅓ cup dried cranberries

¼ cup Apple Cider Vinaigrette (page 212) or store-bought dressing

Most salads wilt with time, but kale is a hearty dark leafy green from the cruciferous family that stands the test of time. You can make this kale salad up to a week in advance. The flavors from the vinaigrette meld with the other ingredients in the refrigerator, so the flavors just keep getting better and better. This recipe serves 2 as an entrée or 4 as a side dish. Leave out the chickpeas if you want to make it a little bit lighter.

1. In a large bowl, massage the kale for 3 minutes, or until tender.

2. Add the chickpeas, almonds, cranberries, and vinaigrette and toss to combine. Serve.

Storage: Store leftover salad in an airtight container in the refrigerator for up to 1 week.

Substitute: If you're allergic to nuts, try swapping in hemp hearts, sunflower seeds, or pumpkin seeds for the almonds. You can also use raisins or halved grapes instead of the dried cranberries if desired.

PER SERVING (AS ENTRÉE): Calories: 660; Total fat: 33g; Carbohydrates: 77g; Fiber: 21g; Protein: 23g; Calcium: 443mg; Vitamin D: 0mcg; Vitamin B_{12}: 0µg; Iron: 8mg; Zinc: 4mg

Vegan Greek Salad with Tofu Feta

MAKES 4 SERVINGS • PREP TIME: 10 MINUTES

DORM-FRIENDLY | GREAT FOR SHARING | MAKES LEFTOVERS | ONE BOWL

2 tablespoons olive oil

1 tablespoon fresh lemon juice

1 teaspoon dried oregano

⅛ teaspoon kosher salt

⅛ teaspoon freshly ground black pepper

½ cup Tofu Feta (page 225) or store-bought tofu

1 pint cherry tomatoes, halved

1 English cucumber, chopped

1 green bell pepper, cored, seeded, and chopped

½ cup sliced red onion

½ cup pitted Kalamata olives

Also known as *horiatiki*, this authentic Greek salad is traditionally a combination of tomatoes, onions, cucumbers, green peppers, olives, and feta cheese dressed with olive oil and sprinkled with oregano. This vegan variation uses a plant-based tofu that mimics feta cheese. Serve this salad as a starter when you're having a communal dinner with friends, especially if the rest of your meal is Mediterranean-inspired.

1. In a large bowl, whisk together the olive oil, lemon juice, oregano, salt, and pepper until well blended.

2. Add the tofu feta, tomatoes, cucumber, green pepper, onion, and olives to the dressing and gently stir until the ingredients are evenly coated. Serve immediately.

Storage: Store leftover salad in an airtight container in the refrigerator for up to 3 days.

Substitute: Use other types of black olives if you can't find Kalamata. Substitute regular feta cheese if you include dairy products in your diet and want to make this recipe easier to prepare.

PER SERVING: Calories: 184; Total fat: 14g; Carbohydrates: 10g; Fiber: 3g; Protein: 8g; Calcium: 211mg; Vitamin D: 0mcg; Vitamin B_{12}: 0µg; Iron: 2mg; Zinc: 1mg

Caprese Pasta Salad

MAKES 2 SERVINGS · PREP TIME: 5 MINUTES · COOK TIME: 20 MINUTES

DORM-FRIENDLY | ONE POT

Kosher salt

**4 ounces dried whole
wheat penne (or other
pasta of choice)**

¼ cup olive oil

**2 tablespoons fresh
lemon juice**

1 teaspoon dried oregano

**⅛ teaspoon freshly ground
black pepper**

**1 cup cherry
tomatoes, halved**

**4 ounces fresh mozzarella
pearls (small balls, or
cut into ½-inch pieces)**

**¾ cup fresh basil leaves
(torn, if large)**

....

Storage: Store leftover
salad in an airtight con-
tainer in the refrigerator for
up to 4 days.

....

Make it easier:
A classic Caprese salad
doesn't usually have pasta,
so leave it out if you want
to try out a more authentic
version of this dish. During
the summer months, I
also love to swap in sliced
heirloom tomatoes.

Caprese salad is a traditional dish featuring red,
white, and green ingredients in honor of the colors of
the Italian flag. Simple Mediterranean ingredients,
including tomatoes, mozzarella, basil, and olive
oil, make this meal delicious and nutrient-packed,
and it's also an excellent source of fiber from the
whole-wheat pasta.

1. Bring an 8-quart stockpot filled three-fourths full
   of water and 1 teaspoon salt to a boil over high
   heat. Pour in the penne and cook for 11 minutes,
   stirring occasionally, or according to package
   instructions, until al dente.

2. Drain the pasta, reserving about 2 tablespoons of
   the cooking liquid in the pot.

3. Return the pasta to the pot over medium heat and
   add the olive oil, lemon juice, oregano, ⅛ teaspoon
   salt, and the pepper. Toss to mix.

4. Add the cherry tomatoes, mozzarella, and fresh
   basil leaves and stir. Cook until the mozzarella
   begins to melt and the liquid is absorbed, about
   3 minutes. Adjust the seasonings, if needed.

5. You can serve the pasta hot, allow it to cool to
   room temperature, or chill and serve cold.

PER SERVING: Calories: 624; Total fat: 40g; Carbohydrates: 48g;
Fiber: 6g; Protein: 21g; Calcium: 326mg; Vitamin D: 0mcg;
Vitamin B$_{12}$: 1μg; Iron: 3mg; Zinc: 3mg

Creamy Greek Yogurt Potato Salad

MAKES 4 SERVINGS · PREP TIME: 5 MINUTES · COOK TIME: 10 MINUTES

DORM-FRIENDLY | GREAT FOR SHARING | MAKES LEFTOVERS | ONE POT

3 medium russet or Yukon Gold potatoes, chopped into 1-inch pieces

1 cup plain Greek yogurt

¼ cup mustard, such as Dijon

2 celery stalks, diced, including leaves

½ cup chopped red onion

Kosher salt

Freshly ground black pepper

Smoked paprika (optional)

Storage: Store leftover salad in an airtight container in the refrigerator for up to 5 days.

Substitute: Looking for a way to make this classic creamy salad vegan and dairy-free? There are a lot of delicious plant-based yogurts available these days. You can also try vegan mayonnaise. Look for both in the refrigerated section near the tofu.

This is the ultimate comforting and shareable salad for a campus picnic. I use Greek yogurt instead of mayonnaise, which is one of my favorite swaps to get a little extra protein into creamy salad recipes. Just make sure you're using plain, unflavored yogurt and opt for unsweetened versions when available. You can use this trick for pretty much every recipe that calls for mayo.

1. Place the potatoes in a 12-quart stockpot and cover with cold water. Bring to a boil over high heat, reduce the heat to medium-low, and simmer for 6 minutes, or until the potatoes are pierced easily with a fork. Drain the water, return the potatoes to the stockpot, and allow them to cool enough to handle.

2. While the potatoes are cooling, in a medium bowl, stir together the yogurt and mustard.

3. Add the celery and red onion and stir to combine.

4. Pour the yogurt mixture over the cooled potatoes and gently toss until thoroughly mixed. Season to taste with salt and pepper.

5. Transfer the salad to a serving dish, top with a sprinkling of smoked paprika (if using), and serve.

PER SERVING: Calories: 272; Total fat: 3g; Carbohydrates: 55g; Fiber: 5g; Protein: 9g; Calcium: 127mg; Vitamin D: 0mcg; Vitamin B$_{12}$: 0µg; Iron: 3mg; Zinc: 1mg

Edamame Mason Jar Salad

MAKES 2 SERVINGS • PREP TIME: 10 MINUTES

DORM-FRIENDLY | MICROWAVABLE

2 tablespoons toasted
  sesame oil

1 tablespoon soy sauce

1 tablespoon rice vinegar

1 teaspoon honey or maple
  syrup (optional)

½ cup shredded
  red cabbage

½ cup shredded carrot

1 small bell pepper, cored,
  seeded, and diced

1 cup frozen shelled
  edamame, thawed

1 cup cooked brown rice
  (see Tip, page 64)

Protein swaps: If
you want to bulk this up,
try adding cooked tofu.
You could also add crunchy
roasted peanuts to the top
of the jar and use Spicy
Peanut Sauce (page 215)
instead of the dressing in
the recipe.

Mason jar salads are a smart way to transport your greens on the go. Because of the way these ingredients are layered, you don't need to worry about delicate veggies getting soggy. Start with the dressing and hearty vegetables and then move up to beans, grains, and more delicate veggies. You can find microwavable packs of edamame and cooked brown rice to make this recipe in your dorm room. It's also a great way to use up any leftover cooked rice.

1. In a medium bowl, whisk together the sesame oil, soy sauce, rice vinegar, and honey until well blended.

2. Divide the dressing between two 1-pint jars with lids (about 3 tablespoons per jar).

3. In the same bowl as you used for the dressing, toss together the red cabbage, carrot, and bell pepper until well mixed, then evenly divide the mixture between the jars.

4. Evenly divide the edamame and cooked brown rice between the jars. To serve, pour the contents of each jar onto a plate.

Storage: Refrigerate the salads for up to 1 week.

PER SERVING: Calories: 364; Total fat: 19g; Carbohydrates: 39g; Fiber: 8g; Protein: 12g; Calcium: 88mg; Vitamin D: 0mcg; Vitamin B$_{12}$: 0µg; Iron: 3mg; Zinc: 2mg

Vegan Caesar Salad

MAKES 2 SERVINGS · PREP TIME: 10 MINUTES

NO COOKING REQUIRED

FOR THE DRESSING

½ cup silken tofu

¼ cup nutritional yeast

3 tablespoons olive oil

3 tablespoons apple
  cider vinegar

5 pitted Kalamata olives

1 teaspoon dried chives

¼ teaspoon garlic powder

⅛ teaspoon kosher salt

⅛ teaspoon freshly ground
  black pepper

FOR THE SALAD

1 head romaine
  lettuce, chopped

1 cup Whole-Grain
  Croutons (page 228) or
  store-bought croutons

½ cup pitted Kalamata
  olives, chopped

Storage: If you have
leftovers, keep the croutons
separate and store them
in an airtight container at
room temperature. Store
the salad in an airtight container in the refrigerator for
up to 1 week.

The rich, creamy texture of Caesar dressing is made
vegan here with the help of silken tofu. Unlike firm and
extra-firm varieties, silken tofu is soft and creamy,
which makes it a great dairy-free alternative for
dressings and sauces. Don't substitute other types of
tofu, as you won't get the same creamy result.

1. **To make the dressing:** Place the tofu, nutritional
   yeast, olive oil, vinegar, whole olives, chives, garlic
   powder, salt, and pepper in a blender or food
   processor and pulse until smooth. If the dressing
   is too thick, add a tablespoon of water and
   pulse again.

2. **To make the salad:** In a large bowl, toss the
   romaine lettuce and dressing until the lettuce is
   evenly coated.

3. Add the croutons and chopped olives to the bowl.
   Serve immediately.

Substitute: If you can't find silken tofu or aren't able to
tolerate soy, substitute with plain yogurt or a plain dairy-free
yogurt alternative. Substitute Parmesan cheese for nutritional
yeast if you include dairy. Substitute black olives or capers for
the kalamata olives.

PER SERVING: Calories: 476; Total fat: 28g; Carbohydrates: 42g;
Fiber: 11g; Protein: 17g; Calcium: 252mg; Vitamin D: 0mcg;
Vitamin B$_{12}$: 0µg; Iron: 7mg; Zinc: 3mg

Sun-Dried Tomato and Farro Salad

MAKES 4 SERVINGS • PREP TIME: 15 MINUTES • COOK TIME: 15 MINUTES

MAKE-AHEAD | ONE POT

1½ cups water

Kosher salt

½ cup farro

2 cups fresh baby spinach

1 (15-ounce) can
    chickpeas, drained
    and rinsed

½ cup chopped sun-dried
    tomatoes

2 tablespoons olive oil

1 tablespoon fresh
    lemon juice

½ teaspoon garlic powder

Freshly ground
    black pepper

Storage: Store leftover salad in an airtight container in the refrigerator for up to 1 week.

This make-ahead grain salad incorporates Mediterranean-inspired flavors, including sun-dried tomatoes, lemon juice, and garlic. It's great for sharing as a side dish at a party, but it's also a nourishing lunch for school. Chickpeas, farro, and ready-to-eat spinach provide a balanced mix of nutrients for long-lasting energy at any time of day.

1. In an 8-quart stockpot, bring the water and ¼ teaspoon salt to a boil and add the farro. Cook the farro for 15 minutes, or until the desired consistency is reached. (You can cook longer for a softer texture.) Drain the excess water and transfer the cooked farro to a large bowl.

2. Add the spinach, chickpeas, sun-dried tomatoes, olive oil, lemon juice, and garlic powder to the farro and toss until well combined. Season with salt and pepper. Serve immediately.

Tip: Look for microwavable farro, which you can often steam right in the package to save on dishes you'll have to clean up. This version is great to save time or if you don't have access to a hot plate or stovetop.

PER SERVING: Calories: 524; Total fat: 18g; Carbohydrates: 77g; Fiber: 18g; Protein: 20g; Calcium: 120mg; Vitamin D: 0mcg; Vitamin B12: 0µg; Iron: 7mg; Zinc: 4mg

Cranberry, Walnut, and Brussels Sprouts Salad

MAKES 2 SERVINGS · PREP TIME: 20 MINUTES · COOK TIME: 1 HOUR

DORM-FRIENDLY | MAKE AHEAD | ONE PAN

3 cups water

Kosher salt

⅓ cup pearled barley

2 tablespoons grapeseed oil

3 cups shredded Brussels sprouts

Freshly ground black pepper

½ cup walnut halves and pieces, toasted if desired

¼ cup dried cranberries

1 tablespoon apple cider vinegar

....

Storage: Store leftover salad in an airtight container in the refrigerator for up to 1 week.

....

Mix it up: Substitute any grain for the barley, such as farro or brown rice. Use crumbled feta or goat cheese instead of walnuts for a nut-free version. Try it with creamy Lemon Tahini Dressing (page 214).

Brussels sprouts are an affordable and nutrient-packed veggie to add to your repertoire during the winter months when they are in season. The sprouts have tons of fiber, and are also a great source of vitamin C. I love sautéing Brussels sprouts in a little oil until they get caramelized and crispy. The veggie makes a hearty and delicious addition to this barley salad accented with walnuts and dried cranberries.

1. In an 8-quart stockpot, bring the water and ¼ teaspoon salt to a boil over high heat. Add the barley, reduce the heat to low, and cook for 55 minutes, or until the grain is chewy and tender. Drain the excess cooking water if needed and fluff with a fork. Transfer the barley to a large bowl.

2. In a large skillet, heat the oil over medium heat. Add the Brussels sprouts and cook for 4 minutes, stirring occasionally, or until the sprouts are lightly browned. Season with salt and pepper and transfer to the bowl with the barley.

3. Add the walnuts, cranberries, and vinegar and toss to combine. Serve.

PER SERVING: Calories: 533; Total fat: 34g; Carbohydrates: 54g; Fiber: 13g; Protein: 12g; Calcium: 96mg; Vitamin D: 0mcg; Vitamin B₁₂: 0μg; Iron: 4mg; Zinc: 2mg

Harvest Butternut Squash and Quinoa Salad

MAKES 4 SERVINGS · PREP TIME: 10 MINUTES · COOK TIME: 20 MINUTES

GREAT FOR SHARING

1 cup water

Kosher salt

⅓ cup quinoa, rinsed

1 medium butternut
squash, peeled, seeded,
and cubed

1 tablespoon grapeseed oil

1 tablespoon maple syrup

Freshly ground
black pepper

1 pound fresh
kale, chopped

¼ cup chopped pecans

¼ cup dried cranberries

¼ cup Apple Cider
Vinaigrette (page 212)
or store-bought
dressing

Every Friendsgiving needs an excellent salad to balance the richer dishes, and this butternut squash recipe is ideal for the occasion. Seasonal winter squash and hearty kale are dressed in an apple cider vinaigrette and topped off with crunchy pecans and tart cranberries. Use cubed squash from the produce section or frozen butternut squash to cut back on the prep time. You can also cook the squash in the toaster oven or in a skillet if you don't have access to an oven.

1. Preheat the oven to 450°F. Line a baking sheet with parchment.

2. In an 8-quart stockpot, bring the water and ⅛ teaspoon salt to a boil. Add the quinoa, reduce the heat to medium-low, and cook for 15 minutes or until the quinoa is tender. Drain any excess cooking liquid if needed and fluff with a fork.

3. While the quinoa is cooking, in a large bowl, toss together the squash, oil, maple syrup, and salt and pepper to taste until the vegetables are well coated. Spread the cubes on the baking sheet. Bake for 20 minutes or until the squash is tender and golden.

4. When the squash is almost done baking, place the kale in a large bowl and massage it with your hands for 5 minutes, or until tender.

5. Add the quinoa, pecans, cranberries, and squash.

6. Pour in the dressing and gently toss until the ingredients are evenly coated. Serve warm.

Storage: Store leftover salad in an airtight container in the refrigerator for up to 1 week.

Substitute: Any type of hearty winter squash works for this recipe. Try substituting acorn or kabocha varieties. Cubed sweet potato will also be delicious if you want to add more sweetness. You can also use toasted pumpkin seeds instead of the pecans.

PER SERVING: Calories: 363; Total fat: 20g; Carbohydrates: 44g; Fiber: 8g; Protein: 9g; Calcium: 237mg; Vitamin D: 0mcg; Vitamin B_{12}: 0µg; Iron: 3mg; Zinc: 2mg

Sesame-Ginger Soba Noodle Salad

MAKES 2 SERVINGS · PREP TIME: 5 MINUTES · COOK TIME: 20 MINUTES

DORM-FRIENDLY | MAKE AHEAD | ONE POT

1 (2.67-ounce) bundle soba noodles (from multi-bundle package)

1 tablespoon coconut oil

2 cups chopped fresh broccoli florets

1 cup frozen shelled edamame

¼ cup chopped scallions, both white and green parts

¼ cup Sesame Ginger Dressing (page 213) or store-bought dressing

Storage: Store leftover salad in an airtight container in the refrigerator for up to 1 week.

Tip: Substitute with udon or rice noodles if you can't find soba. Change the vegetables and use bok choy, snap peas, or mushrooms instead of broccoli. For a plant-based protein swap, use tofu instead of edamame.

Soba (Japanese buckwheat noodles) cook much faster than dried spaghetti, making them convenient for quick lunches. A soba noodle salad is typically a mixture of buckwheat noodles, colorful vegetables, and a soy-based dressing. This salad can be made ahead and tastes great warm, room temperature, or cold. Store it in a mason jar for easy, grab-and-go eating between classes.

1. In an 8-quart stockpot, bring about 6 cups of water to a boil and add the soba noodles. Boil for 6 minutes or according to the package instructions. Drain and transfer to a large bowl.

2. Heat the coconut oil in the same pot over medium heat. Once the oil is melted, add the broccoli and cook for 5 minutes, or until it turns bright green.

3. Add the frozen edamame and scallions and cook for another 5 minutes, or until the edamame is warmed through.

4. Add the cooked noodles and dressing, stirring to combine all the ingredients, then immediately remove from the heat.

PER SERVING: Calories: 315; Total fat: 31g; Carbohydrates: 46g; Fiber: 7g; Protein: 18g; Calcium: 127mg; Vitamin D: 0mcg; Vitamin B$_{12}$: 0µg; Iron: 4mg; Zinc: 2mg

Chili-Lime Taco Salad

MAKES 2 SERVINGS · PREP TIME: 5 MINUTES · COOK TIME: 15 MINUTES

DORM FRIENDLY | GREAT FOR SHARING

2 tablespoons grapeseed oil

¼ cup diced red onion

1 (15-ounce) can black beans, drained and rinsed

1 tablespoon fresh lime juice

2 teaspoons chili powder

2 teaspoons ground cumin

½ cup chopped fresh cilantro

2 cups chopped romaine lettuce

2 large store-bought tortilla bowls (optional)

½ cup Spicy Blender Salsa (page 219) or store-bought salsa

½ cup Chunky Guacamole (page 220) or store-bought guacamole

Protein swaps:
Instead of black beans, use pinto beans, crumbled tempeh, or cubed tofu. You can also add scrambled eggs to turn this into a flavor-packed breakfast salad.

I've always loved the classic taco salad that comes in a crisp tortilla bowl. These bowls are sold already shaped and ready to fill; you can find them where you buy tortillas and tacos. Or, you can skip the tortilla bowl and top your salad with broken tortilla chips.

1. Heat the oil in a medium skillet over medium heat. When the oil is hot, add the onion and cook for 4 minutes or until translucent.

2. Add the beans, lime juice, chili powder, and cumin, and cook for 3 minutes or until beans are warmed through.

3. Add the cilantro and remove the skillet from the heat.

4. Divide the lettuce between the tortilla bowls. Divide the bean mixture between the bowls and top with the salsa and guacamole. Serve.

Tip: You can make your own tortilla bowls if you have time and a 12-cup muffin tin. Preheat the oven to 375°F and microwave 2 large corn tortillas for 20 seconds to make them more flexible (or heat in a skillet). Turn the muffin tin upside down and nestle a tortilla in the space between 4 cups and shape the tortilla to create a bowl. Repeat with the other tortilla. Bake for 15 minutes, or until the tortillas are golden and crispy, then cool on a rack.

PER SERVING: Calories: 571; Total fat: 27g; Carbohydrates: 70g; Fiber: 20g; Protein: 19g; Calcium: 172mg; Vitamin D: 0mcg; Vitamin B$_{12}$: 0µg; Iron: 7mg; Zinc: 3mg

Zucchini Pasta Primavera,
page 108

Chapter Six

Oodles of Noodles

*Whether it's an Asian- or a Mediterranean-*style dish, you can't go wrong with noodles. They're budget-friendly, easy to cook, and have a long shelf life. Pasta is also one of the best vehicles for a vegetable-packed sauce. In this chapter, you'll find everything from quick weeknight dishes to shareable baked pasta casseroles worthy of a communal dinner party. Which will you slurp up first?

Zucchini Pasta Primavera 108

15-Minute Cacio e Pepe 109

One-Pot Pantry Pasta 110

Vegan Pad Thai 112

Garlic and Miso Ramen Noodles 114

Tomato-Basil Orecchiette 116

Ginger Turmeric Rice Noodles 118

Baked Spaghetti Squash Lasagna 119

One-Pot Broccoli Mac and Cheese 121

Five-Spice Noodles 122

One-Pot Creamy Vegan Rigatoni 124

Eggplant Bacon Carbonara 126

Spaghetti and Lentil Balls 128

Creamy Pumpkin-Sage Alfredo 130

Greek Lasagna 132

White Bean and Tomato Stuffed Shells 134

One-Pan Skillet Lasagna 136

Spinach Spaghetti Pie 137

Vegan Cannelloni 138

Cheesy Broccoli Pasta Bake 140

Zucchini Pasta Primavera

MAKES 2 SERVINGS · PREP TIME: 10 MINUTES · COOK TIME: 10 MINUTES

2 tablespoons
   grapeseed oil
1 yellow summer
   squash, diced
1 cup broccoli florets
½ cup frozen green peas
Kosher salt
Freshly ground
   black pepper
½ cup milk (or plain
   unsweetened soy milk)
½ cup shredded
   Parmesan cheese
1 tablespoon fresh
   lemon juice
2½ cups zucchini noodles
Torn basil leaves (optional)

Storage: Store in an airtight container in the refrigerator for up to 3 days.

Substitute: If you don't have soy milk but still want to make this recipe dairy-free, swap in any type of plain, unsweetened, plant-based milk instead. Add a can of chickpeas (drained and rinsed) if you want more protein.

Pasta primavera is a classic spring and summer dish featuring fresh vegetables and a light, creamy lemon sauce. I use zucchini noodles instead of wheat pasta to make this dish even more veggie-packed. *Primavera* means "spring" in Italian, so this dish includes more seasonal green vegetables, including broccoli and peas, to fit the season. Feel free to use fresh, frozen, or canned vegetables for this recipe. I like to serve it with fresh basil leaves to really boost the flavor, but it isn't a necessary component.

1. Heat the oil in a large skillet over medium-low heat. Once the oil shimmers, add the squash, broccoli, and peas. Season with salt and pepper and cook for 4 minutes or until the vegetables are tender.

2. Add the milk, cheese, and lemon juice to the skillet and stir until the cheese is melted, about 3 minutes.

3. Add the zucchini noodles and turn off the heat. Toss until the zucchini noodles are evenly coated with the sauce.

4. Taste and adjust the seasonings. Serve, sprinkled with basil if desired.

PER SERVING: Calories: 338; Total fat: 23g; Carbohydrates: 22g; Fiber: 5g; Protein: 15g; Calcium: 353mg; Vitamin D: 1mcg; Vitamin B_{12}: 1µg; Iron: 2mg; Zinc: 3mg

15-Minute Cacio e Pepe

MAKES 2 SERVINGS · PREP TIME: 5 MINUTES · COOK TIME: 10 MINUTES

DORM-FRIENDLY | ONE POT

Kosher salt

4 ounces whole wheat spaghetti

2 teaspoons olive oil

2 garlic cloves, minced

½ teaspoon freshly ground black pepper

¾ cup grated Pecorino Romano cheese

Fresh herbs, such as parsley or torn basil leaves (optional)

....

Storage: Store the pasta in an airtight container in the refrigerator for up to 5 days.

....

Mix it up: Cacio e pepe is traditionally very simple, but that doesn't mean you can't play with the basic recipe and find ways to get more color and flavor. In addition to fresh herbs, try adding vegetables, such as spinach, green peas, kale, or broccoli.

Cacio e pepe means "cheese and pepper" in Italian. I like to think of it as a grown-up version of mac and cheese. The meal dates back to ancient Roman times, when shepherds would boil pasta, then make the signature creamy sauce by grating fresh cheese into some of the pasta cooking water along with plenty of black pepper. This meal is quick, easy, and comforting, making it ideal for a late-night study session. I like to use whole wheat pasta for extra fiber.

1. Fill an 8-quart stockpot three-fourths full of water and add ⅛ teaspoon salt. Bring to a boil over high heat. Add the spaghetti and cook for 8 minutes, or until al dente.

2. Reserve 2 tablespoons of the pasta cooking liquid and then drain the spaghetti.

3. Reduce the heat to low and return the cooked pasta to the stockpot along with the reserved cooking liquid.

4. Add the olive oil, garlic, black pepper, and cheese.

5. Cook for 2 minutes, or until the cheese is melted and the sauce is thickened, stirring constantly.

6. Taste and season with salt, if needed. Serve with fresh herbs, if desired.

PER SERVING: Calories: 399; Total fat: 16g; Carbohydrates: 49g; Fiber: 5g; Protein: 19g; Calcium: 348mg; Vitamin D: 0mcg; Vitamin B$_{12}$: 1µg; Iron: 2mg; Zinc: 3mg

One-Pot Pantry Pasta

MAKES 2 SERVINGS · PREP TIME: 10 MINUTES · COOK TIME: 30 MINUTES

2 tablespoons
   grapeseed oil

½ cup diced onion

1 tablespoon dried basil

½ teaspoon garlic powder

¼ teaspoon kosher salt

¼ teaspoon freshly ground
   black pepper

4 ounces whole
   wheat penne

1 (15-ounce) can crushed
   tomatoes

1 cup water, or more
   as needed

2 cups frozen
   broccoli florets

1 (15-ounce) can chickpeas
   or white beans, drained
   and rinsed

Grated Parmesan cheese
   or nutritional yeast
   (optional)

There's a big misconception about frozen and canned vegetables. Many people think fresh produce is the only healthy option, but there are actually many beneficial nutrients in the frozen and canned ingredients. I used some of my favorites, including canned tomatoes and frozen broccoli, to make this pantry-friendly pasta recipe. Be sure to stir the sauce occasionally because this will prevent it from burning while the pasta is cooking.

1. Heat the oil in a 12-quart stockpot over medium heat.

2. Once the oil is shiny, add the onion and cook for 4 minutes, or until translucent.

3. Add the basil, garlic powder, salt, and pepper and cook for 1 additional minute.

4. Add the penne, tomatoes, and 1 cup water; add a little more water if needed to fully cover the pasta. Bring the mixture to a boil and cook for 12 minutes, or until most of the liquid is absorbed. Stir occasionally, especially if your pot is not heavy-bottomed, to prevent burning.

5. Add the broccoli and beans and cook until warmed through and the pasta is tender.

6. Serve the pasta with Parmesan cheese or nutritional yeast, if desired.

. . . .

Storage: Store the pasta in an airtight container in the refrigerator for up to 5 days.

. . . .

Protein swaps: If you don't like beans or have trouble digesting them, try making this recipe with lentils, chopped walnuts, or crumbled tempeh instead. You can also leave out the beans out altogether, if preferred.

PER SERVING: Calories: 601; Total fat: 19g; Carbohydrates: 93g; Fiber: 21g; Protein: 24g; Calcium: 210mg; Vitamin D: 0mcg; Vitamin B_{12}: 0µg; Iron: 8mg; Zinc: 4mg

Vegan Pad Thai

MAKES 2 SERVINGS · PREP TIME: 10 MINUTES · COOK TIME: 15 MINUTES

4 ounces rice noodles

2 tablespoons coconut oil, or more as needed

1¼ cups extra-firm tofu, drained, pressed (see Tip, page 50), and cut into 1-inch cubes

2 cups chopped broccoli florets

1 cup Spicy Peanut Sauce (page 215) or store-bought sauce

OPTIONAL TOPPINGS

½ cup roasted peanuts

Fresh Thai basil leaves

Fresh cilantro leaves

Red pepper flakes

Lime wedges

Thailand's national dish is usually made with rice noodles that are stir-fried with eggs, tofu, tamarind paste, fish sauce, and spices. This vegan version is made without the eggs and fish sauce. During World War II, Thailand suffered a shortage of rice, so the Thai government started to promote noodles and created this dish. Opt for brown rice noodles if you want to maximize the fiber and nutritional content.

1. Place an 8-quart stockpot filled three-fourths full of water over high heat and bring to a boil. Cook the pasta according to the package instructions and set aside.

2. Heat the 2 tablespoons coconut oil in a large skillet over medium heat.

3. Once the oil is melted, add the tofu and cook for 7 minutes, or until the tofu easily separates from the pot.

4. Flip the tofu and cook for an additional 3 minutes, or until the other side easily separates and you can stir the tofu without it sticking to the pot. If the tofu is sticking, cook for another minute or so before stirring. Add more oil if needed to coat the pot.

5. Add the broccoli and cook for 3 minutes, or until bright green and lightly browned on the edges. Turn off the heat.

6. Add the cooked rice noodles and the peanut sauce and gently toss until the ingredients are evenly coated.

7. If the noodles are sticking, add a couple tablespoons of water and toss again.

8. Divide the pasta between 2 bowls and serve with the peanuts, Thai basil, cilantro, red pepper flakes, and lime wedges if desired.

....

Storage: Store any leftovers in an airtight container in the refrigerator for up to 3 days.

....

Tip: Instead of tofu, swap in shelled edamame. If you eat eggs, you can also scramble a couple and stir them into the pasta dish for extra protein.

PER SERVING: Calories: 675; Total fat: 36g; Carbohydrates: 67g; Fiber: 6g; Protein: 24g; Calcium: 257mg; Vitamin D: 0mcg; Vitamin B_{12}: 0µg; Iron: 3mg; Zinc: 4mg

Garlic and Miso Ramen Noodles

MAKES 2 SERVINGS · PREP TIME: 5 MINUTES · COOK TIME: 10 MINUTES

2 tablespoons grapeseed oil

1 baby bok choy, chopped into 1-inch pieces

4 garlic cloves, sliced

1 (1-inch) piece of fresh ginger, peeled and grated

1 (3-ounce) package ramen noodles, seasoning packet discarded

1 tablespoon miso paste

OPTIONAL FOR SERVING

2 large fried eggs, kept warm

1 scallion, both white and green parts, chopped

Owing to their convenience and low price point, packages of ramen noodles have been a staple comfort food for college students for decades. Instead of the high-sodium flavor packet that comes with most instant ramen packages, this recipe calls for umami-rich miso paste to provide the salty flavor. Top these ramen noodle bowls with fried eggs if you want to make this meal more filling and satisfying. Either way, this recipe will keep you going when you're studying.

1. Heat the oil in a 12-quart stockpot over medium heat.

2. Add the bok choy, garlic, and ginger and cook for 3 minutes, stirring constantly, or until the bok choy is wilted and the mixture is very aromatic. Transfer the mixture to a plate with a slotted spoon.

3. Fill the stockpot with water, bring to a boil over high heat, and cook the ramen noodles according to the package instructions.

4. In a small bowl, whisk the miso paste with 2 tablespoons of the cooking liquid from the noodles.

5. Drain the noodles and add them to the pot.

6. Add the cooked bok choy mixture and the miso sauce and toss until the noodles and veggies are evenly coated.

7. Divide the ramen mixture between 2 bowls and top each with a fried egg and chopped scallion, if using. Serve immediately.

....

Protein swaps: Instead of a fried egg, serve these ramen noodles with baked tofu or steamed edamame to keep this recipe vegan.

PER SERVING: Calories: 431; Total fat: 23g; Carbohydrates: 48g; Fiber: 4g; Protein: 8g; Calcium: 174mg; Vitamin D: 0mcg; Vitamin B_{12}: 0µg; Iron: 4mg; Zinc: 1mg

Tomato-Basil Orecchiette

MAKES 2 SERVINGS · PREP TIME: 5 MINUTES · COOK TIME: 25 MINUTES

DORM-FRIENDLY | ONE POT

2 tablespoons
  grapeseed oil

¼ cup diced onion

2 garlic cloves, minced

¼ teaspoon kosher salt

¼ teaspoon freshly ground
  black pepper

4 ounces orecchiette pasta

2 cups water, or as
  more needed

1 pint cherry tomatoes

1 cup fresh baby spinach

1 (15-ounce) can white
  beans or chickpeas,
  drained and rinsed
  (optional)

½ cup shredded Parmesan
  cheese (optional)

½ cup torn fresh
  basil leaves

Orecchiette, which means "little ear" in Italian, is a pasta from the Apulia region of southern Italy. I like to use orecchiette to make a simple lunch with classic Mediterranean ingredients, such as spinach, tomatoes, garlic, and fresh basil. For extra staying power, make sure to add the chickpeas or white beans, since they're full of fiber and protein. If you're making this as a side dish, you can leave them out.

1. Heat the oil in a 12-quart stockpot over medium heat.

2. Once the oil is shiny, add the onion and cook for 4 minutes, or until translucent.

3. Add the garlic, salt, pepper, pasta, and the 2 cups water and bring to a boil. Add more water if needed to cover the pasta and cook for 10 minutes.

4. Add the tomatoes, spinach, and beans (if using), and cook for 4 minutes, or until the pasta is al dente and most of the liquid is absorbed. Use a wooden spoon to break open the cherry tomatoes as they cook, if desired. If the pasta cooks before all of the liquid is absorbed, ladle out the excess liquid and discard.

5. Turn off the heat and add the Parmesan cheese and fresh basil leaves, if using.

6. Taste and adjust the seasoning. Serve.

. . . .

Storage: Store the pasta in an airtight container in the refrigerator for up to 5 days.

. . . .

Substitute: If you don't see orecchiette in the pasta aisle at your local grocery store, try making this recipe with penne, rotini, elbows, or small shells instead. Opt for whole wheat pasta to increase the overall fiber content.

PER SERVING: Calories: 371; Total fat: 15g; Carbohydrates: 51g; Fiber: 4g; Protein: 10g; Calcium: 51mg; Vitamin D: 0mcg; Vitamin B_{12}: 0µg; Iron: 2mg; Zinc: 1mg

Ginger-Turmeric Rice Noodles

MAKES 2 SERVINGS · PREP TIME: 5 MINUTES · COOK TIME: 10 MINUTES

1 tablespoon grapeseed oil

2 cups chopped fresh kale

1 cup frozen
   shelled edamame

1 (2-inch) piece of
   fresh ginger, peeled
   and grated

¼ teaspoon freshly ground
   black pepper

4 ounces brown
   rice noodles

1 tablespoon soy sauce

1 teaspoon ground
   turmeric

Fresh Thai basil leaves
   (optional)

Storage: Store the pasta in an airtight container in the refrigerator for up to 3 days.

Mix it up: You can use almost any quick-cooking vegetable in place of the kale in this recipe. Try broccoli, cauliflower, or snap peas. There's no need for the vegetables to be fresh because frozen and canned varieties work well, too.

This 15-minute noodle dish incorporates hearty kale alongside some of my favorite flavors for a nutritious dinner on even your busiest weeknights. Besides the kick of heat, black pepper helps your body absorb more of the anti-inflammatory curcumin compounds found in turmeric. Ginger is another health-promoting ingredient and can help soothe nausea and indigestion. Use ground ginger if you don't have any fresh ginger in your kitchen.

1. Heat the oil in a 12-quart stockpot and add the kale, edamame, ginger, and pepper.

2. Cook for 3 minutes, or until the kale is wilted and the edamame is thawed. Transfer the mixture to a bowl.

3. Fill the pot with water and bring to a boil over high heat. Cook the rice noodles according to package instructions, then drain and return the noodles to the pot.

4. Add the kale mixture, soy sauce, and turmeric and toss to combine. Sprinkle on the basil, if using. Serve immediately.

PER SERVING: Calories: 380; Total fat: 11g; Carbohydrates: 56g; Fiber: 6g; Protein: 13g; Calcium: 89mg; Vitamin D: 0mcg; Vitamin B$_{12}$: 0 µg; Iron: 3mg; Zinc: 2mg

Baked Spaghetti Squash Lasagna

MAKES 2 SERVINGS · PREP TIME: 5 MINUTES · COOK TIME: 55 MINUTES

ONE PAN

1 small spaghetti squash, halved

1 tablespoon grapeseed oil

¼ teaspoon kosher salt

¼ teaspoon freshly ground black pepper

1 (15-ounce) can white beans, drained and rinsed

3 cups Rosemary and Thyme Red Sauce (page 216) or store-bought sauce

1 cup shredded mozzarella cheese

1 teaspoon dried oregano

Red pepper flakes (optional)

Nothing compares to lasagna made with real pasta, but this baked spaghetti squash dish is a fun, lighter twist on the classic. I can't think of anything I'd rather eat on a date night. Once spaghetti squash is cooked, you can use a fork to scrape out the stringy pieces that resemble spaghetti noodles. If you want the cheese to brown faster, turn the broiler on for the last couple of minutes. Just be sure to watch the top carefully to prevent it from burning.

1. Preheat the oven to 450°F.

2. Place the spaghetti squash halves on a parchment-lined baking sheet, brush the squash with the oil, and sprinkle with the salt and pepper.

3. Roast the squash for 45 minutes, or until the inside of the squash begins to easily separate from the skin. Leave the oven on.

4. Remove the squash from the oven and use a fork to loosen the strands in the middle of each half to create 2 bowl shapes.

5. Place the beans in the squash halves and ladle the red sauce on top.

6. Sprinkle each with the mozzarella and oregano.

continues →

Baked Spaghetti Squash Lasagna *continued*

7. Return the squash to the oven and cook until the cheese is melted, about 10 minutes.

8. Garnish with red pepper flakes, if desired. Serve immediately.

. . . .

Storage: Cover the squash halves with plastic or beeswax wrap and refrigerate for up to 5 days.

. . . .

Make it easier: I like to top the cooked squash with the red sauce, but you can also use your favorite jarred pasta sauce to make the prep a little bit easier.

PER SERVING: Calories: 240; Total fat: 14g; Carbohydrates: 28g; Fiber: 10g; Protein: 4g; Calcium: 180mg; Vitamin D: 0mcg; Vitamin B_{12}: 0µg; Iron: 2mg; Zinc: 0mg

One-Pot Broccoli Mac and Cheese

MAKES 2 SERVINGS · PREP TIME: 5 MINUTES · COOK TIME: 15 MINUTES

DORM-FRIENDLY | ONE POT

2½ cups whole milk

2 cups chopped
broccoli florets

4 ounces elbow macaroni
(or other short pasta)

2 tablespoons
unsalted butter

1½ cups shredded
cheddar cheese

¼ teaspoon kosher salt

¼ teaspoon freshly ground
black pepper

Is there anything more comforting than mac and cheese? This one-pot version is easy to make on a hot plate and much tastier than the boxed variety. As always, you can use whole wheat pasta if you want to make this dish a little more nutritious. I prefer to use whole milk because the fat content makes the cheese sauce extra rich and creamy.

1. Pour the milk into an 8-quart stockpot and bring to a simmer over medium heat.

2. Add the broccoli and macaroni and cook for 7 minutes, or until the pasta is tender.

3. Turn off the heat and add the butter, cheese, salt, and pepper.

4. Mix until the butter and cheese are melted, about 2 minutes. Serve immediately.

Storage: Store in an airtight container and refrigerate for up to 5 days.

Mix it up: Change up the vegetable and type of cheese in this recipe to give it a whole new feel. Try spinach or kale with a blend of Parmesan and mozzarella cheeses.

PER SERVING: Calories: 873; Total fat: 51g; Carbohydrates: 64g; Fiber: 4g; Protein: 40g; Calcium: 975mg; Vitamin D: 35mcg; Vitamin B$_{12}$: 2µg; Iron: 2mg; Zinc: 5m

Five-Spice Noodles

MAKES 2 SERVINGS • PREP TIME: 5 MINUTES • COOK TIME: 20 MINUTES

4 ounces rice noodles

2 tablespoons grapeseed oil, or more as needed

1¼ cups extra-firm tofu, drained, pressed (see Tip, page 50), and cut into 1-inch cubes

1 baby bok choy, chopped into 1-inch pieces

1 cup chopped broccoli florets

1 tablespoon toasted sesame oil (or additional grapeseed oil)

1 tablespoon soy sauce or gluten-free tamari

1 teaspoon Chinese five-spice powder

1 teaspoon maple syrup

Red pepper flakes (optional)

Chinese five-spice powder is said to encompass the five elements—wood, fire, earth, metal, and water—with the five flavors: sour, bitter, sweet, pungent, and salty. The standard recipe calls for cinnamon, cloves, fennel, star anise, and Szechuan peppercorns, but blends can vary slightly. The five-spice powder adds flavorful depth to this simple vegetarian noodle dish.

1. Bring a large saucepan filled three-fourths full of water to a boil over high heat and cook the pasta according to the package instructions. Drain.

2. Heat the 2 tablespoons grapeseed oil in a large skillet over medium heat. Once the oil is heated, add the tofu and cook for 7 minutes, or until the tofu easily separates from the pan. Flip and cook for an additional 3 minutes, or until the other side easily separates and you can stir the tofu without it sticking. If the tofu is sticking, cook for another minute or so before stirring. Add more oil as needed to coat the pan.

3. Add the bok choy and broccoli and cook for 3 minutes, or until the vegetables are tender. Turn off the heat.

4. In a small bowl, whisk together the sesame oil, soy sauce, five-spice powder, and maple syrup until blended. Pour the sauce over the tofu and vegetables.

5. Add the rice noodles to the skillet and toss until all the ingredients are coated with the sauce. Serve with the red pepper flakes, if desired.

. . . .

Storage: Store the pasta in an airtight container in the refrigerator for up to 5 days.

. . . .

Substitute: If you can't find five-spice powder, whip together your own simplified version with 1 tablespoon each of cinnamon and ground fennel, ½ teaspoon ground cloves, and freshly ground black pepper to taste.

PER SERVING: Calories: 530; Total fat: 28g; Carbohydrates: 56g; Fiber: 4g; Protein: 17g; Calcium: 258mg; Vitamin D: 0mcg; Vitamin B$_{12}$: 0µg; Iron: 3mg; Zinc: 2mg

One-Pot Creamy Vegan Rigatoni

MAKES 2 SERVINGS · PREP TIME: 10 MINUTES · COOK TIME: 30 MINUTES

ONE POT

Kosher salt

4 ounces rigatoni pasta
(whole wheat, if desired)

2 tablespoons
grapeseed oil

1 small onion, diced

1 teaspoon dried thyme

1 teaspoon dried oregano

2 cups plain oat milk

4 cups chopped fresh kale

¼ cup nutritional yeast
(optional)

¼ teaspoon freshly ground
black pepper

This plant-based pasta dish is my vegan version of the cream-based dishes that originated in Italy. Instead of cream, though, I use oat milk, which has a neutral flavor and lends a similar creamy texture to the sauce. The result is a comforting plate of pasta that you won't even guess is vegan. Don't rinse the pasta after you cook it, because rinsing can remove some of the starch that helps the sauce stick to the noodles.

1. Fill a 12-quart stockpot three-fourths full of water and add a dash of salt. Bring the water to a boil over high heat and cook the pasta according to the package instructions, or until al dente. Drain and transfer to a bowl.

2. Reduce the heat to medium and place the pot back on the heat. Add the oil.

3. Once the oil is shiny, add the onion, thyme, and oregano, and cook for about 5 minutes, stirring often until the onion is translucent.

4. Add the oat milk and cook, uncovered, for 20 minutes, or until the sauce is thickened and reduced to about half its original volume. Add the kale and cook for 5 minutes, or until wilted. Add the nutritional yeast, ¼ teaspoon salt, and the pepper.

5. Turn off the heat and add the pasta, tossing until the sauce fully coats the noodles. Serve.

....

Storage: Store the leftovers in an airtight container in the refrigerator for up to 1 week.

....

Tip: If you don't have oat milk, try substituting regular cow's milk or cream. To keep this recipe vegan, use almond milk; like oat milk, it has a relatively neutral flavor that's ideal for savory applications.

PER SERVING: Calories: 445; Total fat: 15g; Carbohydrates: 61g; Fiber: 4g; Protein: 17g; Calcium: 277mg; Vitamin D: 115mcg; Vitamin B_{12}: 1µg; Iron: 2mg; Zinc: 2mg

Eggplant Bacon Carbonara

MAKES 2 SERVINGS · PREP TIME: 30 MINUTES · COOK TIME: 40 MINUTES

GREAT FOR SHARING

½ medium eggplant, peeled and sliced into thin strips ⅛ inch thick

Kosher salt

1 tablespoon grapeseed oil

1 tablespoon soy sauce

2 teaspoons smoked paprika

2 teaspoons maple syrup

½ teaspoon freshly ground black pepper

2 large eggs

¼ cup grated Parmesan cheese

¼ cup grated Pecorino Romano (or additional Parmesan)

4 ounces whole wheat spaghetti

Freshly ground black pepper

Carbonara is usually made with processed meats such as guanciale, bacon, or pancetta, but this version incorporates eggplant "bacon" instead. It is every bit as crave-worthy as the original, with its salty soy sauce and smoky paprika flavoring. Eggplant retains a lot of water, so don't skip the salting step, which pulls moisture from the slices so they don't get too soggy. I like a blend of Parmesan and Pecorino Romano cheeses, but you can use each interchangeably.

1. Place the eggplant slices in a colander and sprinkle generously with about 1 teaspoon salt. Wait for 30 minutes, rinse, and then pat the eggplant dry.

2. Preheat the oven to 300°F. Line a baking sheet with parchment.

3. In a medium bowl, whisk the oil, soy sauce, smoked paprika, maple syrup, and black pepper until well blended.

4. Add the eggplant to the sauce, toss until evenly coated, and then place the slices on the baking sheet in a single layer.

5. Bake the eggplant for 40 minutes, or until dry and crispy. Let cool for 15 minutes, then chop into bite-size pieces. Let cool for at least 15 minutes.

6. Beat the eggs in a medium bowl. Add the Parmesan and Pecorino Romano, stirring to combine.

7. Fill a large saucepan three-fourths full of water and add a dash of salt. Bring the water to a boil over high heat and cook the spaghetti according to the package instructions until al dente, about 15 minutes. Reserve 1 cup of the cooking liquid, then drain the pasta and put it back into the saucepan.

8. Add the eggplant and the egg-cheese mixture to the pasta. Toss together and gradually add some of the reserved cooking liquid if you want the sauce to be creamier.

9. Taste and season with salt and pepper, if needed. Serve immediately.

Storage: Store leftovers in an airtight container in the refrigerator for up to 5 days.

Substitute: If you want to add more protein to this pasta dish, try swapping in tempeh strips for the eggplant. You can also use portobello mushrooms to mimic the flavor and texture of meat.

PER SERVING: Calories: 509; Total fat: 20g; Carbohydrates: 60g; Fiber: 7g; Protein: 23g; Calcium: 281mg; Vitamin D: 46mcg; Vitamin B_{12}: 1µg; Iron: 4mg; Zinc: 3mg

Spaghetti and Lentil Balls

MAKES 2 SERVINGS · PREP TIME: 10 MINUTES · COOK TIME: 20 MINUTES

Kosher salt

4 ounces whole wheat spaghetti

1 cup cooked lentils

1 (15-ounce) can white beans, drained and rinsed

¼ cup bread crumbs

¼ cup grated Parmesan cheese or nutritional yeast

¼ cup chopped fresh parsley

1 large egg, beaten

½ teaspoon garlic powder

Kosher salt

Freshly ground black pepper

Grapeseed oil or nonstick cooking spray

3 cups Rosemary and Thyme Red Sauce (see page 216) or store-bought sauce

Whenever you need a little extra comfort, these spaghetti and "meatballs" will make you feel at home. Egg and mashed white beans are used to hold the lentil balls together, but you can easily make this recipe vegan, too. Just swap in nutritional yeast for the Parmesan cheese and use a flax egg instead (see page 31). I like to use panko-style bread crumbs for lentil balls, but any type works. Make your own by pulsing stale bread in a food processor until crumbs form.

1. Fill an 8-quart stockpot three-fourths full of water and add a dash of salt. Bring the water to a boil over high heat and cook the spaghetti according to the package instructions until al dente, about 15 minutes. Drain.

2. While the pasta is cooking, in a large bowl, mash the lentils and beans with a potato masher or a fork.

3. Add the bread crumbs, cheese, parsley, egg, garlic powder, and salt and pepper to taste. Use your hands to form the mixture into balls, using about 2 tablespoons to form each ball.

4. Heat the oil in a large skillet over medium heat. Arrange the balls in a single layer in the skillet and cook for 5 minutes, flip, and cook for an additional 3 minutes, or until the balls are browned on all sides.

5. Pour the sauce into the skillet and bring to a simmer.

6. Divide the spaghetti between 2 bowls, top with the "meatballs," and coat with the sauce. Serve.

Storage: Store the leftovers in an airtight container in the refrigerator for up to 5 days.

Make it easier: Swap in your favorite jarred pasta sauce if you don't have time to make the homemade version. You can also use a can of crushed tomatoes or tomato sauce. Just taste and season with salt, pepper, and additional garlic powder if needed.

PER SERVING: Calories: 620; Total fat: 22g; Carbohydrates: 28g; Fiber: 10g; Protein: 31g; Calcium: 638mg; Vitamin D: 0mcg; Vitamin B$_{12}$: 1µg; Iron: 8mg; Zinc: 4mg

Creamy Pumpkin-Sage Alfredo

MAKES 2 SERVINGS · PREP TIME: 5 MINUTES · COOK TIME: 20 MINUTES

ONE POT

Kosher salt

4 ounces fettuccine

1 tablespoon grapeseed oil

2 cups fresh baby spinach

½ cup pumpkin puree

**2 tablespoons minced
    fresh sage**

1 cup plain oat milk

**½ cup shredded
    Parmesan cheese**

**Freshly ground
    black pepper**

As soon as October hits, I add pumpkin to everything. Canned pumpkin puree is used often in desserts, but I like it in savory dishes, too. Canned pumpkin acts as a thickener and flavor enhancer in this creamy, fall-inspired Alfredo sauce. Be sure to use unsweetened pumpkin (not pumpkin pie filling) whenever you're using it in savory applications. If you can't find fresh sage, swap in 2 teaspoons of the dried herb instead.

1. Fill an 8-quart stockpot three-fourths full of water and add a dash of salt. Bring the water to a boil over high heat and cook the fettuccine according to the package instructions or until al dente, about 15 minutes. Reserve 1 cup of the cooking liquid, then drain the pasta and transfer it to a large bowl.

2. Rinse the stockpot, then add the oil and heat it over medium heat.

3. Add the spinach, pumpkin, sage, and milk to the pot and bring to a simmer.

4. Turn off the heat and add the cheese, stirring to combine.

5. Add the pasta to the sauce and toss until it is evenly coated. If the sauce is too thick, add a tablespoon of the reserved cooking liquid and toss it again.

6. Taste and season with salt and pepper. Serve.

....

Storage: Store the leftover pasta in an airtight container in the refrigerator for up to 5 days.

....

Mix it up: Instead of spinach, try this pumpkin Alfredo sauce with kale, broccoli, or cauliflower. You can also use basil or parsley instead of sage to give it a new feel.

PER SERVING: Calories: 454; Total fat: 16g; Carbohydrates: 58g; Fiber: 4g; Protein: 20g; Calcium: 423mg; Vitamin D: 1mcg; Vitamin B$_{12}$: 1µg; Iron: 4mg; Zinc: 3mg

Greek Lasagna

MAKES 8 SERVINGS · PREP TIME: 5 MINUTES · COOK TIME: 1 HOUR

GREAT FOR SHARING | MAKES LEFTOVERS

Grapeseed oil or nonstick
  cooking spray
Kosher salt
12 ounces whole
  wheat penne
1 (28-ounce) can crushed
  tomatoes
1 tablespoon
  dried oregano
2 cups chopped fresh
  baby spinach
2 (8-ounce) blocks tempeh,
  crumbled
1 cup whole milk
1½ cups grated
  Parmesan cheese
½ teaspoon ground
  nutmeg (optional)
⅔ cup plain Greek yogurt
Chopped fresh parsley
  (optional)

Greek lasagna is also known as *pastitsio*, a baked pasta dish with ground meat (often lamb) and creamy white béchamel sauce. This dish is made with protein-packed tempeh and is a hearty and ultra-satisfying entrée to share with friends. (Your study group will love you forever if you meet them with pastitsio in hand.) Serve this Mediterranean-inspired recipe with a green salad to make it a complete meal.

1. Preheat the oven to 350°F. Grease a 9-by-12-inch baking dish.

2. Fill a 12-quart stockpot three-fourths full of water and add a dash of salt. Bring the water to a boil over high heat and cook the penne according to the package instructions or until al dente, about 10 minutes. Drain the pasta.

3. Add the tomatoes, oregano, spinach, and tempeh and transfer the mixture to the baking dish. Add the pasta and stir well.

4. In a large saucepan, heat the milk, cheese, and nutmeg (if using) over medium heat until simmering, then reduce the heat to medium-low and simmer until the cheese is melted, about 10 minutes.

5. Remove the sauce from the heat, allow it to cool for a couple of minutes, and then add the Greek yogurt.

6. Pour the sauce over the pasta mixture in the baking dish and bake for 45 minutes, or until hot and bubbly.

7. Garnish the dish with fresh parsley (if using) and allow it to cool slightly before cutting it into pieces and serving.

....

Storage: Store leftover pasta in an airtight container in the refrigerator for up to 5 days.

....

Protein swaps: If you can't find tempeh, try using lentils or dried peas instead. Opt for precooked packages or prep them ahead of time to make it easier to cook this dish later on.

PER SERVING: Calories: 387; Total fat: 14g; Carbohydrates: 46g; Fiber: 6g; Protein: 24g; Calcium: 347mg; Vitamin D: 0mcg; Vitamin B_{12}: 1µg; Iron: 4mg; Zinc: 3mg

White Bean and Tomato Stuffed Shells

MAKES 8 SERVINGS • PREP TIME: 5 MINUTES • COOK TIME: 30 MINUTES

GREAT FOR SHARING | MAKES LEFTOVERS

Grapeseed oil or nonstick
  cooking spray
Kosher salt
8 ounces jumbo
  pasta shells
1 (8-ounce) package frozen
  spinach, thawed
2 cups ricotta or Almond
  Ricotta (twice the recipe
  on page 224)
2 (15-ounce) cans
  cannellini beans,
  drained and rinsed
¼ cup chopped
  fresh parsley
1 large egg, beaten
1 (28-ounce) can crushed
  tomatoes
1 tablespoon dried
  or finely chopped
  fresh basil
1½ cups shredded
  mozzarella cheese
½ cup grated Parmesan
  or Pecorino
  Romano cheese

These stuffed shells are the type of meal that looks pretty impressive but actually is really quick and easy to make. You can use staple ingredients from your pantry, including canned tomatoes and beans, dried herbs, and frozen spinach. Use regular ricotta to keep it traditional, or swap in plant-based almond cheese for a nutritious twist. In addition to being a great dish to share with friends, this recipe is suitable for future individual meals. Cook the shells and reheat them all week—it doesn't get any better than that.

1. Preheat the oven to 350°F. Grease a 9-by-12-inch baking pan.

2. Place an 8-quart stockpot filled three-fourths full of water and a dash of salt over high heat. Bring to a boil and cook the pasta for half the time on the package instructions, about 5 minutes. Drain.

3. While the shells are cooking, press the liquid from the spinach and transfer the spinach to a large bowl.

4. Add the ricotta, beans, parsley, and egg and stir to combine.

5. Spread one-third of the crushed tomatoes in the baking pan.

6. Stuff the ricotta mixture into the pasta shells and arrange them in a single layer in the pan.

7. Pour the remaining tomatoes over the shells and sprinkle with the basil.

8. Sprinkle the mozzarella and Parmesan cheese on top, and bake the shells for 25 minutes, or until the cheese melts and starts to bubble. Serve immediately.

....

Storage: Store the leftover pasta in an airtight container in the refrigerator for up to 5 days.

....

Protein swaps: You can use canned or dried white beans for this recipe. If you use dried beans, cook them ahead. In addition to cannellini, Great Northern beans and chickpeas work well in this recipe.

PER SERVING: Calories: 419; Total fat: 16g; Carbohydrates: 44g; Fiber: 10g; Protein: 26g; Calcium: 415mg; Vitamin D: 0mcg; Vitamin B$_{12}$: 1µg; Iron: 5mg; Zinc: 3mg

One-Pan Skillet Lasagna

MAKES 2 SERVINGS · PREP TIME: 5 MINUTES · COOK TIME: 25 MINUTES

2 tablespoons grapeseed oil

¼ cup diced onion

1 (8-ounce) block tempeh, crumbled

3 garlic cloves, minced

⅛ teaspoon kosher salt

⅛ teaspoon freshly ground black pepper

1 (28-ounce) can crushed tomatoes

6 lasagna noodles, broken in half

½ cup ricotta or Almond Ricotta (page 224)

½ cup shredded mozzarella cheese

Storage: Store the leftovers in an airtight container in the refrigerator for up to 5 days.

Substitute: If you can't find tempeh, you can either omit it from the recipe or swap in chopped walnuts. Nuts give this dish some added crunchy texture, and walnuts are also a plant-based source of omega-3s.

Lasagna may be delicious, but it's also pretty time-consuming. That's why I love this skillet lasagna. It's super easy, and it only takes about 30 minutes from start to finish. When making traditional lasagna, you boil the noodles, then assemble the ingredients in a dish and bake it. In this quick recipe, all the ingredients (noodles included) are cooked in one pan. Yay for easy cleanup!

1. Heat the oil in a large skillet (one that has a lid) over medium heat.

2. Once the oil is shiny, add the onion and cook for 4 minutes, or until translucent.

3. Add the tempeh, garlic, salt, and pepper and cook for 1 additional minute.

4. Add the tomatoes and lasagna noodles, then press the noodles down into the tomato sauce. Cover the skillet, and simmer for 15 minutes, or until the noodles are tender. (Add some water if needed to fully cover the noodles as they cook.)

5. Spoon the ricotta around the noodles in the pan and sprinkle the mozzarella on top.

6. Cook for 2 minutes more, or until the cheese is melted. Serve immediately.

PER SERVING: Calories: 260; Total fat: 11g; Carbohydrates: 29g; Fiber: 3g; Protein: 14g; Calcium: 124mg; Vitamin D: 0mcg; Vitamin B$_{12}$: 0µg; Iron: 4mg; Zinc: 1mg

Spinach Spaghetti Pie

MAKES 6 SERVINGS · PREP TIME: 5 MINUTES · COOK TIME: 25 MINUTES

GREAT FOR SHARING | MAKES LEFTOVERS | ONE PAN

Grapeseed oil or nonstick cooking spray

1 large egg, lightly beaten

2 cups cooked spaghetti

2 cups chopped fresh baby spinach

2 tablespoons olive oil

1 cup ricotta or Almond Ricotta (page 224)

1 (15-ounce) can crushed tomatoes

1 cup shredded mozzarella cheese

1 teaspoon dried oregano (optional)

½ teaspoon red pepper flakes (optional)

....

Mix it up: Give this spaghetti pie more of a summery feel with traditional Caprese toppings. Top the spaghetti crust with fresh heirloom tomatoes instead of canned and fresh mozzarella instead of shredded. After it's cooked, garnish the pie with chopped fresh basil.

A spaghetti pie is a fun way to change things for a pasta night. Cooked pasta is mixed with an egg (which acts as a binder) and pressed into a pie dish to form the crust. Then the crust is topped with all the classic Italian fixings: spinach, cheese, tomatoes, and oregano. In addition to being a delicious 30-minute dinner, this recipe is a great way to use up leftover cooked pasta.

1. Preheat the oven to 350°F. Lightly grease a 10-inch pie dish.

2. Place the egg, spaghetti, spinach, and olive oil in a large bowl and mix well. Transfer to the pie dish, spreading the mixture out to form a thin layer.

3. Add spoonfuls of the ricotta on top, then add the tomatoes.

4. Sprinkle with the mozzarella, oregano (if using), and red pepper flakes (if using).

5. Bake the dish for 25 minutes, or until the cheese melts and starts to bubble. Serve immediately.

....

Storage: Store leftovers in an airtight container in the refrigerator for up to 5 days.

PER SERVING: Calories: 233; Total fat: 15g; Carbohydrates: 14g; Fiber: 3g; Protein: 12g; Calcium: 213mg; Vitamin D: 0mcg; Vitamin B_{12}: 1µg; Iron: 2mg; Zinc: 2mg

Vegan Cannelloni

MAKES 2 SERVINGS · PREP TIME: 15 MINUTES · COOK TIME: 25 MINUTES

ONE PAN

Kosher salt

4 ounces cannelloni pasta

Grapeseed oil or nonstick
cooking spray

1 (15-ounce) can crushed
tomatoes

1 (8-ounce) package frozen
spinach, thawed

1 cup Almond Ricotta
(page 224) or
store-bought
vegan ricotta

1 garlic clove, minced (or
use garlic powder)

¼ teaspoon freshly ground
black pepper

Chopped fresh basil
(optional)

Cannelloni refers to the cylindrical shape of this pasta. It is often served stuffed and baked with spinach and ricotta. This vegan version is made with frozen spinach and almond-based dairy-free ricotta, which you can make in just a few minutes in a food processor. Instead of a piping bag to stuff the pasta tubes, I use a zippered plastic bag with one of the corner tips snipped off. You can also use a knife to fill the pasta tubes. If you can't find cannelloni, try this recipe with manicotti tubes instead.

1. Fill a large saucepan three-fourths full of water, add a dash of salt, and bring to a boil over high heat. Add the pasta and cook according to the package instructions. Drain.

2. Preheat the oven to 350°F. Lightly grease an 8-by-11-inch baking pan.

3. Spread a layer of crushed tomatoes in the baking pan.

4. Squeeze out the extra water from the spinach, then transfer the spinach to a large bowl and add the almond ricotta, garlic, ¼ teaspoon salt, and the pepper, stirring to combine.

5. Cut a corner tip off the bottom of a zippered plastic bag and fill the bag with the spinach-ricotta mixture. Pipe the mixture into the pasta tubes and arrange the tubes in the baking pan.

6. Spoon the remaining tomatoes over the pasta and bake for 25 minutes, or until warmed through.

7. Garnish the dish with chopped fresh basil, if desired, and serve.

Storage: Store the leftovers in an airtight container in the refrigerator for up to 5 days.

Tip: Stir a can of white beans into the tomato sauce for extra protein. Just be sure to drain and rinse the beans first.

PER SERVING: Calories: 591; Total fat: 32g; Carbohydrates: 40g; Fiber: 5g; Protein: 35g; Calcium: 609mg; Vitamin D: 1mcg; Vitamin B$_{12}$: 1µg; Iron: 5mg; Zinc: 4mg

Cheesy Broccoli Pasta Bake

MAKES 8 SERVINGS · PREP TIME: 5 MINUTES · COOK TIME: 40 MINUTES

GREAT FOR SHARING

3 tablespoons grapeseed
   oil, plus more for the
   baking dish
Kosher salt
12 ounces whole
   wheat rotini
½ medium onion, diced
2 (8-ounce) blocks tempeh,
   crumbled
1 teaspoon dried oregano
1 teaspoon dried basil
¼ teaspoon freshly ground
   black pepper
4 cups chopped
   broccoli florets
1 (28-ounce) can crushed
   tomatoes
1 cup shredded
   mozzarella cheese
½ cup shredded Parmesan
   cheese (or additional
   mozzarella)

Having friends over for dinner or working on a group project? This baked pasta is my favorite thing to make when I'm cooking for a group. You'll get extra credit if you have this dish prepped and ready to pop in the oven around dinnertime. You only need one pot if you make it in a Dutch oven. Otherwise, you can sauté the ingredients in a large skillet and then transfer them to a baking dish to finish it off.

1. Preheat the oven to 350°F. Lightly grease a 9-by-12-inch baking dish (if you are not using a Dutch oven).

2. Bring a large saucepan filled three-fourths full of water with a dash of salt to a boil over high heat. Add the pasta and cook for 8 minutes, or according to the package instructions. Drain.

3. Heat the 3 tablespoons oil in a Dutch oven (or large skillet) over medium heat.

4. Once the oil is shiny, add the onion and cook for 4 minutes or until translucent.

5. Add the tempeh, oregano, basil, ¼ teaspoon salt, the pepper, and broccoli and cook for 3 minutes, or until the broccoli is bright green. Turn off the heat.

6. Add the tomatoes, stirring to combine, then add the pasta, stirring until it is evenly coated with the sauce.

7. Transfer the mixture to the baking dish (if you're not using a Dutch oven). Sprinkle the mixture with the mozzarella and Parmesan.

8. Bake the casserole for 25 minutes, or until the cheese is melted and bubbling. Move the dish to the broiler during the final couple of minutes, if desired (do not move a Dutch oven to the broiler). Allow to cool for 5 minutes, then serve.

....

Storage: Store the leftovers in an airtight container in the refrigerator for up to 5 days.

....

Protein swap: Omit the tempeh, if desired. You can also swap in white beans or cooked lentils for another source of plant-based protein.

PER SERVING: Calories: 427; Total fat: 17g; Carbohydrates: 51g; Fiber: 7g; Protein: 25g; Calcium: 249mg; Vitamin D: 0mcg; Vitamin B$_{12}$: 0µg; Iron: 5mg; Zinc: 3mg

**Sesame Tofu
and Broccoli,**
page 154

Chapter Seven

Other Entrées

Do you want to ratchet things up and make a meal that's completely different from your regular sandwich, salad, and pasta routine? You'll find everything from a simple naan pizza to Moroccan-inspired couscous and lentil curry in this chapter. All these meals are a fun way to break out of a cooking rut, they're all packed with healthy ingredients, and they are quick enough to prep and cook on a busy weeknight.

Watermelon Poke Bowls 144

Moroccan-Inspired Chickpea Couscous 145

Pinto Bean Tostadas with Red Cabbage and Cilantro Slaw 147

Vegan Garlic-Mushroom Naan Pizzas 149

Easy Edamame Stir-Fry 151

Roasted Chickpea and Carrot Dinner 152

Sesame Tofu and Broccoli 154

Black Bean Burrito Bowl 156

Jerked Tempeh with Herb Rice 157

Lentil and Pumpkin Curry 159

Better-than-Takeout Orange Tofu 160

Tempeh-Stuffed Peppers 161

Vegan Loaded Sweet Potatoes 163

Chimichurri Baked Tofu Bowls 165

Mushroom Taco Bake 166

Watermelon Poke Bowls

MAKES 2 SERVINGS · PREP TIME: 10 MINUTES, PLUS 30 MINUTES TO MARINATE

ONE POT | NO COOK

2 tablespoons soy sauce

1 tablespoon toasted sesame oil

2 teaspoons rice vinegar

¼ teaspoon ground ginger

2 cups cubed seedless watermelon

1 scallion, both white and green parts, chopped

1 cup cooked brown rice (see Tip, page 64)

1 cup steamed shelled edamame

1 nori sheet, torn into pieces

1 avocado, peeled, pitted, and sliced

Storage: Store leftovers in an airtight container in the refrigerator for up to 2 days.

Protein swaps: Instead of the steamed edamame in these bowls, try swapping in crispy tofu, which has been sautéed in a lightly greased skillet for 4 minutes on each side, or until golden and crisp.

Poke (pronounced POH-keh) is the latest food trend. *Poke* means "to slice or cut" in Hawaiian. It consists of marinated fish, usually raw tuna, which is tossed with rice and vegetables in a bowl. But this version uses marinated watermelon cubes instead. Watermelon is a hydrating fruit that's a rich source of antioxidants and phytonutrients, including beta-carotene, vitamin C, and lycopene. Here it is marinated in soy sauce, sesame, and ginger and served in a rice bowl with steamed edamame for protein and avocado for healthy fats. The nori in these bowls is a type of seaweed that's commonly used for sushi; look for it in the Asian section of your local grocery store.

1. In a medium bowl, whisk the soy sauce, sesame oil, vinegar, and ginger until well combined.

2. Add the watermelon and scallion and marinate for at least 30 minutes or cover and chill in the refrigerator overnight.

3. Divide the rice into 2 bowls and add the edamame, nori, and avocado.

4. Top with the marinated watermelon.

5. Drizzle the remaining marinade over the bowls, if desired. Serve.

PER SERVING: Calories: 505; Total fat: 27g; Carbohydrates: 56g; Fiber: 15g; Protein: 16g; Calcium: 96mg; Vitamin D: 0mcg; Vitamin B$_{12}$: 0µg; Iron: 3mg; Zinc: 3mg

Moroccan-Inspired Chickpea Couscous

MAKES 2 SERVINGS · PREP TIME: 5 MINUTES · COOK TIME: 20 MINUTES

ONE POT

1½ cups water

1 cup traditional couscous

1 tablespoon grapeseed oil

¼ cup diced onion

1 teaspoon ground cumin

½ teaspoon ground turmeric

¼ teaspoon kosher salt

¼ teaspoon freshly ground black pepper

2 teaspoons olive oil

1 (15-ounce) can chickpeas, drained and rinsed

2 tablespoons chopped fresh cilantro

2 tablespoons chopped fresh mint

¼ cup slivered almonds

¼ cup raisins

This staple food of North Africa has become popular in the United States, as well. It's an ideal weeknight dinner for two busy college students, since it is easy, affordable, and takes less than 30 minutes to prep and cook. Here, the grain dish is balanced with a mix of nutrients for long-lasting energy, including plant-based protein and fiber from chickpeas. I like to add fresh herbs for lots of color and flavor, but you could also use dried versions in a pinch.

1. In a medium saucepan, bring the water to a boil over high heat, remove it from the heat, stir in the couscous, cover, and let stand for 10 minutes. Fluff with a fork and set aside.

2. Heat the grapeseed oil in a large skillet (that has a lid) over medium heat.

3. Once the oil is shiny, add the onion and cook for 4 minutes or until the onion is translucent.

4. Add the cumin, turmeric, salt, and pepper and cook for 1 minute or until aromatic.

5. Turn off the heat and add the olive oil, the couscous, the chickpeas, cilantro, mint, almonds, and raisins.

6. Taste and adjust the seasoning, if needed. Serve.

continues →

Moroccan-Inspired Chickpea Couscous *continued*

. . . .

Storage: Store any leftovers in an airtight container in the refrigerator for up to 1 week.

. . . .

Substitute: Many different kinds of dried fruits would be delicious in this recipe. Instead of raisins, try dried cherries, currants, apricots, or dates. If you want to try fresh fruit, use halved grapes or pitted cherries.

PER SERVING: Calories: 723; Total fat: 22g; Carbohydrates: 108g; Fiber: 16g; Protein: 25g; Calcium: 133mg; Vitamin D: 0mcg; Vitamin B_{12}: 0µg; Iron: 6mg; Zinc: 3mg

Pinto Bean Tostadas with Red Cabbage and Cilantro Slaw

MAKES 2 SERVINGS · PREP TIME: 5 MINUTES · COOK TIME: 10 MINUTES

ONE POT

4 (4-inch) corn tortillas

1 teaspoon grapeseed oil

Kosher salt

1 (15-ounce) can pinto beans, drained and rinsed

¼ cup vegetable broth or water

1 teaspoon ground cumin

1 teaspoon chili powder

½ teaspoon garlic powder

⅛ teaspoon cayenne (optional)

1 cup Red Cabbage and Cilantro Slaw (page 93)

Tostadas are a quick and easy lunch to enjoy between classes. Even if you only have 15 minutes, you can still fill up on lots of protein from the pinto beans and fiber from the zesty cabbage slaw. Bake the tortillas and prep the slaw a few days in advance, if you want. Then on the day of, you need only warm the beans and assemble the tostada. If you don't have a full-size oven, you can make these in a toaster oven instead.

1. Preheat the oven or toaster oven to 400°F. Line a baking sheet with parchment.

2. Brush the tortillas with the oil, sprinkle with salt, and spread on the baking sheet in a single layer.

3. Bake the tortillas for 8 minutes, flipping halfway through, or until crispy. Cool the tortillas on a rack for 15 minutes.

4. While the tortillas are baking, in a large saucepan, stir together the pinto beans, broth or water, cumin, chili powder, and garlic powder over medium heat.

5. Cook for 5 minutes, or until warmed through and the broth is absorbed.

continues →

Pinto Bean Tostadas with Red Cabbage and Cilantro Slaw *continued*

6. Taste and season with salt, if needed.

7. Mash the bean mixture with a potato masher or a fork and divide it evenly among the tortillas, spreading it out.

8. Spoon the Red Cabbage and Cilantro Slaw on top. Serve immediately.

....

Make it easier: Crispy tostada shells are often available at the supermarket; look for them near the tortillas. You can also use a premixed vegetable slaw instead of the prepared slaw.

PER SERVING: Calories: 324; Total fat: 5g; Carbohydrates: 58g; Fiber: 15g; Protein: 15g; Calcium: 165mg; Vitamin D: 0mcg; Vitamin B$_{12}$: 0μg; Iron: 5mg; Zinc: 2mg

Vegan Garlic-Mushroom Naan Pizzas

MAKES 2 SERVINGS · PREP TIME: 5 MINUTES · COOK TIME: 15 MINUTES

GREAT FOR SHARING

1 tablespoon grapeseed oil, plus more as needed

½ cup sliced fresh mushrooms

4 garlic cloves, sliced

1 teaspoon balsamic vinegar

2 tablespoons nutritional yeast

¼ teaspoon kosher salt

⅛ teaspoon freshly ground black pepper

2 vegan naan flatbreads

½ cup tomato sauce

1 teaspoon dried oregano

½ teaspoon red pepper flakes (optional)

The hardest part of homemade pizza is making the dough, but this recipe handily solves that problem by using store-bought naan instead. Naan is an oven-baked flatbread that's a staple of Indian cooking. It works perfectly as a base for the meaty sautéed mushrooms and spicy garlic, or you can use any of your favorite pizza toppings. Many naan flatbreads are naturally vegan, but check the label first if you want to ensure the recipe is dairy-free.

1. Preheat the oven or toaster oven to 400°F. Grease a baking sheet or line it with parchment.

2. Heat the 1 tablespoon oil in a large skillet over medium heat.

3. Add the mushrooms and garlic and cook for 4 minutes or until the mushrooms are tender and darker in color.

4. Turn off the heat and add the vinegar, nutritional yeast, salt, and pepper, stirring to combine.

5. Lay the naan on the baking sheet and spread half the tomato sauce on each bread, leaving about ½ inch space around the edge.

6. Divide the mushroom mixture between the breads.

continues →

Vegan Garlic-Mushroom Naan Pizzas *continued*

7. Sprinkle the pizzas with the oregano and red pepper flakes (if using) and bake for 10 minutes, or until the crusts are golden. Serve immediately.

....

Substitute: Nutritional yeast is a delicious vegan alternative to cheese. Look for it in the bulk section or natural foods aisle. If you can't find nutritional yeast, try subbing with a nut-based cheese, such as the Almond Ricotta on page 224. You can also top the breads with fresh or shredded mozzarella, if you include dairy foods.

PER SERVING: Calories: 386; Total fat: 12g; Carbohydrates: 56g; Fiber: 5g; Protein: 15g; Calcium: 117mg; Vitamin D: 0mcg; Vitamin B_{12}: 0µg; Iron: 5mg; Zinc: 2mg

Easy Edamame Stir-Fry

MAKES 2 SERVINGS · PREP TIME: 10 MINUTES · COOK TIME: 10 MINUTES

DORM-FRIENDLY | ONE PAN

2 tablespoons soy sauce

1 tablespoon rice vinegar

1 tablespoon toasted
sesame oil

1 teaspoon ground ginger

1 teaspoon maple syrup

½ teaspoon garlic powder

2 tablespoons
grapeseed oil

4 cups chopped
broccoli florets

1 cup frozen
shelled edamame

OPTIONAL TOPPINGS

1 scallion, both white and
green parts, chopped

1 tablespoon sesame seeds

Mix it up: The nice thing about a stir-fry is that you can use pretty much any vegetable you have in your kitchen. I often make this recipe with whatever fresh produce I need to use up before it goes bad. Try bok choy, cauliflower, carrots, or bell peppers.

A veggie stir-fry is a staple dish to make when you don't have a lot of time or fresh ingredients on hand. Keep bags of shelled edamame and frozen broccoli in your kitchen at all times, and you'll always be able to make simple yet nutritious meals in minutes. I like to serve this vegan stir-fry over rice (which you can also buy precooked in the frozen section) for a quick, easy, and ultra-satisfying meal. Opt for brown rice to maximize the fiber and nutritional benefits of this dish.

1. In a small bowl, whisk together the soy sauce, vinegar, sesame oil, ginger, maple syrup, and garlic powder.

2. Heat the grapeseed oil in a large skillet or wok over medium-high heat.

3. Add the broccoli and cook for 3 minutes or until bright green.

4. Add the edamame and the soy sauce mixture and cook until warmed through.

5. Garnish the dish with the scallions and sesame seeds, if desired.

PER SERVING: Calories: 361; Total fat: 25g; Carbohydrates: 24g; Fiber: 9g; Protein: 15g; Calcium: 145mg; Vitamin D: 0mcg; Vitamin B$_{12}$: 0µg; Iron: 4mg; Zinc: 2mg

Roasted Chickpea and Carrot Dinner

MAKES 2 SERVINGS · PREP TIME: 10 MINUTES · COOK TIME: 30 MINUTES

ONE PAN

2 tablespoons grapeseed
   oil, plus more
   for greasing the
   baking sheet
1 tablespoon apple
   cider vinegar
1 teaspoon ground cumin
½ teaspoon onion powder
½ teaspoon garlic powder
¼ teaspoon kosher salt
¼ teaspoon freshly ground
   black pepper
1 (15-ounce) can
   chickpeas, drained
   and rinsed
1 pound fresh carrots,
   halved (5 medium)

OPTIONAL FOR SERVING

½ cup chopped fresh
   cilantro
¾ cup Lemon Tahini
   Dressing (page 214) or
   store-bought sauce
Cooked brown rice

A simple roasted vegetable dinner is the ultimate convenience meal, since you can cook the whole thing on a single rimmed baking sheet. The trick is to choose a protein and vegetables that cook in about the same amount of time. The chickpeas and carrots in this recipe are an ideal pairing, since both roast to perfection in about 30 minutes. Don't skip drying the chickpeas off with a towel before you mix them with the rest of the ingredients—it helps them get crispy while they are roasting in the oven.

1. Preheat the oven to 450°F. Grease or line a rimmed baking sheet with parchment.

2. In a large bowl, whisk together the 2 tablespoons oil, the vinegar, cumin, onion powder, garlic powder, salt, and pepper until well blended.

3. Dry the chickpeas with a clean towel and add them along with the carrots to the bowl with the dressing, and stir until evenly coated.

4. Spread the mixture on the baking sheet and bake for 30 minutes or until the carrots are tender and the chickpeas are golden and crispy.

5. Divide the mixture between 2 bowls and serve with the cilantro, tahini dressing and brown rice, if desired.

Storage: Store any leftovers in an airtight container in the refrigerator for up to 1 week. Reheat in the oven for best results.

Mix it up: My favorite way to serve this dish is to drizzle it with the creamy and tangy tahini dressing but you can also try it with a vinaigrette or salsa and guacamole for a Mexican-inspired twist. Instead of brown rice, serve the dish over cooked farro, quinoa, or barley.

PER SERVING: Calories: 425; Total fat: 18g; Carbohydrates: 57g; Fiber: 16g; Protein: 13g; Calcium: 149mg; Vitamin D: 0mcg; Vitamin B$_{12}$: 0µg; Iron: 5mg; Zinc: 3mg

Sesame Tofu and Broccoli

MAKES 2 SERVINGS · PREP TIME: 10 MINUTES · COOK TIME: 15 MINUTES

DORM-FRIENDLY | ONE PAN

1 tablespoon grapeseed oil

½ (14-ounce) block extra-firm tofu, drained, pressed (see Tip, page 50), and cubed

4 cups chopped broccoli florets

1 (1-inch) piece of fresh ginger, peeled and grated

2 garlic cloves, sliced

¼ cup vegetable broth

2 tablespoons soy sauce

1 tablespoon rice vinegar

1 tablespoon toasted sesame oil

1 teaspoon maple syrup

1 tablespoon sesame seeds, toasted if desired

Most people think of citrus fruits as providing the most vitamin C, but broccoli, a humble member of the cruciferous family, actually contains even more of the immune-boosting antioxidant than oranges. Use fresh or frozen broccoli to make this easy Asian-inspired dish, which is hearty and satisfying when served over a scoop of brown rice. For the crispiest tofu, press out all the liquid before chopping it into cubes.

1. Heat the grapeseed oil in a large skillet or wok over medium heat.

2. Add the tofu and cook for 4 minutes each side, or until golden. Transfer to a plate.

3. Add the broccoli, ginger, garlic, and broth to the skillet and cook for 5 minutes or until the broccoli is tender.

4. In a small bowl, whisk together the soy sauce, vinegar, sesame oil, maple syrup, and sesame seeds until well blended.

5. Pour the sauce into the skillet. Add the cooked tofu, toss, and serve warm.

Storage: Store the leftovers in an airtight container in the refrigerator for up to 1 week.

Protein swaps: Shelled edamame, which is another soy-based food like tofu, makes an ideal substitute in Asian-inspired dishes like this one. For a soy-free alternative, try making this dish with scrambled eggs instead. Scramble the eggs, transfer them to a plate, and cook the rest of the recipe as usual, stirring the cooked eggs back in just before serving.

PER SERVING: Calories: 321; Total fat: 22g; Carbohydrates: 20g; Fiber: 6g; Protein: 17g; Calcium: 279mg; Vitamin D: 0mcg; Vitamin B$_{12}$: 0µg; Iron: 4mg; Zinc: 2mg

Black Bean Burrito Bowl

MAKES 2 SERVINGS · PREP TIME: 5 MINUTES · COOK TIME: 6 MINUTES

DORM-FRIENDLY | ONE PAN

1 tablespoon grapeseed oil

¼ cup diced red onion

1 (15-ounce) can black
beans, drained
and rinsed

1 cup frozen or canned
corn kernels

1 cup chopped fresh kale
or fresh baby spinach

1 tablespoon fresh
lime juice

2 teaspoons ground cumin

1 teaspoon chili powder

¼ teaspoon kosher salt

⅛ teaspoon freshly ground
black pepper

OPTIONAL FOR SERVING

Cooked brown rice
Fresh cilantro
Sliced avocado

School-day lunches don't get any easier than these burrito bowls. Prep the rice in advance (or look for pre-cooked options in the store's frozen section), and you can make this vegan meal in less than 15 minutes. Burrito bowls are tasty warm or at room temperature, so even if you don't have access to a microwave, this is still a convenient meal to pack for a lunch on the go. Slice the avocado just before serving or squeeze a bit of lime juice on top to prevent browning if you're preparing this in advance.

1. Heat the oil in a large skillet over medium heat.

2. Once the oil is shiny, add the onion and cook for 3 minutes, or until translucent.

3. Add the black beans, corn, kale, lime juice, cumin, chili powder, salt, and pepper and cook for 3 minutes, or until warmed through and the kale is wilted.

4. Serve with brown rice, cilantro, and avocado, if desired.

Storage: Store leftovers in an airtight container and refrigerate for up to 1 week. Wait to slice the avocado until immediately before serving.

Protein swaps: Canned black beans are a convenient staple for adding protein to Mexican-inspired dishes. Dried beans also work great, and you can swap in pinto or red kidney varieties to change the flavor. For another twist, try lentils or scrambled eggs.

PER SERVING: Calories: 353; Total fat: 9g; Carbohydrates: 57g; Fiber: 17g; Protein: 17g; Calcium: 167mg; Vitamin D: 0mcg; Vitamin B_{12}: 0µg; Iron: 6mg; Zinc: 3mg

Jerked Tempeh with Herb Rice

MAKES 2 SERVINGS · PREP TIME: 10 MINUTES · COOK TIME: 10 MINUTES

DORM-FRIENDLY | ONE PAN

1 (8-ounce)
    package tempeh
1 tablespoon coconut oil,
    melted, plus more for
    greasing the skillet
2 tablespoons jerk
    seasoning
1 cup cooked brown rice
    (see Tip, page 64)
½ cup shredded
    green cabbage
½ cup chopped fresh
    cilantro
1 tablespoon olive oil,
    or more as needed
1 tablespoon fresh lime
    juice, or more as needed
Kosher salt

Jamaican jerk preparations may have originated in the tropics, but it's so prevalent in the United States now that you can find the seasoning blend in most supermarkets. This Caribbean preparation typically includes a sweet and spicy blend of cumin, allspice, ginger, nutmeg, chili pepper, thyme, and brown sugar. Combined with the nutty flavors of melted coconut oil, the seasoning makes a flavorful coating for pan-fried tempeh strips. It's the ideal meal to make when you should be studying but are actually dreaming about your next spring break.

1. Brush the tempeh with the 1 tablespoon melted coconut oil and sprinkle all over with the jerk seasoning.

2. Lightly grease a large skillet and preheat it over medium heat.

3. Arrange the seasoned tempeh in a single layer in the skillet and cook for 4 minutes on each side, or until golden and warmed through.

4. Transfer the tempeh to a cutting board, cut it into strips, and place the strips in a large bowl.

continues →

Jerked Tempeh with Herb Rice *continued*

5. Add the brown rice, cabbage, cilantro, 1 tablespoon olive oil, and 1 tablespoon lime juice.

6. Taste the mixture and season with salt, and add more oil or lime juice if needed.

....

Storage: Store the leftovers in an airtight container in the refrigerator for up to 5 days.

....

Mix it up: Fresh cilantro adds an herbaceous punch to the rice salad served with these Jamaican jerk tempeh strips. If you're not a fan of cilantro, try swapping in fresh parsley instead.

PER SERVING: Calories: 484; Total fat: 27g; Carbohydrates: 41g; Fiber: 4g; Protein: 24g; Calcium: 149mg; Vitamin D: 0mcg; Vitamin B$_{12}$: 0µg; Iron: 4mg; Zinc: 2mg

Lentil and Pumpkin Curry

MAKES 4 SERVINGS • PREP TIME: 10 MINUTES • COOK TIME: 30 MINUTES

DORM-FRIENDLY | GREAT FOR SHARING | MAKES LEFTOVERS | ONE PAN

2 tablespoons
   grapeseed oil
½ cup diced onion
2 medium carrots, diced
¼ teaspoon kosher salt
¼ teaspoon freshly ground
   black pepper
2 tablespoons
   curry powder
1 cup dried lentils, rinsed
1 (13-ounce) can
   unsweetened
   coconut milk
1 (15-ounce) can
   pumpkin puree
1 cup vegetable broth
1 scallion, both white and
   green parts, chopped
Fresh cilantro (optional)

Protein swaps:

Instead of dried lentils, use cooked white beans, cubed tofu, or canned chickpeas to get your protein. Dried split peas are another budget-friendly protein option. Just adjust the cooking time and add water as needed to simmer the peas until they're tender.

The pumpkin puree acts as a natural thickener in this plant-based curry recipe, which requires only one pan to cook the dried lentils and flavorful coconut curry sauce. Be sure to use unsweetened pumpkin (not pumpkin pie filling), and serve the finished dish over brown rice for a hearty and satisfying autumnal dinner with friends.

1. Heat the oil in a large skillet (that has a lid) over medium heat.

2. Once the oil is shiny, add the onion, carrots, salt, and pepper, and cook for 5 minutes or until the onion is translucent.

3. Add the curry powder and cook for 1 minute. Add the lentils, coconut milk, pumpkin, and broth. Cover the skillet, and bring the liquid to a boil.

4. Reduce the heat to low and simmer for for 20 minutes, stirring occasionally, or until the lentils are tender and the curry is thickened. Add ¼ to ½ cup water if the curry is thickened before the lentils are tender.

5. Garnish with the chopped scallion and the cilantro, if desired. Serve.

Storage: Store the leftovers in an airtight container in the refrigerator for up to 5 days.

PER SERVING: Calories: 330; Total fat: 27g; Carbohydrates: 22g; Fiber: 6g; Protein: 6g; Calcium: 82mg; Vitamin D: 0mcg; Vitamin B$_{12}$: 0µg; Iron: 6mg; Zinc: 1mg

Better-than-Takeout Orange Tofu

MAKES 2 SERVINGS · PREP TIME: 5 MINUTES · COOK TIME: 5 MINUTES

DORM-FRIENDLY | ONE PAN

1 tablespoon grated
orange zest

3 tablespoons fresh
orange juice

1 tablespoon rice vinegar

1 tablespoon toasted
sesame oil

1 tablespoon soy sauce

2 tablespoons maple syrup
or honey

1 teaspoon cornstarch

1 teaspoon ground ginger

1 recipe Tofu Nuggets
(page 183), or 1 cup
store-bought equivalent

Red pepper flakes
(optional)

....

Make it easier:
Breaded tofu nuggets
mimic the crispy fried
poultry that's often used
for this dish. To make it
easier, use plain cubed tofu
instead. The texture may
be less crispy, but you'll still
get all the sweet and tart
citrusy flavors.

Orange chicken may seem like a classic Chinese dish, but it was actually developed in the United States when Chinese restaurants began catering to the sweeter palates of Americans in the mid-1900s. This version is made with tofu and is flavored with fresh citrus, sesame oil, soy sauce, and a little bit of maple syrup or honey for sweetness. This recipe isn't overpoweringly sweet, so it tastes even better than takeout. Serve it with rice and steamed veggies, such as broccoli, bok choy, or carrots.

1. In a medium bowl, whisk together the orange zest, orange juice, vinegar, sesame oil, soy sauce, maple syrup, cornstarch, and ginger until blended.

2. Pour the sauce into a large skillet over medium heat. Once it is simmering, add the tofu nuggets and cook for 5 minutes, or until warmed through and the sauce is thickened.

3. Garnish with the red pepper flakes, if desired, and serve.

....

Storage: Store leftovers in an airtight container in the refrigerator for up to 1 week.

PER SERVING: Calories: 450; Total fat: 27g; Carbohydrates: 40g; Fiber: 3g; Protein: 14g; Calcium: 240mg; Vitamin D: 0mcg; Vitamin B$_{12}$: 0µg; Iron: 3mg; Zinc: 2mg

Tempeh-Stuffed Peppers

MAKES 2 SERVINGS · PREP TIME: 10 MINUTES · COOK TIME: 35 MINUTES

GREAT FOR SHARING

2 bell peppers (any color)

2 tablespoons grapeseed oil

¼ cup diced onion

1 teaspoon ground cumin

1 teaspoon ground coriander

½ teaspoon smoked paprika

¼ teaspoon kosher salt

¼ teaspoon freshly ground black pepper

1 (16-ounce) package tempeh, crumbled

⅔ cup cooked brown rice (see Tip, page 64)

½ cup frozen corn kernels

1 cup chopped fresh or frozen spinach

½ cup shredded pepper jack cheese (optional)

Stuffed bell peppers are a classic dish in many cultures. This recipe uses a mix of American and Mexican-inspired ingredients, along with protein-packed tempeh crumbles instead of the more traditional ground beef. To reduce your waste, snap off the stems and discard, then dice the tops of the bell peppers and put them in the skillet along with the rest of the filling ingredients. This is also a great way to make use of leftover cooked rice.

1. Preheat the oven to 375°F.

2. Cut the tops off the bell peppers, scoop out the seeds, and transfer the peppers to an 8-inch glass baking dish.

3. Heat the oil in a large skillet over medium heat.

4. Once the oil is shiny, add the onion and cook for 3 minutes, or until translucent.

5. Add the cumin, coriander, smoked paprika, salt, and pepper and cook for 1 minute.

6. Add the crumbled tempeh, brown rice, corn, and spinach. Cook for 5 minutes, or until warmed through.

7. Use the mixture to stuff the bell peppers. Top each pepper with the pepper jack cheese (if using) and bake for 25 minutes, or until the cheese is melted. Serve immediately.

continues →

Tempeh-Stuffed Peppers *continued*

Storage: Store leftovers in an airtight container in the refrigerator for up to 1 week.

Substitute: To make these stuffed peppers vegan, just leave out the pepper jack cheese—there's still plenty of flavor from the tempeh filling on its own. For cheesy flavor without any dairy, try stirring a couple tablespoons of nutritional yeast into the tempeh filling before you stuff the peppers.

PER SERVING: Calories: 617; Total fat: 33g; Carbohydrates: 51g; Fiber: 8g; Protein: 38g; Calcium: 322mg; Vitamin D: 0mcg; Vitamin B_{12}: 0µg; Iron: 8mg; Zinc: 3mg

Vegan Loaded Sweet Potatoes

MAKES 2 SERVINGS · PREP TIME: 5 MINUTES · COOK TIME: 45 MINUTES

ONE PAN

2 medium sweet potatoes, scrubbed

2 tablespoons grapeseed oil

¼ cup diced onion

1 teaspoon ground cumin

1 teaspoon ground coriander

½ teaspoon smoked paprika

¼ teaspoon kosher salt

¼ teaspoon freshly ground black pepper

1 (15-ounce) can black beans, drained and rinsed

2 cups chopped fresh or frozen spinach

1 avocado, peeled, pitted, and diced

Spicy Blender Salsa (page 219) or store-bought salsa (optional)

The bright orange hue of a standard sweet potato is one indicator of its high antioxidant content. These compounds are essential for fighting the free radicals that can otherwise cause damage to the body. As a starchy vegetable, sweet potatoes make a tasty alternative to grains such as rice or barley, since they also provide gut-boosting fiber and energizing carbohydrates. Stuff the baked sweet potatoes with protein-packed black beans, dark leafy greens, and diced avocado for a simple and satisfying school-night meal. I like to add salsa, but experiment with other sauces to find a new favorite.

1. Preheat the oven to 450°F.

2. Pierce the sweet potatoes a few times with a fork and place them on a foil-lined baking sheet. Bake for 45 minutes, or until softened and easily pierced with a fork.

3. While the potatoes are baking, heat the oil in a large skillet over medium heat.

4. Once the oil is shiny, add the onion and cook for 3 minutes, or until translucent.

5. Add the cumin, coriander, smoked paprika, salt, and pepper and cook for 1 minute.

continues →

Vegan Loaded Sweet Potatoes *continued*

6. Add the black beans and spinach and cook for 5 minutes, or until warmed through.

7. Cut the sweet potatoes open lengthwise without cutting through the bottom skin.

8. Open the potatoes and mash the insides with a fork to create bowls in the center of each half.

9. Divide the bean mixture between the sweet potatoes. Top with the avocado and serve with the salsa, if desired.

. . . .

Storage: Store leftovers in an airtight container in the refrigerator for up to 1 week.

. . . .

Make it easier: Cook the sweet potatoes in the microwave to speed up the cooking time. Pierce the sweet potatoes a few times with a fork, arrange them on a microwave-safe plate, and cook for 5 minutes or until fork-tender.

PER SERVING: Calories: 573; Total fat: 26g; Carbohydrates: 71g; Fiber: 25g; Protein: 21g; Calcium: 299mg; Vitamin D: 0mcg; Vitamin B_{12}: 0μg; Iron: 8mg; Zinc: 3mg

Chimichurri Baked Tofu Bowls

MAKES 2 SERVINGS · PREP TIME: 5 MINUTES · COOK TIME: 30 MINUTES

ONE PAN

½ (14-ounce) block firm
   tofu, drained and
   pressed
2 medium carrots,
   quartered
2 cups fresh
   cauliflower florets
2 tablespoons
   grapeseed oil
1 tablespoon apple
   cider vinegar
¼ teaspoon kosher salt
¼ teaspoon freshly ground
   black pepper
1½ cups cooked brown rice
   (see Tip, page 64)
½ cup Chimichurri
   Sauce (page 217) or
   store-bought sauce

Mix it up: The great
thing about sauces is that
they add tons of flavor to an
otherwise neutral dish. This
means you can swap out
the chimichurri and choose
any of all sorts of different
tastes. Try sesame oil, rice
vinegar, and soy sauce for
an Asian-inspired tofu bowl.

Zesty and herbaceous chimichurri originated in
Argentina, where it was served on meat. Here the
parsley-based sauce is used to flavor crispy baked
tofu and vegetables. In this recipe, you bake the tofu,
carrots, and cauliflower all on the same baking sheet,
so cleanup is simple. Cut the carrots and cauliflower
into large pieces that are about the same size as the
tofu—that helps all the ingredients to roast evenly in
the oven.

1. Preheat the oven to 450°F. Line a rimmed baking
    sheet with parchment or a silicone baking mat.

2. Cut the tofu into 8 pieces and place in a large bowl.

3. Add the carrots, cauliflower, oil, vinegar, salt, and
    pepper to the bowl and toss to combine.

4. Spread the mixture in an even layer on the baking
    sheet and bake for 30 minutes, flipping halfway
    through, or until the tofu is golden and crispy.

5. Place the rice in 2 bowls and add the tofu mixture.
    Spoon the sauce over each and serve.

Storage: Store the leftovers in an airtight container in the
refrigerator for up to 1 week.

PER SERVING: Calories: 896; Total fat: 70g; Carbohydrates: 49g;
Fiber: 7g; Protein: 12g; Calcium: 199mg; Vitamin D: 0mcg;
Vitamin B$_{12}$: 0µg; Iron: 5mg; Zinc: 2mg

Mushroom Taco Bake

MAKES 6 SERVINGS · PREP TIME: 10 MINUTES · COOK TIME: 40 MINUTES

GREAT FOR SHARING | MAKES LEFTOVERS

2 tablespoons grapeseed oil, plus more for greasing the baking dish

½ cup diced red onion

6 garlic cloves, chopped

1 tablespoon ground cumin

1 tablespoon ground coriander

¼ teaspoon kosher salt

⅛ teaspoon freshly ground black pepper

2 portobello mushroom caps (about 6 ounces), chopped

3 cups cooked black beans

1 (28-ounce) can crushed tomatoes

12 (4-inch) corn tortillas, halved

1½ cups shredded pepper jack cheese

Next time you have friends over for dinner, try this crowd-pleasing casserole. What's not to love about mushrooms, beans, tortillas, and cheese, all layered and baked until hot and melty. To make this recipe as budget-friendly as possible, cook a large batch of dried black beans (you can prepare them up to 3 days in advance) and buy a block of pepper jack cheese to shred yourself. Canned beans and bags of shredded cheese save time, but you'll usually pay a little bit extra for that convenience.

1. Preheat the oven to 425°F and grease an 8-by-11-inch baking dish.

2. Heat the 2 tablespoons oil in a large skillet over medium heat.

3. Once the oil is shiny, add the onion and cook for 3 minutes or until translucent.

4. Add the garlic, cumin, coriander, salt, and pepper and cook for 1 minute.

5. Add the mushroom caps and cook for 3 minutes, or until darkened.

6. Add the beans and tomatoes and cook for 5 minutes, or until warmed through.

7. Spread one-fourth of the bean mixture in the bottom of the baking dish.

8. Arrange 8 of the tortilla halves on top of the sauce and cover with another one-fourth of the bean mixture.

9. Sprinkle ½ cup of the cheese on top.

10. Repeat layering the ingredients 2 more times, until all the ingredients are used.

11. Transfer the dish to the oven and bake for 25 minutes, or until the cheese is melted. Serve.

. . . .

Storage: The leftovers can be covered and refrigerated for up to 1 week.

. . . .

Protein swaps: Instead of black beans, substitute pinto beans, red kidney beans, lentils, crumbled tempeh, or walnuts.

PER SERVING: Calories: 77; Total fat: 15g; Carbohydrates: 45g; Fiber: 13g; Protein: 19g; Calcium: 359mg; Vitamin D: 0mcg; Vitamin B_{12}: 0µg; Iron: 4mg; Zinc: 3mg

Baked Potato Skins,
page 189

Chapter Eight

Snacks and Sides

When you're a college student, it often feels like you don't ever have time to sit down for a full meal. You know you need energy to keep you going, but cooking and grocery shopping just aren't going to happen. On weekends, university life comes with plenty of opportunities for shareable party snacks. Either way, you need simple, energizing, and great-tasting noshes in order to thrive while you're away at school. These recipes make up my favorite midday bites for every college occasion.

Blended Golden Milk Latte 170

Granny Smith Green Smoothie 171

Energizing Matcha Smoothie 172

Curried Kale Chips 173

Quick Pickled Carrots and Vegetables 174

Apple Chips with Cinnamon-Yogurt Dip 175

Fruit and Nut Energy Bites 176

No-Bake Chocolate–Peanut Butter Bars 177

Sesame-Ginger Edamame 178

Cheesy Vegan Popcorn 179

Chili-Lime Tortilla Chips 180

Roasted Potatoes with Lemon-Chive Yogurt Dip 181

Vegetable Spring Rolls 182

Tofu Nuggets 183

Buffalo Cauliflower 184

Garlicky Roasted Chickpeas 186

Black Bean Quesadillas 187

Pan-Roasted Nachos 188

Baked Potato Skins 189

Vegan Party Platter 190

Blended Golden Milk Latte

MAKES 2 SERVINGS · PREP TIME: 5 MINUTES

3 cups plain Creamy Oat Milk (page 210) (or milk of choice)

1 teaspoon ground turmeric

½ teaspoon ground cinnamon

¼ teaspoon ground ginger

⅛ teaspoon freshly ground black pepper

1 teaspoon maple syrup (optional)

½ teaspoon vanilla extract (optional)

Ice cubes, for serving (optional)

Whenever I want to treat myself to something cool and spicy, I make this blended turmeric drink. The blender mixes the ingredients while frothing the oat milk into a barista-worthy beverage in no time. Make these drinks while you're taking a study break or on the morning after you accidentally stayed out too late.

1. Place the oat milk, turmeric, cinnamon, ginger, black pepper, and maple syrup and vanilla (if using) in a blender.

2. Blend on high for 30 seconds, or until the ingredients are well mixed and the oat milk is frothy. Serve over ice, if desired.

Mix it up: Heat the oat milk in the microwave or on the stovetop before you add it to the blender if you want to make this latte hot. Pour in the warm milk carefully and be sure the cover is completely secure whenever you blend hot ingredients.

PER SERVING: Calories: 161; Total fat: 4g; Carbohydrates: 20g; Fiber: 1g; Protein: 13g; Calcium: 467mg; Vitamin D: 4mcg; Vitamin B$_{12}$: 2µg; Iron: 1mg; Zinc: 2mg

Granny Smith Green Smoothie

MAKES 2 SERVINGS • PREP TIME: 5 MINUTES

1 cup frozen spinach

1 medium Granny Smith apple, cored and diced

1 cup frozen mango chunks

1 cup plain Greek yogurt, or more as desired

½ teaspoon ground ginger

½ teaspoon ground cinnamon

½ cup plain Creamy Oat Milk (page 210) (or milk of choice)

Smoothies aren't always the most satisfying snack, but Greek yogurt adds protein and plenty of creamy texture to this midday beverage. You can peel the apple, but I like to leave on the skin for the fiber and antioxidants. The thickness of this smoothie will depend on the thickness of your yogurt. Start with the indicated amount in the recipe and gradually add more if needed. Add a little maple syrup or honey if you want the flavor to be sweeter.

1. Place the spinach, apple, mango, yogurt, ginger, cinnamon, and oat milk in a blender container.

2. Blend on high for 1 minute or until smooth and creamy. Serve immediately.

Substitute: Any type of frozen fruit works, but I like to use a light-colored variety to keep the color green. Try pineapple or banana if you don't have mango. To make it vegan, use a dairy-free yogurt alternative or mashed avocado in place of the Greek yogurt.

PER SERVING: Calories: 229; Total fat: 6g; Carbohydrates: 36g; Fiber: 6g; Protein: 10g; Calcium: 342mg; Vitamin D: 1mcg; Vitamin B_{12}: 1µg; Iron: 2mg; Zinc: 2mg

Energizing Matcha Smoothie

MAKES 2 SERVINGS • PREP TIME: 5 MINUTES

NO COOKING REQUIRED

**2 cups frozen
  mango chunks**
½ cup frozen spinach
2 tablespoons chia seeds
1 tablespoon matcha
**2 cups plain Creamy Oat
  Milk (page 210) (or milk
  of choice)**
**1 teaspoon vanilla extract
  (optional)**
**2 teaspoons maple syrup
  or sweetener of choice
  (optional)**

Green tea contains caffeine and L-theanine, which have been shown to improve alertness and focus. With the addition of matcha, this smoothie is ideal for sipping on while you're studying for exams. I like to add spinach to brighten the green hue and provide an extra kick of fiber and micronutrients. Not yet a fan of green tea? Try halving the matcha for a fruity smoothie with a milder flavor.

1. Place the mango, spinach, chia seeds, matcha, oat milk, and vanilla and maple syrup (if using) in a blender.

2. Blend on high for 1 minute, or until smooth and creamy. Serve.

Substitute: If you don't have oat milk, try this smoothie with whatever type of milk you have on hand. Opt for soy or cow's milk if you want to add more protein. For an additional boost, try this recipe with a tablespoon of ground flaxseed.

PER SERVING: Calories: 282; Total fat: 8g; Carbohydrates: 44g; Fiber: 9g; Protein: 13g; Calcium: 463mg; Vitamin D: 3mcg; Vitamin B_{12}: 1µg; Iron: 2mg; Zinc: 2mg

Curried Kale Chips

MAKES 4 SERVINGS · PREP TIME: 10 MINUTES · COOK TIME: 50 MINUTES

ONE PAN

¼ cup tahini

1 tablespoon curry powder

1 teaspoon maple syrup

¼ teaspoon kosher salt

4 tablespoons water

1 pound fresh kale

Storage: Store the chips in an airtight container at room temperature for up to 1 week.

Mix it up: You can use all sorts of spice blends to flavor kale chips. Try sweet and spicy Jamaican jerk seasoning, cheesy nutritional yeast, or Cajun spices. Instead of tahini, use peanut butter or any nut butter you happen to have on hand.

One of my favorite ways to increase my dark leafy green intake is by making these curry-spiced kale chips. Kale is a nutrient-dense member of the cruciferous family. It's packed with fiber and micronutrients, including vitamins A, C, and E. These baked veggie chips are a crunchy alternative to potato chips and are perfect for when you're looking for something lighter to snack on. Keep a bowl by your side during movie nights and late-night study sessions for a feel-good snack that'll keep you satisfied.

1. Preheat the oven to 275°F. Line 2 baking sheets with parchment.

2. In a large bowl, whisk together the tahini, curry powder, maple syrup, and salt until blended. Gradually add the water until the sauce is thinned.

3. Tear the kale leaves from the stems and toss them in the bowl with the tahini sauce. Use your hands to toss the kale pieces until they're evenly coated. Spread the kale in a single layer on the baking sheets.

4. Bake the chips for 50 minutes or until dry and crispy. Cool them on a rack.

PER SERVING: Calories: 154; Total fat: 9g; Carbohydrates: 15g; Fiber: 6g; Protein: 8g; Calcium: 244mg; Vitamin D: 0mcg; Vitamin B_{12}: 0µg; Iron: 3mg; Zinc: 1mg

Quick Pickled Carrots and Vegetables

MAKES 4 SERVINGS · PREP TIME: 10 MINUTES

DORM-FRIENDLY | MAKES LEFTOVERS | NO COOKING REQUIRED

1 cup thinly sliced carrots

2 jalapeño peppers,
   thinly sliced

1 tablespoon kosher salt

1 tablespoon sugar

1 tablespoon cumin seeds
   (optional)

½ cup water

½ cup rice vinegar

Storage: The pickles
will keep in the covered
jar, refrigerated, for up to
3 months.

Mix it up: If you're
not a fan of jalapeños, try
making pickled vegetables
with radishes, cucumbers,
beets, or red onions. You
can also change the pickling
spices. Try adding herbs,
such as chives or dill, or
coriander seeds.

When you're craving something salty, give these pickled vegetables a try. They're a flavorful way to get more veggies and are also packed with electrolytes. Besides being a crunchy snack all on their own, you can serve pickled carrots and jalapeños on soups, sandwiches, bowls, and tacos. Making your own pickles instead of buying them can save money, and they will last for months. You can quickly prep a large batch to keep on hand for whenever the mood strikes.

1. Place the carrots and jalapeños in a pint glass jar with a lid. Add the salt, sugar, cumin seeds (if using), water, and vinegar. Cover the jar and shake to mix.

2. Refrigerate the mixture for at least 30 minutes, or until the vegetables have softened and are flavored by the pickling liquid. Taste and add more salt or sugar as needed.

3. Cover the jar again and refrigerate until ready to use.

PER SERVING: Calories: 29; Total fat: 0g; Carbohydrates: 6g; Fiber: 1g; Protein: 0g; Calcium: 14mg; Vitamin D: 0mcg; Vitamin B$_{12}$: 0µg; Iron: 0mg; Zinc: 0mg

Apple Chips with Cinnamon-Yogurt Dip

MAKES 2 SERVINGS · PREP TIME: 5 MINUTES · COOK TIME: 50 MINUTES

ONE PAN

1 apple, cored and sliced ⅛ inch thick

1 cup plain Greek yogurt

2 teaspoons maple syrup

½ teaspoon ground cinnamon

½ teaspoon vanilla extract (optional)

⅛ teaspoon kosher salt

2 tablespoons chopped nuts (optional)

Storage: Store the dip in an airtight container in the refrigerator for up to 1 week. Store the apple chips in an airtight container at room temperature for up to 6 months.

Substitute: For a vegan alternative to this Greek yogurt dip, substitute a plain dairy-free yogurt alternative. You can find vegan yogurts made from coconut, soy, almond, or oat milk in the dairy section of most grocery stores.

Crunchy baked apple chips with a protein-rich Greek yogurt dip makes the best midday snack when you don't have time for a full meal. Be sure to line the pan with parchment or a reusable silicone baking mat to prevent the thinly sliced apples from burning in the oven. Watch them closely at the end to prevent any mishaps. I like to use full-fat Greek yogurt, but any type works. Top the dip with chopped pecans, walnuts, or almonds for a little extra crunch.

1. Preheat the oven or toaster oven to 275°F. Line a baking sheet with parchment or baking mat.

2. Spread the apple slices in a single layer on the baking sheet and bake for 50 minutes, or until golden and crispy. Cool the chips on a rack. The apples will continue to get crispy as they cool.

3. While the chips are baking, in a small bowl, stir together the yogurt, maple syrup, cinnamon, vanilla (if using), and salt until blended.

4. Top the dip with chopped nuts (if using) and serve with the baked apple chips.

PER SERVING: Calories: 141; Total fat: 5g; Carbohydrates: 23g; Fiber: 3g; Protein: 5g; Calcium: 167mg; Vitamin D: 0mcg; Vitamin B$_{12}$: 0µg; Iron: 0mg; Zinc: 1mg

Fruit and Nut Energy Bites

MAKES 8 SERVINGS • PREP TIME: 10 MINUTES

MAKE AHEAD | MAKES LEFTOVERS | NO COOKING REQUIRED

1¼ cups pitted
   dates, chopped
¾ cup walnut halves
   and pieces
½ cup blanched almonds
2 tablespoons ground
   flaxseed
1 teaspoon ground
   cinnamon
1 teaspoon vanilla extract
¼ teaspoon kosher salt

There's a reason hikers turn to the classic mix of dried fruit and nuts to keep them going for miles. These plant-based ingredients offer a balanced blend of carbohydrates, fats, and protein for feel-good energy and real staying power. Even if you're not the outdoorsy type, you can benefit from this easy recipe. Vegan energy bites are perfect for stashing in your bookbag or snacking on while you walk to the gym.

1. Place the dates, walnuts, almonds, flaxseed, cinnamon, vanilla, and salt in a food processor and pulse until a sticky dough forms. It should stick together when pressed between your fingers.

2. Take about 2 tablespoons of the dough and use your hands to roll it into a ball. Repeat with the remaining dough. Enjoy.

Storage: Store the balls in an airtight container in the refrigerator for up to 2 weeks or freeze for up to 3 months.

Protein swaps: You can use any combination of nuts to make these plant-based energy bites. For a nut-free alternative, try a mix of pumpkin and sunflower seeds.

PER SERVING: Calories: 200; Total fat: 12g; Carbohydrates: 22g; Fiber: 4g; Protein: 4g; Calcium: 52mg; Vitamin D: 0mcg; Vitamin B_{12}: 0µg; Iron: 1mg; Zinc: 1mg

No-Bake Chocolate-Peanut Butter Bars

MAKES 4 SERVINGS • PREP TIME: 10 MINUTES

MAKE AHEAD | MAKES LEFTOVERS | NO COOKING REQUIRED

1½ cups chopped
    pitted dates

1 cup walnut halves
    and pieces

¼ cup peanut butter

2 tablespoons
    unsweetened
    cocoa powder

2 teaspoons vanilla extract

Storage: Store the bars in an airtight container in the refrigerator for up to 2 weeks or freeze for up to 3 months.

Substitute: If you're looking for an alternative to peanuts, try making these energy bars with sunflower seed butter or tahini. Instead of walnuts, try almonds, pecans, or cashews.

You can find plant-based energy bars in most supermarkets these days, but many are way too expensive to fit a college student's food budget. One way you can get around this is by making your own bars using some simple pantry ingredients. The trick is getting the right mix of the crunchy walnuts with the dates and peanut butter, both of which act as binders. If the mixture isn't sticking together when you press it between your fingers, add more dates or peanut butter and process again.

1. Place the dates, walnuts, peanut butter, cocoa powder, and vanilla in food processor and pulse until a sticky dough forms. It should stick together when pressed between your fingers.

2. Line a loaf pan with parchment paper and press the dough into the pan evenly.

3. Chill the mixture in the refrigerator for at least 1 hour.

4. Remove the chilled dough from the pan by lifting it out using the parchment paper and transfer to a cutting board. Cut into 4 bars.

PER SERVING: Calories: 455; Total fat: 27g; Carbohydrates: 51g; Fiber: 8g; Protein: 10g; Calcium: 61mg; Vitamin D: 0mcg; Vitamin B$_{12}$: 0µg; Iron: 2mg; Zinc: 2mg

Sesame-Ginger Edamame

MAKES 2 SERVINGS · PREP TIME: 2 MINUTES · COOK TIME: 5 MINUTES

ONE PAN

Grapeseed oil or nonstick cooking spray
2¼ cups frozen edamame, in pods
1-inch piece of ginger, peeled and grated
1 tablespoon toasted sesame oil
1 teaspoon rice vinegar
1 teaspoon soy sauce
1 teaspoon maple syrup
Kosher salt

Maybe you've tried edamame in the pod at a sushi restaurant, but if not, here's what you need to know. Edamame is a protein-rich snack option that's completely plant-based; it's the young, edible part of the soybean that is inside the pod. To eat edamame, use your teeth to squeeze the bean out of the pod and directly into your mouth. The salt and sesame-ginger coating adds to the flavor experience even though you're not actually consuming the pod.

1. Lightly oil a large skillet or wok and heat it over medium heat.

2. Add the frozen edamame and cook until thawed.

3. Add the ginger, sesame oil, vinegar, soy sauce, and maple syrup and cook for 3 minutes, or until warmed through.

4. Season the mixture with salt and serve.

Storage: Store the leftovers in an airtight container in the refrigerator for up to 1 week.

Mix it up: Switch up the spices when you're making edamame for snacking. Try garlic powder or cayenne pepper for a spicy twist.

PER SERVING: Calories: 286; Total fat: 16g; Carbohydrates: 20g; Fiber: 9g; Protein: 19g; Calcium: 114mg; Vitamin D: 0mcg; Vitamin B$_{12}$: 0µg; Iron: 4mg; Zinc: 2mg

Cheesy Vegan Popcorn

MAKES 2 SERVINGS · PREP TIME: 2 MINUTES · COOK TIME: 5 MINUTES

ONE POT

1 tablespoon coconut oil

¼ cup popcorn kernels

2 tablespoons nutritional yeast

½ teaspoon garlic powder

½ teaspoon onion powder

¼ teaspoon kosher salt

⅛ teaspoon freshly ground black pepper

....

Storage: Store the popcorn in an airtight container for up to 1 day.

....

Mix it up: Popcorn is a healthy snack that tastes good all on its own or with just a sprinkle of salt. For a change, try using Cajun seasoning, curry powder, or a little hot sauce.

Nutritional yeast is a deactivated type of yeast that you can use to add cheesy flavor to vegan dishes. This recipe is my all-time favorite way to use this ingredient, which you can typically find in the bulk section or natural foods aisle of your supermarket. This mix of nutritional yeast, garlic powder, and onion powder is the best way to snack on popcorn. Give it a try next time you're hosting a movie night.

1. Heat the coconut oil in a 12-quart stockpot over medium heat.

2. When the oil is melted, pour in the popcorn kernels and cover the pot.

3. Cook for 5 minutes, shaking the pot occasionally to promote even cooking, or until all of the popcorn kernels are popped.

4. Add the nutritional yeast, garlic powder, onion powder, salt, and pepper and shake the pot to mix. Serve.

PER SERVING: Calories: 165; Total fat: 8g; Carbohydrates: 18g; Fiber: 4g; Protein: 2g; Calcium: 15mg; Vitamin D: 0mcg; Vitamin B$_{12}$: 0µg; Iron: 1mg; Zinc: 0mg

Chili-Lime Tortilla Chips

MAKES 4 SERVINGS · PREP TIME: 5 MINUTES · COOK TIME: 10 MINUTES

GREAT FOR SHARING | MAKE AHEAD | MAKES LEFTOVERS

8 (4-inch) corn tortillas
¼ cup grapeseed oil
2 tablespoons fresh lime juice (from 1 medium)
1 teaspoon chili powder
Kosher salt

Storage: Store the chips in an airtight container for up to 1 week.

Make it easier: Want to make this homemade snack super simple and easy? Leave out the lime juice and chili powder, and you'll still get a great-tasting crunchy corn chip that's perfect for dipping into salsa or guacamole.

One of the best ways to save money during college is by skipping packaged foods for homemade versions of snack foods whenever it fits your lifestyle. One of the easiest options is to make your own tortilla chips, which you can flavor with spices and lime juice for an extra lift. You'll either need to cook this in batches or use 2 baking sheets to make all the chips at once.

1. Preheat the oven or toaster oven to 400°F. Line 2 baking sheets with parchment.

2. Cut the tortillas into triangles and spread them in a single layer on the baking sheets.

3. In a small bowl, whisk together the oil, lime juice, and chili powder and brush the mixture on each side of the tortilla chips.

4. Sprinkle the tortilla chips with salt and transfer the baking sheets to the oven. Bake for 10 minutes, flipping halfway through, or until the chips are golden and crispy.

5. Cool the chips on a rack before serving. The chips will continue to get crispier as they cool.

PER SERVING: Calories: 177; Total fat: 14g; Carbohydrates: 12g; Fiber: 2g; Protein: 1g; Calcium: 23mg; Vitamin D: 0mcg; Vitamin B$_{12}$: 0µg; Iron: 0mg; Zinc: 0mg

Roasted Potatoes with Lemon-Chive Yogurt Dip

MAKES 4 SERVINGS · PREP TIME: 5 MINUTES · COOK TIME: 25 MINUTES

GREAT FOR SHARING

4 medium russet or Yukon Gold potatoes, cut into 1-inch cubes

2 tablespoons grapeseed oil

½ teaspoon onion powder

½ teaspoon garlic powder

¼ teaspoon kosher salt

¼ teaspoon freshly ground black pepper

1 cup plain Greek yogurt

2 tablespoons chopped fresh chives

1 tablespoon fresh lemon juice

¼ teaspoon maple syrup

Storage: Store the leftovers in an airtight container in the refrigerator for up to 5 days.

Substitute: This recipe will work with any type of chopped root vegetable, including Yukon Gold potatoes, Red Bliss potatoes, parsnips, carrots, or sweet potatoes.

Starchy russet (baking) potatoes are often overlooked in the nutrition world, but don't underestimate these humble vegetables. Potatoes pack more potassium than a banana, and they're a great source of vitamin B_6 and vitamin C. This balanced snack is a good way to stay energized during a study group, and you can always use dairy-free yogurt alternatives if you want to make this recipe vegan.

1. Preheat the oven to 450°F. Line a baking sheet with parchment.

2. In a large bowl, toss together the potatoes, oil, onion powder, garlic powder, salt, and pepper, and spread out in a single layer on the baking sheet.

3. Bake the potatoes for 25 minutes, stirring halfway through, or until golden and crispy. Set aside until cooled enough to handle, about 15 minutes.

4. While the potatoes are baking, in a small bowl, stir together the yogurt, chives, lemon juice, and maple syrup until blended. Season the dip with salt and pepper.

5. Serve the dip with the roasted potatoes.

PER SERVING: Calories: 266; Total fat: 9g; Carbohydrates: 41g; Fiber: 5g; Protein: 7g; Calcium: 103mg; Vitamin D: 0mcg; Vitamin B_{12}: 0μg; Iron: 2mg; Zinc: 1mg

Vegetable Spring Rolls

MAKES 6 SERVINGS · PREP TIME: 20 MINUTES

DORM-FRIENDLY | GREAT FOR SHARING | MAKES LEFTOVERS | NO COOKING REQUIRED

6 spring roll wrappers

1 cup thinly sliced cucumber

1 cup shredded carrots

½ cup fresh cilantro

¼ cup Sesame Ginger Dressing (page 213) or store-bought sauce

Mix it up: Cabbage, bell peppers, fresh basil, scallions, and pickled vegetables all make delicious additions to the spring rolls. Use whatever you have in your refrigerator to help reduce food waste.

Spring rolls are an easy no-cook snack to make when you don't have access to cooking equipment. You can find the rice paper wrappers in the Asian aisle of many supermarkets. They come hard and brittle, but soften and become easy to fold and wrap once they're dipped in water. Lay the softened rice paper on a nonstick smooth surface, such as a cutting board or piece of parchment, to prevent it from sticking.

1. Dip a wrap in water until it's flexible and lay it on a flat surface.

2. Arrange one-sixth of the cucumber, carrots, and cilantro in the center of the rice paper.

3. Fold up the side edges and roll up the wrapper from the far end to form a sealed roll.

4. Repeat with the remaining wrappers, using all of the vegetable mix.

5. Serve the rolls with the sauce for dipping.

Storage: Store the leftovers in an airtight container in the refrigerator for up to 2 days.

PER SERVING: Calories: 120; Total fat: 6g; Carbohydrates: 13g; Fiber: 1g; Protein: 2g; Calcium: 13mg; Vitamin D: 0mcg; Vitamin B$_{12}$: 0µg; Iron: 0mg; Zinc: 0mg

Tofu Nuggets

MAKES 2 SERVINGS · PREP TIME: 5 MINUTES · COOK TIME: 40 MINUTES

ONE PAN

¼ cup whole wheat flour (or other flour of choice)

2 tablespoons cornstarch

½ teaspoon onion powder

½ teaspoon garlic powder

½ teaspoon kosher salt

½ (14-ounce) block extra-firm tofu, drained and pressed (see Tip, page 50)

2 tablespoons grapeseed oil

Storage: Store the leftovers in an airtight container in the refrigerator for up to 1 week.

Mix it up: Tofu is a blank slate when it comes to flavor, so you have lots of opportunities to add spices to the breading to take things up a notch. Try dried basil, Jamaican jerk seasoning, or nutritional yeast for a cheesy flavor.

Were chicken tenders your favorite food when you were a kid? If you're looking for a poultry-free alternative, try these crispy tofu nuggets, which are a rich source of plant-based protein. They are breaded with whole wheat flour, cornstarch, and onion and garlic powders for a crunchy texture and satisfying flavor. You can serve these tofu bites just like chicken tenders, with a side of ketchup, mustard, barbecue sauce, or ranch dressing.

1. Preheat the oven to 450°F. Line a baking sheet with parchment or a silicone baking mat.

2. In a large bowl, stir together the flour, cornstarch, onion powder, garlic powder, and salt until blended.

3. Tear the tofu into bite-size pieces and add to the bowl.

4. Add the oil to the bowl and use your hands to toss the tofu until it's evenly coated.

5. Dust off the extra flour and spread the tofu on the baking sheet.

6. Bake the tofu for 40 minutes, or until golden and crispy.

7. Cool the tofu on a rack before serving.

PER SERVING: Calories: 310; Total fat: 20g; Carbohydrates: 21g; Fiber: 2g; Protein: 13g; Calcium: 208mg; Vitamin D: 0mcg; Vitamin B$_{12}$: 0µg; Iron: 3mg; Zinc: 2mg

Buffalo Cauliflower

MAKES 4 SERVINGS · PREP TIME: 5 MINUTES · COOK TIME: 40 MINUTES

¼ **cup whole wheat flour (or other flour of choice)**

2 **tablespoons cornstarch**

½ **teaspoon onion powder**

½ **teaspoon garlic powder**

½ **teaspoon kosher salt**

1 **medium head of cauliflower, cut into large florets**

¼ **cup grapeseed oil**

¼ **cup buffalo-style hot sauce**

1 **scallion, both white and green parts, chopped (optional)**

For a tailgating party, you can't beat this vegetarian appetizer made from cauliflower, which belongs to the nutrient-packed cruciferous family. The cauliflower florets are coated in flour and cornstarch for a crispy texture. Then they're roasted until golden and crispy and tossed in spicy buffalo-style hot sauce. Serve these "wings" with carrot and celery spears and ranch or blue cheese dressing for a party-worthy platter.

1. Preheat the oven to 450°F. Line a baking sheet with parchment or a silicone baking mat.

2. In a large bowl, stir together the flour, cornstarch, onion powder, garlic powder, and salt until well mixed. Add the cauliflower and toss to combine.

3. Add the oil to the bowl and use your hands to toss the cauliflower until it's evenly coated.

4. Spread the cauliflower in a single layer on the baking sheet.

5. Roast the cauliflower for 40 minutes, or until golden and crispy.

6. While the cauliflower is baking, pour the hot sauce into a large bowl.

7. Cool the cauliflower on a rack for 5 minutes.

8. Add the cooked cauliflower to the sauce and toss until it is evenly coated with sauce.

9. Garnish with the scallion, if desired, and serve immediately.

....

Storage: Store any leftovers in an airtight container in the refrigerator for up to 1 week.

....

Make it easier: If you don't care a lot about getting crunchy texture, you can easily make this recipe without the flour, cornstarch, and onion and garlic powders. The cauliflower will still get golden and roasted without the breading, and it'll have plenty of flavor from the hot sauce.

PER SERVING: Calories: 202; Total fat: 14g; Carbohydrates: 17g; Fiber: 4g; Protein: 4g; Calcium: 38mg; Vitamin D: 0mcg; Vitamin B_{12}: 0μg; Iron: 1mg; Zinc: 1mg

Garlicky Roasted Chickpeas

MAKES 2 SERVINGS · PREP TIME: 5 MINUTES · COOK TIME: 20 MINUTES

ONE PAN

1 (15-ounce) can
    chickpeas, drained
    and rinsed
2 tablespoons
    grapeseed oil
1 teaspoon garlic powder
½ teaspoon onion powder
¼ teaspoon kosher salt
¼ teaspoon freshly ground
    black pepper

Storage: Store the chickpeas in an airtight container for up to 1 week.

Mix it up: Try roasted chickpeas with any of your favorite seasoning blends. Try taco seasoning, curry powder, Cajun seasoning, or a Jamaican jerk spice blend.

If you're looking for a savory snack that acts as an alternative to expensive packaged snack foods, try these delectable chickpeas. Chickpeas belong to the pulse (legume) family, which is a sustainable source of protein that's also rich in fiber. When they're roasted in the oven, they turn golden brown and crispy on the edges. I like them best right out of the oven, but they still taste delicious up to a week later, too.

1. Preheat the oven or toaster oven to 400°F. Line a baking sheet with parchment.

2. Use paper towels to dry the chickpeas and then transfer them to a large bowl.

3. Add the oil, garlic powder, onion powder, salt, and pepper to the bowl and toss to combine.

4. Spread the chickpeas in a single layer on the baking sheet and bake for 20 minutes, or until golden and crispy. Serve.

PER SERVING: Calories: 329; Total fat: 17g; Carbohydrates: 35g; Fiber: 10g; Protein: 11g; Calcium: 64mg; Vitamin D: 0mcg; Vitamin B_{12}: 0µg; Iron: 4mg; Zinc: 2mg

Black Bean Quesadillas

MAKES 2 SERVINGS · PREP TIME: 5 MINUTES · COOK TIME: 10 MINUTES

DORM-FRIENDLY | ONE PAN

1 cup cooked black beans

1 cup chopped fresh baby spinach

½ cup chopped fresh cilantro

1 jalapeño pepper, sliced

¼ teaspoon kosher salt

Grapeseed oil or nonstick cooking spray

4 (10-inch) flour tortillas

1 cup shredded pepper jack cheese

....

Storage: Store any leftovers in an airtight container and refrigerate for up to 5 days.

....

Protein swap: If you don't want to use black beans, fill these quesadillas with cooked lentils, crumbled tempeh, or pinto beans. You could also try scrambled eggs to make these for brunch over the weekend.

There are sure to be days when you feel like having a hearty snack that's satisfying and filling enough to hold you over for hours, until your next meal. These quesadillas are a convenient option since you can make them in about 15 minutes, and they provide a balanced blend of energy from carbohydrates, fats, and protein. Dip these bean quesadillas into salsa, guacamole, or plain Greek yogurt, if desired.

1. In a medium bowl, combine the beans, spinach, cilantro, jalapeño, and salt.

2. Lightly oil a large skillet and preheat it on medium heat.

3. Place 1 tortilla in the skillet and spread one-fourth of the bean filling on one side of the tortilla. Sprinkle the filling with one-fourth of the cheese, and fold over the tortilla to cover the filling.

4. Cook for 5 minutes or until the bottom turns golden brown, and then flip the tortilla over and cook for an additional 5 minutes, or until both sides are golden brown and the cheese is melted.

5. Repeat with remaining tortillas, cooking in batches as needed. Serve.

PER SERVING: Calories: 513; Total fat: 21g; Carbohydrates: 53g; Fiber: 10g; Protein: 26g; Calcium: 523mg; Vitamin D: 0mcg; Vitamin B$_{12}$: 0µg; Iron: 5mg; Zinc: 3mg

Pan-Roasted Nachos

MAKES 4 SERVINGS · PREP TIME: 5 MINUTES · COOK TIME: 10 MINUTES

GREAT FOR SHARING | ONE PAN

1 (12-ounce) bag corn
   tortilla chips
1 (15-ounce) can black
   beans, drained
   and rinsed
1 jalapeño pepper, sliced
   (optional)
1 tablespoon ground cumin
1 tablespoon chili powder
1 tablespoon fresh
   lime juice
¼ teaspoon kosher salt
1½ cups shredded pepper
   jack cheese
1 avocado, peeled, pitted,
   and diced

Nachos are a classic tailgating party snack, and this version is simple enough to make on one baking sheet. Be sure to spread the chips out as much as possible so they're not overlapping. This helps them cook evenly and get uniformly coated with cheese and all of the other toppings. Serve with salsa, hot sauce, pickled vegetables, or any of your favorite nacho toppings.

1. Preheat the oven to 400°F. Line a rimmed baking sheet with parchment.

2. Spread the tortilla chips in a single layer on the baking sheet.

3. In a medium bowl, stir together the beans, jalapeño (if using), cumin, chili powder, lime juice, and salt until well combined, and top the tortilla chips evenly with the mixture.

4. Sprinkle the chips with the cheese and bake for 10 minutes, or until the cheese is melted.

5. Top the nachos with diced avocado and serve immediately.

Change it Up: For a milder flavor, omit the jalapeño and use shredded cheddar cheese instead of pepper jack. You can also try nachos with cotija cheese if you see it at your supermarket.

PER SERVING: Calories: 775; Total fat: 40g; Carbohydrates: 82g; Fiber: 15g; Protein: 24g; Calcium: 472mg; Vitamin D: 0mcg; Vitamin B$_{12}$: 0µg; Iron: 5mg; Zinc: 4mg

Baked Potato Skins

MAKES 4 SERVINGS · PREP TIME: 10 MINUTES · COOK TIME: 20 MINUTES

GREAT FOR SHARING | ONE PAN

4 medium russet potatoes

1 tablespoon grapeseed oil, plus extra for greasing the skillet

¼ teaspoon kosher salt

½ cup shredded pepper jack or cheddar cheese

¼ cup chopped fresh chives

Plain Greek yogurt, for dipping (optional)

....

Storage: Wrap leftover potatoes in plastic or beeswax wrap and refrigerate up to 5 days.

....

Protein swaps: To make these potato skins dairy-free, sprinkle with nutritional yeast instead of using pepper jack or cheddar cheese. Top with diced avocado for a plant-based fat alternative, or dip potato skins in guacamole instead of Greek yogurt.

Crispy baked potato skins are always a party favorite, especially when topped with melted cheese. Make sure the potatoes are baked to prepare them for this recipe. You can pierce whole potatoes and cook them in the oven or microwave until you can easily pierce them with a fork.

1. Preheat the oven to 450°F. Pierce the potatoes with a fork, transfer them to a baking sheet, and bake for 30 minutes, or until you can easily pierce them with a fork.

2. Make sure the baked potatoes are cooled, then slice them in half lengthwise, and use a spoon to scoop out about half the potato in each half. Reserve the scooped-out potato for another recipe.

3. Brush the potato skins with the oil and sprinkle with the salt.

4. Lightly oil a large skillet and preheat it over medium heat. Arrange the potatoes, cut-side down, in the skillet and cook for 15 minutes, or until the bottoms turn golden brown.

5. Flip the potatoes over, sprinkle with the cheese, and cook until the cheese is melted.

6. Top the potato skins with the chopped chives and serve with the yogurt for dipping, if desired.

PER SERVING: Calories: 214; Total fat: 8g; Carbohydrates: 30g; Fiber: 4g; Protein: 7g; Calcium: 127mg; Vitamin D: 0mcg; Vitamin B$_{12}$: 0µg; Iron: 1mg; Zinc: 1mg

Vegan Party Platter

MAKES 8 SERVINGS · PREP TIME: 10 MINUTES · COOK TIME: 5 MINUTES

GREAT FOR SHARING

1 cup whole almonds

¼ cup olive oil

2 tablespoons balsamic vinegar

1 teaspoon dried thyme

Kosher salt

Freshly ground black pepper

1 cup olives of choice

1 cup Tofu Feta (page 225) or store-bought tofu

1½ cups Classic Hummus (page 222) or store-bought hummus

Crackers or fresh bread

Fresh fruit, such as berries or grapes

Whether it's for a birthday party, game night, or pre-finals study group, you can't go wrong with this Mediterranean platter. This vegan snack plate is full of brain-boosting ingredients, and it's ideal for grazing while you're working on a group project or studying. For a satisfying snack platter, include crunchy nuts, dips, vegan "cheese," and a flavorful bowl of marinated olives. Add antioxidant-rich fresh fruits for a sweet finish.

1. Preheat the oven to 350°F. Line a baking sheet with parchment.

2. Spread the almonds on the baking sheet and bake for 5 minutes or until aromatic. Transfer the almonds to a large bowl and set aside.

3. In a small bowl, whisk together the olive oil, vinegar, thyme, and salt and pepper to taste.

4. Add the olives to the bowl and mix to fully coat.

5. On a large platter, arrange the toasted almonds, marinated olives, tofu feta, hummus, crackers or fresh bread, and fresh fruit. Serve.

Storage: Store the crackers and bread in a bag or airtight container at room temperature. Cover the rest of the platter with plastic or beeswax wrap and refrigerate for up to 5 days. You can also transfer individual portions to smaller airtight containers.

Change it Up: If you like the concept of a party-friendly snack platter, but want to feature more Mexican flavors, assemble a plate with tortilla chips, salsa, guacamole, pickled vegetables, and queso sauce.

PER SERVING: Calories: 390; Total fat: 33g; Carbohydrates: 20g; Fiber: 7g; Protein: 14g; Calcium: 212mg; Vitamin D: 0mcg; Vitamin B_{12}: 0µg; Iron: 5mg; Zinc: 3mg

**Strawberry-Banana
Ice Cream,**
page 195

Chapter Nine

Desserts

The best way to satisfy a sweet craving is to eat dessert! Nourishing yourself should never feel boring or restrictive, and for most people, there's no reason to completely shun white flour or granulated sugar. The treats in this chapter range from quick and easy bites to a shareable cheesecake that's ideal for a summer birthday party. Some recipes incorporate healthy ingredients, such as whole grains and nuts, while others are more traditional. Neither is better than the other. Treating yourself is all about celebration, balance, and paying attention to your body.

Chocolate-Covered Mangos 194

Strawberry-Banana
Ice Cream 195

Chickpea Cookie Dough 196

Yogurt-Dipped
Strawberries 197

Chocolate-Avocado
Pudding 198

Snickerdoodle Skillet
Cookie 199

Chocolate–Peanut
Butter Cups 201

Chai Tea Mug Cake 203

Pumpkin Pie Parfait Jars 204

Vegan No-Bake Blueberry
Cheesecake 205

Chocolate-Covered Mangos

MAKES 8 SERVINGS • PREP TIME: 10 MINUTES, PLUS 10 MINUTES TO CHILL • COOK TIME: 2 MINUTES

GREAT FOR SHARING | MAKES LEFTOVERS

¼ cup coconut oil

2 tablespoons unsweetened cocoa powder

2 tablespoons Vanilla Almond Milk (page 211) (or milk of choice)

1 tablespoon maple syrup

2 cups dried mangos

Flaky salt or chili powder (optional)

Mix it up: There are endless ways to enjoy chocolate-dipped fruit. Try dried pineapple rings or fresh strawberries. You can also sprinkle the fruit with finely chopped nuts, coconut flakes, or cacao nibs for extra flavor and texture. The toppings will stick to the fruit as the chocolate coating hardens.

Dried mango covered in chocolate is a treat that's actually very simple to make. Just heat up a quick chocolate coating and dip in the dried fruit. You can also make the chocolate sauce in a microwave. Heat the ingredients in a microwave-safe dish in 30-second increments until the coconut oil is melted, stirring in between.

1. In a small saucepan, stir together the coconut oil, cocoa powder, almond milk, and maple syrup over low heat. Cook for 2 minutes, stirring constantly, until a uniform sauce forms. Turn off the heat.

2. Dip a piece of dried mango into the chocolate sauce and transfer it to a baking dish or container with a lid. Repeat with remaining mango pieces, arranging them in a single layer. Sprinkle the dipped mango with flaky salt or chili powder (if using) and chill the fruit in the refrigerator for at least 10 minutes, or until the chocolate is set.

Storage: Store the coated fruit in an airtight container in the refrigerator for up to 1 week. If you have leftover chocolate sauce, allow it to harden on a piece of parchment or a silicone baking mat. Then transfer it to a bag or container and store it in the refrigerator for up to 1 week.

PER SERVING: Calories: 145; Total fat: 7g; Carbohydrates: 22g; Fiber: 2g; Protein: 1g; Calcium: 19mg; Vitamin D: 0mcg; Vitamin B$_{12}$: 0µg; Iron: 0mg; Zinc: 0mg

Strawberry-Banana Ice Cream

MAKES 2 SERVINGS · PREP TIME: 5 MINUTES

NO COOKING REQUIRED

2 cups frozen banana slices (from 4 small bananas)
1 cup frozen strawberries
¼ cup Vanilla Almond Milk (page 211) (or milk of choice), or more as needed
⅛ teaspoon kosher salt

OPTIONAL FOR SERVING

¾ cup Vegan Chocolate Sauce (page 229)
Chopped nuts

. . . .

Mix it up: Frozen bananas provide the creamy, cool texture for this vegan treat, but you can swap in all sorts of ingredients to change the flavor. Try cocoa powder, peanut butter, pitted cherries, or even matcha. Add any toppings you usually like to have on ice cream sundaes.

When you have extra bananas that are starting to turn brown, slice them and spread in a single layer on a freezer-safe plate or baking sheet. The next day, transfer the banana slices to a bag and store in the freezer for up to 3 months. Frozen bananas are ideal for smoothies, and you can also use them to make a fruity alternative to store-bought ice cream. It's similar to the texture of soft-serve ice cream, and you can make it in just a few minutes with a blender or food processor.

1. Place the bananas, strawberries, almond milk, and salt in a blender or food processor and blend for 1 minute, or until smooth and creamy, scraping down the sides with a spatula as needed. If the mixture isn't blending well, add a little more almond milk and process again. The blend should be similar to the consistency of soft-serve ice cream.

2. Serve immediately with the chocolate sauce and chopped nuts, if desired.

PER SERVING: Calories: 184; Total fat: 1g; Carbohydrates: 46g; Fiber: 6g; Protein: 2g; Calcium: 82mg; Vitamin D: 0mcg; Vitamin B$_{12}$: 0µg; Iron: 1mg; Zinc: 1mg

Chickpea Cookie Dough

MAKES 2 SERVINGS · PREP TIME: 5 MINUTES

1 (15-ounce) can chickpeas, drained and rinsed
¼ cup creamy peanut butter
¼ cup maple syrup
1 teaspoon vanilla extract
¼ teaspoon kosher salt
¼ cup chocolate chips or chocolate chunks (optional)

We all know that sampling bits of dough is the best thing about baking cookies. Unlike traditional cookie dough, this recipe doesn't use eggs, so it's naturally vegan and safe to eat. The secret ingredient is chickpeas, which are a nutrient-packed source of fiber, carbohydrates, and protein. Eat it by the spoonful or use it as a dip with fruit or graham crackers. Love cookie dough ice cream? Try adding a couple spoonfuls to your next scoop.

1. Place the chickpeas, peanut butter, maple syrup, vanilla, and salt in a food processor and process for 1 minute, or until smooth and creamy.

2. Transfer the mixture to a medium bowl and add the chocolate chips, if desired.

Storage: Store the dough in an airtight container in the refrigerator for up to 1 week.

Protein swaps: Instead of peanut butter, use sunflower seed butter or tahini to make this nut-free. Creamy Almond Butter (page 227) is another tasty option if you don't have any peanut butter on hand.

PER SERVING: Calories: 503; Total fat: 20g; Carbohydrates: 68g; Fiber: 11g; Protein: 18g; Calcium: 117mg; Vitamin D: 0mcg; Vitamin B$_{12}$: 0µg; Iron: 4mg; Zinc: 3mg

Yogurt-Dipped Strawberries

MAKES 2 SERVINGS • PREP TIME: 15 MINUTES, PLUS 30 MINUTES TO CHILL

MAKE AHEAD | NO COOKING REQUIRED

2 cups fresh strawberries, rinsed

½ cup vanilla Greek yogurt (whole milk)

¼ cup finely chopped nuts, such as pecans or walnuts

Storage: Store leftovers in an airtight container and refrigerate for up to 1 week.

Make it easier: Use pre-chopped nuts or omit the nuts completely to make this recipe a little bit easier. You can also use flavored yogurt to add interest without any additional ingredients.

Yogurt-dipped fruit is a quick, easy, and nutritious dessert. Thick, strained varieties of full-fat yogurt work best for this recipe, since thinner types with less fat won't cover the fruit as easily. The fats in the yogurt and nuts also work to balance the natural sugars in strawberries, so you're less likely to experience a crash in your energy levels later on. This makes the dipped strawberries ideal for a study snack. Don't skip the chilling step; the chilling helps the yogurt coating harden and stick to the fruit.

1. Dry the strawberries with a clean towel or paper towel.

2. Dip three-fourths of a strawberry into the yogurt. Place the dipped berry on a clean plate and sprinkle with some of the nuts. Repeat with the remaining strawberries.

3. Chill in the refrigerator for at least 30 minutes.

PER SERVING: Calories: 178; Total fat: 12g; Carbohydrates: 16g; Fiber: 4g; Protein: 4g; Calcium: 107mg; Vitamin D: 0mcg; Vitamin B$_{12}$: 0µg; Iron: 1mg; Zinc: 1mg

Chocolate-Avocado Pudding

MAKES 2 SERVINGS • PREP TIME: 5 MINUTES, PLUS 2 HOURS TO CHILL

DORM-FRIENDLY | NO COOKING REQUIRED

**2 avocados, peeled
and pitted**

**¼ cup unsweetened
cocoa powder**

¼ cup maple syrup

**½ teaspoon vanilla extract
(optional)**

⅛ teaspoon kosher salt

OPTIONAL FOR SERVING

Whipped cream

**Chocolate chips or
cacao nibs**

Fresh fruit

Mix it up: Add any ingredients that pair well with chocolate to give this plant-based pudding a little more flavor appeal. Try blending in a little fresh mint, instant espresso powder, or fresh raspberries.

Looking for a romantic date-night dessert for two? This pudding is rich and creamy, thanks to all the healthy fats from the avocado. Be sure to fully blend the ingredients to get the smoothest, most pudding-like texture. I like this pudding best after it's been chilled in the refrigerator for at least a couple of hours. You can also prepare it a few days in advance so it's ready to eat as soon as you're finished with dinner.

1. Place the avocados, cocoa powder, maple syrup, vanilla, and salt in a blender or food processor and blend on high for 1 minute, or until smooth and creamy.

2. Transfer the pudding to 6-ounce ramekins or small bowls, cover, and chill in the refrigerator for at least 2 hours.

3. Serve with whipped cream, chocolate chips or cacao nibs, or fresh fruit, if desired.

Storage: Cover the pudding with plastic wrap and refrigerate for up to 3 days.

PER SERVING: Calories: 491; Total fat: 32g; Carbohydrates: 56g; Fiber: 20g; Protein: 9g; Calcium: 83mg; Vitamin D: 0mcg; Vitamin B_{12}: 0µg; Iron: 2mg; Zinc: 2mg

Snickerdoodle
Skillet Cookie

MAKES 8 SERVINGS · PREP TIME: 5 MINUTES · COOK TIME: 40 MINUTES

**Grapeseed oil or nonstick
   cooking spray**
**½ cup (packed)
   brown sugar**
**½ cup granulated sugar,
   plus additional for
   topping (optional)**
**¼ cup (½ stick) salted
   butter, melted**
**1 tablespoon ground
   cinnamon, plus extra for
   topping (optional)**
1 large egg
1 teaspoon vanilla extract
1 cup all-purpose flour
¼ teaspoon baking soda

Mix this cinnamon-spiced cookie dough in one bowl and bake it in a single skillet. Serve the cookie right out of the pan or slice it into wedges. Either way, this dessert is easy to make and ideal for sharing. Freshly baked, it has a crispy outside and chewy inside, so you get the best of both cookie textures. Pro tip: The cinnamon flavor pairs perfectly with a scoop of vanilla ice cream.

1. Preheat the oven to 375°F. Grease a 10-inch oven-safe (cast iron or stainless steel) skillet.

2. In a large bowl, stir together the brown sugar, granulated sugar, butter, and cinnamon until there aren't any large lumps.

3. Add the egg and vanilla, stirring to combine.

4. Add the flour and baking soda and stir until a thick dough forms. Use your hands to mix at the end, if needed.

5. Press the dough firmly into the skillet, and sprinkle with additional granulated sugar and cinnamon, if desired.

continues →

Snickerdoodle Skillet Cookie *continued*

6. Bake the cookie for 20 minutes, or until the edges are golden and the center is baked through. Allow the cookie to cool. Then serve it in the skillet or turn the skillet over to release to cookie and slice it into 8 wedges.

....

Storage: Wrap the cookie in plastic wrap or beeswax wrap and store in an airtight container at room temperature for up to 1 week.

....

Mix it up: Instead of cinnamon, try swapping in ½ cup chocolate chips. During the fall months, substitute pumpkin pie spice, which is made with cinnamon along with other warming spices such as ginger, nutmeg, and cloves.

PER SERVING: Calories: 221; Total fat: 7g; Carbohydrates: 39g; Fiber: 1g; Protein: 3g; Calcium: 29mg; Vitamin D: 0mcg; Vitamin B_{12}: 0µg; Iron: 1mg; Zinc: 0mg

Chocolate-Peanut Butter Cups

MAKES 12 SERVINGS · PREP TIME: 15 MINUTES, PLUS 1 HOUR TO CHILL

GREAT FOR SHARING | MAKES LEFTOVERS

¼ cup sugar

1 teaspoon cornstarch

1 cup peanut butter

2½ cups chocolate chips, melted (dairy-free, if desired)

Flaky salt (optional)

There's no need to buy candy when you can make these easy cups. They're made with just a few simple ingredients and a muffin tin. Before you assemble the cups, you'll need to melt the chocolate chips. Pour them into a microwave-safe bowl and heat in 30-second increments, stirring in between, until the chocolate is completely melted. Then layer the melted chocolate with the peanut butter filling inside the cups of the muffin tin. Once they're chilled, you can remove the peanut butter cups by running a butter knife along the edges to release them.

1. Line a 12-cup muffin tin with paper liners and set it aside.

2. Place the sugar, cornstarch, and peanut butter in a food processor and process on high for 30 seconds or until the mixture is smooth and creamy.

3. Evenly divide half the melted chocolate among the muffin cups, spreading it evenly in the bottom of each one, about 1½ tablespoons in each cup.

4. Divide the peanut butter mixture among the cups, spooning it on top of the chocolate. Evenly divide the remaining melted chocolate among the cups to cover the peanut butter mixture.

continues →

Chocolate–Peanut Butter Cups *continued*

5. Sprinkle the cups with flaky salt (if using) and chill them in the refrigerator for at least 1 hour, or until the chocolate is set.

6. Pull out the liners or run a knife around the edges to release each of the peanut butter cups.

....

Storage: Place the cups in an airtight container and store in the refrigerator for up to 1 month or freeze for up to 3 months.

....

Tip: Instead of peanut butter, use sunflower seed butter for a nut-free alternative. This recipe will also work with any type of nut butter, so try cashew or almond butter.

PER SERVING: Calories: 339; Total fat: 22g; Carbohydrates: 31g; Fiber: 4g; Protein: 7g; Calcium: 30mg; Vitamin D: 0mcg; Vitamin B_{12}: 0µg; Iron: 3mg; Zinc: 1mg

Chai Tea Mug Cake

MAKES 1 SERVING · PREP TIME: 5 MINUTES · COOK TIME: 2 MINUTES

DORM-FRIENDLY

⅓ cup Vanilla Almond Milk (page 211) (or milk of choice)

1 tea bag chai tea

⅓ cup whole wheat pastry flour (or other flour of choice)

1 tablespoon sugar

¼ teaspoon baking powder

¼ teaspoon ground cinnamon, plus additional for topping

Pinch of salt

1½ tablespoons grapeseed oil

Substitute: If you don't have chai tea, mimic the flavors by adding ⅛ teaspoon each of ground cardamom and ground ginger to the warmed milk. You can also make this chocolate flavored by omitting the chai tea and cinnamon and instead adding a spoonful of cocoa powder to the warmed milk.

Masala chai is a traditional Indian drink of black tea and aromatic spices, including cardamom and ginger. This mug cake, which you can "bake" in your microwave in a coffee cup, incorporates the flavors of chai tea for a quick and cozy weeknight dessert. Try to use a large mug with straight sides to promote even cooking of the cake. Top it off with a dollop of whipped cream or the cinnamon yogurt dip on page 175.

1. Heat the milk in a 14-ounce or larger mug in the microwave for 30 seconds, or until hot.

2. Steep the chai tea in the warmed milk for 5 minutes.

3. While the tea is steeping, in a small bowl, stir together the flour, sugar, baking powder, cinnamon, and salt until blended.

4. Squeeze the tea bag into the mug, discard the tea bag, and stir the oil into the mug. Gradually add the flour mixture to the mug, stirring until just mixed. Sprinkle the batter with additional cinnamon, if desired. Microwave the mug cake for 1 minute, or until the cake is cooked through. Serve.

PER SERVING: Calories: 364; Total fat: 22g; Carbohydrates: 39g; Fiber: 5g; Protein: 6g; Calcium: 226mg; Vitamin D: 1mcg; Vitamin B$_{12}$: 1μg; Iron: 2mg; Zinc: 2mg

Pumpkin Pie Parfait Jars

MAKES 2 SERVINGS · PREP TIME: 10 MINUTES

1 (15-ounce) can
    pumpkin puree
¼ cup Vanilla Almond
    Milk (page 211) (or milk
    of choice)
2 tablespoons maple
    syrup, plus additional
    for serving
1 tablespoon pumpkin
    pie spice
⅛ teaspoon kosher salt
1 cup vanilla Greek yogurt
    (dairy or dairy-free)
1 cup granola, such as
    Apple Pie Granola
    (page 23)

No Friendsgiving is complete without pumpkin, but you don't have to bake an entire pie to satisfy seasonal cravings. These luscious parfaits are quick and easy to make with canned pumpkin, yogurt, and granola. Any type of granola or yogurt works; use dairy-free yogurt alternatives to make them vegan. For the best crunchy granola texture, serve immediately, but if you don't mind a consistency that's more like overnight oats, you can also make these up to 3 days in advance.

1. In a medium bowl, stir together the pumpkin puree, almond milk, maple syrup, pumpkin pie spice, and salt until well blended.

2. Layer ¼ cup of the pumpkin mixture in the bottom of 2 pint glass jars. Add a spoonful of the vanilla yogurt to each jar and sprinkle ¼ cup of the granola on top. Repeat layering until all the ingredients are used.

3. Serve immediately or cover and refrigerate the parfait jars for up to 3 days.

Substitute: For a sweeter and less tart flavor, use whipped cream instead of yogurt. Blend canned coconut milk for 5 minutes, or until thickened, to make a dairy-free alternative to whipped cream.

PER SERVING: Calories: 381; Total fat: 6g; Carbohydrates: 75g; Fiber: 11g; Protein: 12g; Calcium: 318mg; Vitamin D: 0mcg; Vitamin B$_{12}$: 1μg; Iron: 5mg; Zinc: 3mg

Vegan No-Bake Blueberry Cheesecake

MAKES 8 SERVINGS · PREP TIME: 40 MINUTES, PLUS 8 HOURS TO CHILL · COOK TIME: 10 MINUTES

GREAT FOR SHARING | MAKES LEFTOVERS

2 cups raw cashews (about 10 ounces)

2 cups frozen blueberries

2 tablespoons sugar

1 teaspoon grated lemon zest

2 cups chopped pitted dates

1⅕ cups walnut halves and pieces

½ cup unsweetened coconut flakes

½ cup Vanilla Almond Milk (page 211) (or milk of choice)

¼ cup fresh lemon juice

¼ cup maple syrup

¼ teaspoon salt

You don't even need an oven to make this crowd-pleasing cheesecake. The crust is made with nuts and dates, the filling is a tart and creamy mixture of lemon and cashews, and it's all topped with simmered blueberries. This dairy-free cheesecake requires a little planning since it needs to set overnight in the freezer. On the day of your party, take the cheesecake out of the freezer and allow it to thaw for at least 15 minutes before slicing it into pieces.

1. Place the cashews in a medium bowl and cover by about 2 inches with water. Set aside to soak for 30 minutes.

2. In a large saucepan, heat the blueberries, sugar, and lemon zest over medium heat until softened, stirring often, about 10 minutes. Remove the saucepan from the heat.

3. Place the dates, walnuts, and coconut flakes in a blender or food processor and pulse until the ingredients are finely chopped and the mixture sticks together when pressed between your fingers.

4. Firmly press the dough into the bottom of a freezer-safe, 10-inch pie dish, spreading it to evenly cover the bottom.

continues →

Vegan No-Bake Blueberry Cheesecake *continued*

5. Drain the cashews, rinse, and transfer them to a blender or food processor along with the almond milk, lemon juice, maple syrup, and salt. Cover and blend for 1 minute, or until smooth and creamy. Spread the cashew mixture evenly over the crust.

6. Spread the cooked blueberries on top of the cashew mixture. Cover with plastic or beeswax wrap and freeze the pie overnight. Thaw the pie for 15 minutes or more before cutting it into 8 slices and serving.

Storage: Cover the leftovers with plastic wrap or beeswax wrap and freeze for up to 3 weeks.

Mix it up: Skip the blueberries and make the cheesecake plain. You can also top it with Vegan Chocolate Sauce (page 229) or chopped nuts and maple syrup. Stir chocolate chips into the cashew filling for extra flavor and texture.

PER SERVING: Calories: 508; Total fat: 30g; Carbohydrates: 58g; Fiber: 7g; Protein: 11g; Calcium: 88mg; Vitamin D: 0mcg; Vitamin B$_{12}$: 0µg; Iron: 4mg; Zinc: 3mg

Spicy Peanut Sauce (shown
with Tofu Nuggets, page 183),
page 215

Chapter Ten

Staples, Sauces, and Dressings

If you want to save big on your grocery bill, skip as many packaged foods as possible and instead learn how to make your own staples, sauces, and dressings at home. Plant-based milk, pasta sauce, salad dressing, and croutons can all be made without too much extra time or effort. Don't feel like you have to overhaul your entire kitchen overnight. Start with DIYing one of your most-used packaged foods and go from there. Beyond the financial savings, you'll benefit from the natural ingredients and homemade flavor.

Creamy Oat Milk 210

Vanilla Almond Milk 211

Apple Cider Vinaigrette 212

Sesame Ginger Dressing 213

Lemon Tahini Dressing 214

Spicy Peanut Sauce 215

Rosemary and Thyme Red Sauce 216

Chimichurri Sauce 217

Carrot-Top Pesto 218

Spicy Blender Salsa 219

Chunky Guacamole 220

Vegan Queso Dip 221

Classic Hummus 222

White Bean Sandwich Spread 223

Almond Ricotta 224

Tofu Feta 225

Blueberry Chia Jam 226

Creamy Almond Butter 227

Whole-Grain Croutons 228

Vegan Chocolate Sauce 229

Creamy Oat Milk

MAKES 4 SERVINGS (ABOUT 4 CUPS TOTAL) • PREP TIME: 10 MINUTES

DORM-FRIENDLY | MAKES LEFTOVERS | NO COOKING REQUIRED

1 cup old-fashioned rolled oats, rinsed

4 cups water

⅛ teaspoon salt

You can buy a dozen or more different plant-based milk alternatives, but if you want to save money and reduce packaging waste, there's nothing like homemade. Oat milk is my go-to for everyday use, since it has a neutral flavor and creamy texture that works in both sweet and savory applications. After making the milk, you will have leftover oat pulp that can be used in oatmeal or any type of baked good.

1. Place the oats, water, and salt in a blender and blend on high for 1 minute.

2. Strain the mixture through a cheesecloth or nut milk bag into a pitcher or quart jar. Squeeze at the end to extract all the liquid.

Storage: Cover the pitcher or seal the jar and refrigerate for up to 5 days. Shake well before using.

Mix it up: Add ½ teaspoon of vanilla extract or 2 cups of strawberries to flavor the milk. If you typically like sweetened plant-based milk, add a spoonful of sugar, maple syrup, or honey to the blender.

PER SERVING: Calories: 80; Total fat: 3g; Carbohydrates: 11g; Fiber: 1g; Protein: 2g; Calcium: 460mg; Vitamin D: 4mcg; Vitamin B$_{12}$: 0µg; Iron: 1mg; Zinc: 0mg

Vanilla Almond Milk

MAKES 4 SERVINGS (ABOUT 4 CUPS TOTAL) • PREP TIME: 10 MINUTES

DORM-FRIENDLY | MAKES LEFTOVERS | NO COOKING REQUIRED

1 cup slivered almonds

4 cups water

½ teaspoon vanilla extract

1 teaspoon maple syrup (optional)

⅛ teaspoon salt

Nutty almonds and vanilla are a match made in heaven and are ideal for any sweet recipe that calls for milk. Try vanilla-flavored plant milk with cereal or granola or incorporate it into cakes and smoothies. Once you strain the blended milk through cheesecloth or a nut milk bag, you'll have leftover almond pulp, which you can incorporate into baked goods or pancake batter. Don't be alarmed if the ingredients separate in the refrigerator. Just shake the jar, and the almond milk will come back together.

1. Place the almonds, water, vanilla, maple syrup (if using), and salt in a blender and blend on high for 1 minute.

2. Strain the mixture through a cheesecloth or nut milk bag into a pitcher or quart jar. If you're using a nut milk bag, squeeze the bag with your hands to extract as much liquid as possible.

Storage: Cover the pitcher or seal the jar and refrigerate for up to 5 days. Shake well before using.

Protein swaps: Use another type of nut, such as cashews, walnuts, or macadamia nuts, to make this milk.

PER SERVING: Calories: 60; Total fat: 3g; Carbohydrates: 8g; Fiber: 0g; Protein: 1g; Calcium: 451mg; Vitamin D: 3mcg; Vitamin B$_{12}$: 0µg; Iron: 1mg; Zinc: 1mg

Apple Cider Vinaigrette

MAKES 2 SERVINGS (ABOUT ¼ CUP TOTAL) · PREP TIME: 5 MINUTES

3 tablespoons olive oil

1 tablespoon apple
cider vinegar

1 teaspoon maple syrup
or honey

3 garlic cloves, minced
(about 1 tablespoon)

½ teaspoon onion powder

¼ teaspoon kosher salt

¼ teaspoon freshly ground
black pepper

Vinaigrette is a classic sauce made from oil and something acidic, such as vinegar or citrus juice. It's most commonly used as a salad dressing, but it can also function as a marinade. If you don't have a whisk (or just don't want to bother with extra dishes), you can mix and store vinaigrettes in one jar. Add all the ingredients, cover, and shake. Feel free to double or triple the recipe, since you can save it for a couple of weeks.

1. In a small bowl, whisk together the olive oil, vinegar, maple syrup, garlic, onion powder, salt, and pepper until well blended.

2. Pour into a cruet to serve.

Storage: Store the vinaigrette in an airtight container in the refrigerator for up to 2 weeks.

Make it easier: Cut down on the prep time and skip the knife and cutting board by using 1 ½ teaspoons of garlic powder in place of the fresh cloves. Every ½ teaspoon of garlic powder is roughly equivalent to 1 garlic clove.

PER SERVING: Calories: 198; Total fat: 20g; Carbohydrates: 4g; Fiber: 0g; Protein: 0g; Calcium: 14mg; Vitamin D: 0mcg; Vitamin B$_{12}$: 0µg; Iron: 0mg; Zinc: 0mg

Sesame Ginger Dressing

MAKES 2 SERVINGS (ABOUT ¼ CUP TOTAL) • PREP TIME: 5 MINUTES

3 tablespoons toasted sesame oil

1 tablespoon rice vinegar

1 teaspoon soy sauce

1 teaspoon maple syrup or honey

1 (2-inch) piece of fresh ginger, peeled and grated

3 garlic cloves, minced

1 scallion, both white and green parts, chopped (optional)

1 teaspoon sesame seeds (optional)

With sesame oil, rice vinegar, soy sauce, and ginger, this vinaigrette is a flavorful component to add to any Asian-inspired dish. Try it with edamame salads, stir-fries, baked tofu, rice bowls, or as a dipping sauce for fresh spring rolls. To cut back on kitchen mess, mix and store the dressing in the same glass jar. You can store this in an airtight container for up to 2 weeks.

1. In a small bowl, whisk together the sesame oil, vinegar, soy sauce, maple syrup, ginger, garlic, and the scallion and sesame seeds (if using) until blended.

2. Pour into a cruet to serve.

Storage: Store the dressing in an airtight container in the refrigerator for up to 2 weeks.

Make it easier: If you want to whip up this dressing without having to make an extra trip to the store, use dry ingredients instead of fresh. Swap in ground ginger, garlic powder, and onion powder to get similar flavors from pantry staples.

PER SERVING: Calories: 200; Total fat: 20g; Carbohydrates: 4g; Fiber: 0g; Protein: 1g; Calcium: 13mg; Vitamin D: 0mcg; Vitamin B_{12}: 0µg; Iron: 0mg; Zinc: 0mg

Lemon Tahini Dressing

MAKES 2 SERVINGS (ABOUT ¾ CUP TOTAL) • PREP TIME: 5 MINUTES

DORM-FRIENDLY | NO COOKING REQUIRED

2 tablespoons tahini

1 teaspoon grated lemon
zest (optional)

1 tablespoon fresh
lemon juice

3 garlic cloves, minced

1 teaspoon maple syrup
or honey

¼ teaspoon kosher salt

⅛ teaspoon freshly ground
black pepper

2 tablespoons water, or
more as needed

The sauce I crave most often is this creamy dressing, which adds texture and flavor to salads, grain bowls, and roasted vegetables. The exact amount of water needed to make this dressing varies depending on the consistency of your tahini paste. Gradually whisk in 1 tablespoon of water at a time until it's thinned to the consistency you like. Tahini dressing tends to thicken in the refrigerator, so you may need to whisk in additional water if you make this recipe in advance.

1. In a small bowl, whisk together the tahini, lemon zest (if using), lemon juice, garlic, maple syrup, salt, and pepper until blended. Gradually add the water as needed until the dressing thins to your desired consistency.

2. Pour into a cruet to serve.

Storage: Store the dressing in an airtight container in the refrigerator for up to 10 days.

Protein swaps: Including nuts and seeds in salad dressings is a convenient way to get more protein. Any nut or seed butter can be substituted for the tahini in this recipe. Try it with sunflower seed, almond, cashew, or peanut butter.

PER SERVING: Calories: 106; Total fat: 8g; Carbohydrates: 7g; Fiber: 2g; Protein: 3g; Calcium: 76mg; Vitamin D: 0mcg; Vitamin B$_{12}$: 0µg; Iron: 1mg; Zinc: 1mg

Spicy Peanut Sauce

MAKES 4 SERVINGS (ABOUT 1½ CUPS TOTAL) • PREP TIME: 10 MINUTES

DORM-FRIENDLY | MAKES LEFTOVERS | NO COOKING REQUIRED

¼ cup creamy
    peanut butter
2 tablespoons rice vinegar
1 tablespoon soy sauce
1 tablespoon maple syrup
½ teaspoon garlic powder
½ teaspoon ground ginger
¼ teaspoon cayenne
2 tablespoons water, or
    more as needed

Peanut sauce originated in Indonesia, where it accompanies satay, a grilled meat kebab. My version of this creamy sauce, which is also popular in Southeast Asian countries such as Thailand and Vietnam, is balanced with a mix of protein, fats, and carbohydrates. Serve it over grain bowls or baked tofu or toss it with Asian-inspired noodles and salads.

1. In a medium bowl, whisk together the peanut butter, vinegar, soy sauce, maple syrup, garlic powder, ginger, and cayenne until blended.

2. Gradually whisk in the water as needed until the desired consistency is reached.

3. Pour into a bowl, ready to serve.

Storage: Store the sauce in an airtight container in the refrigerator for up to 1 week.

Tip: If you don't have peanut butter, substitute almond butter, cashew butter, or tahini. Instead of maple syrup, use sugar, honey, or agave nectar. If you prefer, you can also omit the sweetener completely.

PER SERVING: Calories: 116; Total fat: 8g; Carbohydrates: 7g; Fiber: 1g; Protein: 4g; Calcium: 15mg; Vitamin D: 0mcg; Vitamin B$_{12}$: 0µg; Iron: 0mg; Zinc: 1mg

Rosemary and Thyme Red Sauce

MAKES 4 SERVINGS (ABOUT 3 CUPS TOTAL) • PREP TIME: 5 MINUTES • COOK TIME: 15 MINUTES

DORM-FRIENDLY | MAKES LEFTOVERS | ONE POT

2 tablespoons grapeseed oil

½ cup diced onion (1 small)

6 garlic cloves, minced (or 3 teaspoons garlic powder)

1 tablespoon crushed fresh rosemary

1 tablespoon dried thyme

½ teaspoon kosher salt

¼ teaspoon freshly ground black pepper

1 (28-ounce) can crushed tomatoes, with juice

1 tablespoon maple syrup

Storage: Refrigerate the sauce for up to 4 days or place it in a freezer-save container and freeze for up to 6 months.

Mix it up: Add umami flavor to this Italian-inspired tomato sauce with a handful of grated Parmesan cheese. Instead of rosemary and thyme, try seasoning the sauce with basil, oregano, marjoram, or sage.

Switching to homemade pasta sauce is a simple way to save money and cut back on packaged foods. Many jarred tomato sauces are loaded with sugar, so another benefit of homemade is that you can reduce the sweetness. This Italian-inspired red sauce is packed with herbaceous flavor from rosemary and thyme. Use it in pasta dishes, on pizza, or as a dipping sauce for fresh bread. If you don't have maple syrup, substitute honey or sugar.

1. Heat the oil in a large saucepan over medium heat.

2. Once the oil is shiny, add the onion and cook for 4 minutes, or until translucent.

3. Add the garlic, rosemary, thyme, salt, and pepper and cook for 1 minute.

4. Add the tomatoes and maple syrup and bring the sauce to a boil. Reduce the heat to low and simmer the sauce for 10 minutes, stirring occasionally.

5. Cool the sauce for 5 minutes, then transfer to a quart jar with a lid.

PER SERVING: Calories: 120; Total fat: 7g; Carbohydrates: 14g; Fiber: 5g; Protein: 2g; Calcium: 90mg; Vitamin D: 0mcg; Vitamin B$_{12}$: 0µg; Iron: 1mg; Zinc: 0mg

Chimichurri Sauce

MAKES 2 SERVINGS (ABOUT ½ CUP TOTAL) • PREP TIME: 15 MINUTES

DORM-FRIENDLY | NO COOKING REQUIRED

¼ cup olive oil

2 tablespoons finely chopped fresh parsley

2 tablespoons finely chopped fresh cilantro

2 tablespoons red wine vinegar

2 garlic cloves, minced

¼ teaspoon red pepper flakes

¼ teaspoon kosher salt

¼ teaspoon freshly ground black pepper

Zippy chimichurri sauce originated in Argentina, where it's commonly used as a condiment for meat. The combination of herbaceous parsley and cilantro with oil, vinegar, and aromatic garlic makes this sauce ideal for topping pretty much any protein (think tofu, tempeh, or beans) or vegetable (try it with potatoes or carrots). I like to chop the herbs and garlic with a knife and cutting board, but you can also do that in a small food processor.

1. In a medium bowl, whisk together the olive oil, parsley, cilantro, vinegar, garlic, red pepper flakes, salt, and pepper until well mixed.

2. Pour into a bowl, ready to serve.

Storage: Store the sauce in an airtight container in the refrigerator for up to 3 weeks.

Mix it up: For extra texture, along with some additional gut-boosting fiber, essential fatty acids, and satisfying protein, try stirring in a spoonful of hemp hearts or finely chopped walnuts.

PER SERVING: Calories: 248; Total fat: 27g; Carbohydrates: 1g; Fiber: 0g; Protein: 0g; Calcium: 13mg; Vitamin D: 0mcg; Vitamin B$_{12}$: 0µg; Iron: 1mg; Zinc: 0mg

Carrot-Top Pesto

MAKES 4 SERVINGS (ABOUT 1¼ CUPS TOTAL) • PREP TIME: 5 MINUTES

DORM-FRIENDLY | MAKES LEFTOVERS | NO COOKING REQUIRED

½ cup carrot greens

½ cup fresh basil

¼ cup walnut halves
   and pieces

4 garlic cloves, chopped

¼ cup shredded
   Parmesan cheese

1 tablespoon fresh
   lemon juice

1 teaspoon maple syrup

¼ teaspoon kosher salt

¼ teaspoon freshly ground
   black pepper

6 tablespoons olive oil

Did you know you can eat the greens that have been growing on top of your bunch of carrots? Root-to-stem cooking, or using the entire vegetable, is a great way to save money and make your kitchen more environmentally friendly. Raw carrot tops can be bitter, but when balanced with sweet fresh basil and a little maple syrup, they taste delicious. Use this classic Italian sauce for pasta, sandwiches, and pizza.

1. Place the carrot greens, basil, walnuts, garlic, Parmesan, lemon juice, maple syrup, salt, and pepper in a food processor and process until the ingredients are finely chopped.

2. Pour in the olive oil and pulse until the desired consistency is reached.

3. Pour into a jar with a lid until ready to serve.

Storage: Store the pesto in an airtight container in the refrigerator for up to 4 days or freeze for up to 4 months.

Substitute: Use nutritional yeast instead of Parmesan cheese to make this pesto vegan and dairy-free. Use sunflower seeds instead of walnuts to make it nut-free. If you don't have carrot tops, substitute with additional basil or fresh parsley.

PER SERVING: Calories: 264; Total fat: 27g; Carbohydrates: 4g; Fiber: 1g; Protein: 3g; Calcium: 76mg; Vitamin D: 0mcg; Vitamin B$_{12}$: 0µg; Iron: 1mg; Zinc: 1mg

Spicy Blender Salsa

MAKES 8 SERVINGS (ABOUT 3 CUPS TOTAL) · PREP TIME: 10 MINUTES

DORM-FRIENDLY | GREAT FOR SHARING | MAKES LEFTOVERS | NO COOKING REQUIRED

3 ripe medium tomatoes (1 pound)
½ cup chopped onion
4 garlic cloves, chopped
⅓ cup chopped fresh cilantro
1 jalapeño pepper, chopped (optional)
¼ lime
¼ teaspoon kosher salt

My favorite thing about Mexican restaurants is that you get to start each meal with fresh chips and salsa. When I'm making tacos or burritos at home, I like to re-create the spicy condiment. This recipe is convenient for meal prep, since you can use salsa in so many different ways, and it stays fresh for a week in the refrigerator. Restaurant-style blender salsa is also a crowd-pleasing favorite to make any time you're invited to a last-minute tailgating party. Leave out the jalapeño pepper for a mild salsa flavor.

1. Place the tomatoes, onion, garlic, cilantro, jalapeño, lime, and salt in a blender and blend on high for 15 seconds or until the desired consistency is reached.

2. Pour into a jar with a lid.

Storage: Store in an airtight container in the refrigerator for up to 2 weeks.

Substitute: Substitute a 28-ounce can of tomatoes for the fresh tomatoes to make this salsa during the winter months. You can also make salsa verde (green salsa) by substituting fresh tomatillos for the tomatoes.

PER SERVING: Calories: 15; Total fat: 0g; Carbohydrates: 3g; Fiber: 1g; Protein: 1g; Calcium: 10mg; Vitamin D: 0mcg; Vitamin B$_{12}$: 0µg; Iron: 0mg; Zinc: 0mg

Chunky Guacamole

MAKES 8 SERVINGS (ABOUT 3 CUPS TOTAL) · PREP TIME: 10 MINUTES

DORM-FRIENDLY | GREAT FOR SHARING | NO COOKING REQUIRED | ONE BOWL

4 medium avocados,
   peeled and pitted

1 ripe medium
   tomato, diced

⅓ cup chopped fresh
   cilantro

¼ cup minced red onion

1 jalapeño pepper, minced

1 teaspoon grated
   lime zest

1 tablespoon fresh
   lime juice

¼ teaspoon kosher salt

Whether it's for a study group, tailgating party, or topping off tacos on a weeknight, there's no wrong time to eat guacamole. I like the texture to be extra chunky, so I always make guacamole by hand (versus mixing it in a food processor), and I only mash the avocado partly to keep more large pieces intact. Serve it with freshly baked tortilla chips (page 180) and salsa for a platter worthy of any college party.

1. In a medium bowl, mash the avocados with a potato masher or a fork until they are the desired consistency.

2. Add the tomato, cilantro, red onion, jalapeño, lime zest, lime juice, and salt and stir to combine. Best served immediately.

Mix it up: For a crunchy twist, try mixing in chopped jicama. Jicama is a white tuber that has a crisp texture and sweet, nutty flavor. You can also use jicama strips for dipping in guacamole.

PER SERVING: Calories: 189; Total fat: 15g; Carbohydrates: 13g; Fiber: 9g; Protein: 4g; Calcium: 19mg; Vitamin D: 0mcg; Vitamin B$_{12}$: 0µg; Iron: 0mg; Zinc: 1mg

Vegan Queso Dip

MAKES 2 SERVINGS (ABOUT 1 CUP TOTAL) · PREP TIME: 35 MINUTES · COOK TIME: 5 MINUTES

DORM-FRIENDLY | ONE-POT

¼ cup raw sunflower seeds

½ cup plain unsweetened oat milk (or milk of choice)

1 tablespoon nutritional yeast

2 chipotle chiles in adobo sauce

½ teaspoon onion powder

½ teaspoon garlic powder

¼ teaspoon kosher salt

⅛ teaspoon freshly ground black pepper

2 tablespoons water, or more as needed

Mix it up: If you don't have canned chipotle peppers in adobo sauce, substitute with 1 teaspoon of chili powder and cayenne to taste. You can also add black beans, sliced jalapeño peppers, or fresh cilantro.

Even cheese lovers won't be able to resist this plant-based cheesy queso sauce. This Mexican-inspired dip is made with sunflower seeds and oat milk, so it's naturally free of common allergens like nuts and dairy. Use it for dipping tortilla chips, nachos, tostadas, or tacos. Don't bother rinsing the canned chipotle chiles before you add them to the blender or food processor. The adobo sauce they're stored in adds tons of spicy flavor to this dairy-free queso dip.

1. Place the sunflower seeds in a small bowl and cover with water by about 1 inch. Set aside to soak for 30 minutes.

2. Drain the sunflower seeds and transfer them to a blender or food processor. Add the milk, nutritional yeast, chipotle chiles, onion powder, garlic powder, salt, and pepper. Blend for 1 minute, or until the sauce is smooth and creamy. If the mixture is too thick, add the water and blend again.

3. Transfer the sauce to a small saucepan and place it over medium heat. Cook the sauce for 5 minutes, or until warmed through.

4. Pour into a bowl, ready to serve.

PER SERVING: Calories: 168; Total fat: 10g; Carbohydrates: 14g; Fiber: 3g; Protein: 8g; Calcium: 103mg; Vitamin D: 1mcg; Vitamin B$_{12}$: 1µg; Iron: 2mg; Zinc: 2mg

Classic Hummus

MAKES 4 SERVINGS (ABOUT 1½ CUPS TOTAL) · PREP TIME: 5 MINUTES

DORM-FRIENDLY | GREAT FOR SHARING | MAKES LEFTOVERS | NO COOKING REQUIRED

1¼ cups cooked or canned chickpeas

¼ cup tahini

3 garlic cloves, chopped

1 tablespoon grated lemon zest

2 tablespoons fresh lemon juice

2 tablespoons olive oil, or more as needed

¼ teaspoon kosher salt

⅛ teaspoon freshly ground black pepper

Smoked paprika (optional)

Protein swaps:
Traditional hummus is made with chickpeas, but you can use any type of pulse to make a protein-packed dip or sandwich spread like this one. Try substituting lentils, cannellini beans, or navy beans.

Hummus is a classic Middle Eastern dip made with fiber- and protein-rich chickpeas. The word *hummus* even translates to "chickpeas" in Arabic. Hummus is usually made with chickpeas, tahini (sesame seed paste), garlic, and lemon. This version also incorporates olive oil and smoked paprika for topping. Whether you use dried or canned chickpeas, this vegan dip is perfect for sharing on game night. Serve it with pita bread, crackers, or fresh vegetables. You can also use hummus as a sandwich spread for a quick lunch.

1. Place the chickpeas, tahini, garlic, lemon zest, lemon juice, olive oil, salt, and pepper in a food processor and process for 1 minute or until smooth and creamy. If the mixture is too thick or isn't mixing, add another tablespoon of olive oil and process again.

2. Transfer the hummus to a bowl and sprinkle it with smoked paprika, if desired, and serve.

Storage: Store the hummus in an airtight container in the refrigerator for up to 1 week.

PER SERVING: Calories: 239; Total fat: 16g; Carbohydrates: 19g; Fiber: 4g; Protein: 7g; Calcium: 94mg; Vitamin D: 0mcg; Vitamin B$_{12}$: 0µg; Iron: 3mg; Zinc: 2mg

White Bean Sandwich Spread

MAKES 2 SERVINGS (ABOUT 1 CUP TOTAL) • PREP TIME: 5 MINUTES

1 (15-ounce) can cannellini beans, drained and rinsed

1 teaspoon grated lemon zest

1 tablespoon fresh lemon juice

1 tablespoon olive oil, or more as needed

1 tablespoon nutritional yeast (optional)

1 teaspoon onion powder

2 garlic cloves, minced

¼ teaspoon kosher salt

¼ teaspoon freshly ground black pepper

Mix it up: Nutritional yeast adds a cheesy flavor to this white bean spread, but you can also flavor it with basil, oregano, Jamaican jerk, Cajun seasoning, or curry powder. If you don't have cannellini beans, try substituting navy beans or lentils.

A protein-rich sandwich spread made with cannellini beans is an essential plant-based recipe for any busy college student. Serve it on any type of bread (use whole grain to get more fiber) and garnish with lettuce, tomato, onion, or any of your other favorite sandwich toppings. Add avocado, roasted sweet potato, or cheese to make it more filling. For breakfast, try this spread on a bagel or English muffin with a scrambled or fried egg.

1. Place the beans, lemon zest, lemon juice, olive oil, nutritional yeast (if using), onion powder, garlic, salt, and pepper in the food processor and process for 1 minute, or until smooth and creamy.

2. If the mixture is too thick, add a tablespoon of olive oil or water and process again.

3. Pour into a jar with a lid.

Storage: Store the spread in an airtight container in the refrigerator for up to 1 week.

PER SERVING: Calories: 239; Total fat: 7g; Carbohydrates: 33g; Fiber: 9g; Protein: 12g; Calcium: 58mg; Vitamin D: 0mcg; Vitamin B$_{12}$: 0µg; Iron: 3mg; Zinc: 1mg

Almond Ricotta

MAKES 4 SERVINGS (ABOUT 1 CUP TOTAL) · PREP TIME: 5 MINUTES

DORM-FRIENDLY | GREAT FOR SHARING | MAKES LEFTOVERS | NO COOKING REQUIRED

2 cups slivered almonds

1 tablespoon nutritional yeast

2 tablespoons fresh lemon juice

¼ teaspoon onion powder

¼ teaspoon garlic powder

½ teaspoon kosher salt

Ricotta is a popular Italian ingredient for lasagna, stuffed pasta, and casseroles. It's also sometimes used in desserts. This dairy-free version is made with blanched almonds and nutritional yeast and only takes a few minutes to prepare. In addition to using this in Italian recipes, you can use it as a dip for crackers and vegetables or as a spread for whole-grain toast at breakfast.

Place the almonds, nutritional yeast, lemon juice, onion powder, garlic powder, and salt in a blender and blend on high for 1 minute, pausing to scrape down the sides with a spatula as needed, or until smooth and creamy.

Storage: Store the ricotta in an airtight container in the refrigerator for up to 1 week.

Mix it up: Try stirring in fresh or dried herbs, such as basil, oregano, rosemary, thyme, marjoram, or sage. You can also mix in dried Italian seasoning to give this plant-based cheese some extra herbaceous flavor.

PER SERVING: Calories: 324; Total fat: 27g; Carbohydrates: 13g; Fiber: 7g; Protein: 13g; Calcium: 149mg; Vitamin D: 0mcg; Vitamin B$_{12}$: 0μg; Iron: 2mg; Zinc: 2mg

Tofu Feta

MAKES 2 SERVINGS (ABOUT 1 CUP TOTAL) · PREP TIME: 5 MINUTES, PLUS 30 MINUTES TO MARINATE

DORM-FRIENDLY | NO COOKING REQUIRED | ONE BOWL

1 (14-ounce) block
    firm tofu
3 tablespoons olive oil
1 teaspoon grated
    lemon zest
1 tablespoon fresh
    lemon juice
1 tablespoon
    nutritional yeast
1 teaspoon garlic powder
1 teaspoon dried oregano
¼ teaspoon kosher salt
⅛ teaspoon freshly ground
    black pepper

Feta cheese originated in Greece and is typically made from sheep's milk. It has a crumbly texture and briny flavor that's delicious with Mediterranean ingredients, including olives, tomatoes, and cucumber. This version of plant-based feta cheese is made from firm tofu, so it's naturally high in protein and contains less fat than traditional feta cheese. Firm tofu best mimics the texture of conventional feta, but you can also use extra-firm, if that's what you have on hand already.

1. Use your hands to crumble the tofu into a large bowl.

2. Add the olive oil, lemon zest, lemon juice, nutritional yeast, garlic powder, dried oregano, salt, and pepper to the bowl, mixing to combine.

3. Marinate the tofu for at least 30 minutes at room temperature or in the refrigerator overnight.

Storage: Store the tofu feta in an airtight container in the refrigerator for up to 3 days.

Mix it up: This vegan feta cheese is marinated with dried oregano for herbaceous Mediterranean flavor. Omit the oregano if you'd like this tofu feta to be unflavored. You can also add additional herbs and spices, such as basil, thyme, or red pepper flakes.

PER SERVING: Calories: 385; Total fat: 32g; Carbohydrates: 8g; Fiber: 2g; Protein: 22g; Calcium: 365mg; Vitamin D: 0mcg; Vitamin B$_{12}$: 0µg; Iron: 4mg; Zinc: 3mg

Blueberry Chia Jam

MAKES 8 SERVINGS (ABOUT 2 CUPS TOTAL) · PREP TIME: 5 MINUTES · COOK TIME: 15 MINUTES

DORM-FRIENDLY | MAKES LEFTOVERS | ONE POT

**2 cups fresh or frozen
   blueberries**

½ cup maple syrup

2 tablespoons chia seeds

**1 tablespoon fresh
   lemon juice**

⅛ teaspoon salt

Chia seeds are a natural plant-based thickener that also happens to contain satisfying fiber and brain-boosting fatty acids. Use them to make a quick and easy fruit jam with nearly any type of fresh or frozen fruit. The sweet blueberries and tart lemon in this recipe is a classic combination for breakfast. Slather this antioxidant-loaded jam onto whole-grain toast, add a spoonful to your next bowl of oats, or stir it into a chia pudding. Both fresh and frozen blueberries work, so use whichever is available to you.

1. In a large saucepan, stir together the blueberries, maple syrup, chia seeds, lemon juice, and salt over medium heat.

2. Cook the mixture for 15 minutes or until the blueberries are softened and the jam is thickened. The jam will continue to thicken as it cools.

Storage: Store the cooled jam in an airtight container in the refrigerator for up to 1 month.

Mix it up: Instead of blueberries, make homemade chia jam with blackberries, strawberries, or raspberries during the spring and summer. In fall and winter months, try making this jam with apples or pears.

PER SERVING: Calories: 90; Total fat: 1g; Carbohydrates: 20g; Fiber: 2g; Protein: 1g; Calcium: 45mg; Vitamin D: 0mcg; Vitamin B$_{12}$: 0μg; Iron: 0mg; Zinc: 0mg

Creamy Almond Butter

MAKES 8 SERVINGS (ABOUT 1 CUP TOTAL) • PREP TIME: 15 MINUTES • COOK TIME: 5 MINUTES

MAKES LEFTOVERS

1 cup blanched almonds
1 tablespoon coconut oil
¼ teaspoon kosher salt

Mix it up: Use this creamy nut butter recipe as the base for all types of sweet flavors. Some of my favorite ingredients to mix into this creamy almond butter are cocoa powder, vanilla, and cinnamon. Add any of these with the coconut oil and salt at the end of processing.

If you're looking for another way to buy fewer packaged foods, try making your own nut butters at home. You only need a food processor to make them. I like to toast the nuts in the oven first because it brings out their natural oils and flavors. Skip this step if you don't have access to an oven. Once they are toasted, transfer the almonds to the food processor and process until the nuts first break down into small pieces and then thicken into a creamy paste. The recipe itself is simple but requires some patience.

1. Preheat the oven or toaster oven to 350°F. Line a baking sheet with parchment.

2. Spread the almonds on the baking sheet and bake for 5 minutes, or until golden and aromatic.

3. Transfer the almonds to a food processor and process for 10 minutes, or until smooth, creamy, and thickened. Pause to scrape down the sides with a spatula as needed. Once the almond butter is thick, add the coconut oil and salt and process for 15 seconds to mix.

Storage: Store the almond butter in an airtight container in the refrigerator for up to 1 month.

PER SERVING: Calories: 118; Total fat: 11g; Carbohydrates: 4g; Fiber: 2g; Protein: 4g; Calcium: 48mg; Vitamin D: 0mcg; Vitamin B_{12}: 0µg; Iron: 1mg; Zinc: 1mg

Whole-Grain Croutons

MAKES 4 SERVINGS (ABOUT 1 CUP TOTAL) · PREP TIME: 5 MINUTES · COOK TIME: 15 MINUTES

MAKES LEFTOVERS

2 cups torn whole-
grain bread
2 tablespoons grapeseed
oil, or other oil of choice
1 tablespoon nutritional
yeast (optional)
1 teaspoon dried thyme
½ teaspoon onion powder
½ teaspoon garlic powder
½ teaspoon kosher salt
¼ teaspoon freshly ground
black pepper

There aren't many things in life that taste better than freshly baked bread, but it can be challenging to make use of a full loaf when you're living on your own. Whenever I have leftover bread that's getting stale, I like to tear it into bite-size pieces and bake them to make homemade croutons that are delicious on salads and soups. Whole-grain bread is an excellent choice if you want to make these croutons higher in satisfying fiber.

1. Preheat the oven or toaster oven to 375°F. Line a baking sheet with parchment.

2. In a large bowl, toss together the bread, oil, nutritional yeast (if using), thyme, onion powder, garlic powder, salt, and pepper, and spread the mixture out in a single layer on the baking sheet.

3. Bake the croutons for 15 minutes or until golden and crispy. Cool them on a rack before serving.

Storage: Store the croutons in an airtight container at room temperature for up to 1 week.

Make it easier: To make plain whole-grain croutons, skip the nutritional yeast, thyme, onion powder, and garlic powder. Toss the torn bread pieces with oil, salt, and pepper, and bake as described.

PER SERVING: Calories: 114; Total fat: 8g; Carbohydrates: 9g; Fiber: 2g; Protein: 3g; Calcium: 22mg; Vitamin D: 0mcg; Vitamin B_{12}: 0µg; Iron: 1mg; Zinc: 0mg

Vegan Chocolate Sauce

MAKES 4 SERVINGS (ABOUT ¾ CUP TOTAL) · PREP TIME: 5 MINUTES · COOK TIME: 5 MINUTES

DORM-FRIENDLY | GREAT FOR SHARING | MAKES LEFTOVERS | ONE POT

½ cup Vanilla Almond Milk (page 211) (or milk of choice)
½ cup unsweetened cocoa powder
¼ cup maple syrup
⅛ teaspoon salt

Life is just better with a drizzle of chocolate. Serve this plant-based chocolate sauce over any type of dessert, including ice cream (page 195), fresh fruit, or even Vegan No-Bake Blueberry Cheesecake (page 205). It's made without any dairy or refined oils and is naturally sweetened with maple syrup. You can even eat it at breakfast by pouring it over pancakes or stirring it into chia pudding, oatmeal, or overnight oats.

1. In a medium saucepan, whisk together the almond milk, cocoa powder, maple syrup, and salt over medium-low heat.

2. Simmer the sauce for 5 minutes, or until warmed through, stirring constantly. Remove the sauce from the heat.

Storage: Store the sauce in an airtight container in the refrigerator for up to 1 week. Shake well before using.

Substitute: Instead of almond milk, substitute oat milk, hemp milk, or flax milk to make this chocolate sauce nut-free. If you include dairy products in your lifestyle, you can also make this recipe with cow's milk.

PER SERVING: Calories: 88; Total fat: 2g; Carbohydrates: 21g; Fiber: 3g; Protein: 3g; Calcium: 68mg; Vitamin D: 0mcg; Vitamin B$_{12}$: 0μg; Iron: 2mg; Zinc: 1mg

Measurement Conversions

VOLUME EQUIVALENTS (LIQUID)

US STANDARD	US STANDARD (OUNCES)	METRIC (APPROXIMATE)
2 tablespoons	1 fl. oz.	30 mL
¼ cup	2 fl. oz.	60 mL
½ cup	4 fl. oz.	120 mL
1 cup	8 fl. oz.	240 mL
1½ cups	12 fl. oz.	355 mL
2 cups or 1 pint	16 fl. oz.	475 mL
4 cups or 1 quart	32 fl. oz.	1 L
1 gallon	128 fl. oz.	4 L

OVEN TEMPERATURES

FAHRENHEIT	CELSIUS (APPROXIMATE)
250°F	120°C
300°F	150°C
325°F	165°C
350°F	180°C
375°F	190°C
400°F	200°C
425°F	220°C
450°F	230°C

VOLUME EQUIVALENTS (DRY)

US STANDARD	METRIC (APPROXIMATE)
⅛ teaspoon	0.5 mL
¼ teaspoon	1 mL
½ teaspoon	2 mL
¾ teaspoon	4 mL
1 teaspoon	5 mL
1 tablespoon	15 mL
¼ cup	59 mL
⅓ cup	79 mL
½ cup	118 mL
⅔ cup	156 mL
¾ cup	177 mL
1 cup	235 mL
2 cups or 1 pint	475 mL
3 cups	700 mL
4 cups or 1 quart	1 L

WEIGHT EQUIVALENTS

US STANDARD	METRIC (APPROXIMATE)
½ ounce	15 g
1 ounce	30 g
2 ounces	60 g
4 ounces	115 g
8 ounces	225 g
12 ounces	340 g
16 ounces or 1 pound	455 g

Resources

Websites for Recipes

Budget Bytes: BudgetBytes.com

Delicious Knowledge by Alexandra Caspero, RD: DelishKnowledge.com

Dishing Out Health by Jamie Vespa, RD: DishingOutHealth.com

The Foodie Dietitian by Kara Lydon, RD: KaraLydon.com

Grateful Grazer by Stephanie McKercher, RDN: GratefulGrazer.com

Half Baked Harvest by Tieghan Gerard: HalfBakedHarvest.com

Happy Cow: HappyCow.net (vegetarian restaurants)

The Plant-Powered Dietitian by Sharon Palmer, RD: SharonPalmer.com

Websites for Food and Nutrition Information

Academy of Nutrition and Dietetics: EatRight.org

Champagne Nutrition by Ginger Hultin, RD: ChampagneNutrition.com

Jack Norris, RD: JackNorrisRD.com

Natural Resources Defense Council: NRDC.org (information about food waste)

Nutrition à la Natalie by Natalie Rizzo, RD: NutritionalaNatalie.com (vegetarian sports nutrition)

The Vegan RD by Virginia Messina, RD: TheVeganRD.com

Vegetarian Nutrition Dietetic Practice Group of the Academy of Nutrition and Dietetics: VegetarianNutrition.net

The Vegetarian Resource Group: VRG.org

Books

Cooking Scrappy by Joel Gamoran

The Easy Superfoods Cookbook by Emily Cooper

Fresh Italian Cooking for the New Generation by Alexandra Caspero Lenz

Half Baked Harvest Super Simple by Tieghan Gerard

The Healing Soup Cookbook by Cara Harbstreet and Julie Harrington

How to Cook Everything Vegetarian by Mark Bittman

Intuitive Eating by Evelyn Tribole and Elyse Resch

The Plant-Powered Diet by Sharon Palmer

Plant-Powered for Life by Sharon Palmer

The Vegetarian Flavor Bible by Karen Page

References

Caspero, A. "Easy Tofu Recipe: Vegan Baked Tofu Nuggets (Chick-fil-A Copycat!)." Delish Knowledge. https://www.delishknowledge.com/vegan-tofu-nuggets/. Published 2018. Accessed April 5, 2020.

Cookie and Kate (blog). "Healthy Carrot Muffins Recipe." https://cookieandkate.com/healthy-carrot-muffins-recipe/. Accessed April 5, 2020.

Derbyshire, E. "Brain Health across the Lifespan: A Systematic Review on the Role of Omega-3 Fatty Acid Supplements." *Nutrients*. 2018;10(8):1094. doi:10.3390/nu10081094

Flynn, M. and A. Schiff. "Economical Healthy Diets (2012): Including Lean Animal Protein Costs More Than Using Olive Oil." *J Hunger Environ Nutr*. 2015;10(4):467-482. doi:10.1080/19320248.2015.1045675

FoodData Central. https://fdc.nal.usda.gov/. Published 2020. Accessed March 6, 2020.

Melina, V., W. Craig, and S. Levin. "Position of the Academy of Nutrition and Dietetics: Vegetarian Diets." *J Acad Nutr Diet*. 2016;116(12):1970-1980. doi:10.1016/j.jand.2016.09.025

Minimalist Baker (blog). "5-Ingredient Vegan Almond Ricotta." https://minimalistbaker.com/whipped-almond-ricotta-5-ingredients/. Accessed April 5, 2020.

Nikkhah Bodagh M., I. Maleki, A. Hekmatdoost. "Ginger in gastrointestinal disorders: A systematic review of clinical trials." *Food Sci Nutr*. 2018;7(1):96-108. doi:10.1002/fsn3.807

Soret , S., A. Mejia, M. Batech, K. Jaceldo-Siegl, H. Harwatt, and J. Sabaté. "Climate change mitigation and health effects of varied dietary patterns in real-life settings throughout North America." *Am J Clin Nutr*. 2014;100(suppl_1):490S-495S. doi:10.3945/ajcn.113.071589

Thug Kitchen. New York: Rodale; 2014:98.

Willett W., J. Rockström, B. Loken B et al. "Food in the Anthropocene: the EAT–Lancet Commission on healthy diets from sustainable food systems." *The Lancet.* 2019;393(10170):447-492. doi:10.1016/s0140-6736(18)31788-4

Williams, J., J. Everett, N. D. Cunha et al. "The Effects of Green Tea Amino Acid L-Theanine Consumption on the Ability to Manage Stress and Anxiety Levels: a Systematic Review." *Plant Foods for Human Nutrition.* 2019;75(1):12-23. doi:10.1007/s11130-019-00771-5

Index

A

Almonds
    Almond Ricotta, 224
    Creamy Almond
        Butter, 227
    Fruit and Nut Energy
        Bites, 176
    Make-Ahead Kale
        Salad, 94
    Moroccan-Inspired
        Chickpea
        Couscous, 145–146
    No-Bake Green Tea
        Energy Bars, 20–21
    Vanilla Almond Milk, 211
    Vegan Party
        Platter, 190–191
Aluminum foil, 13
Apple Cider Vinaigrette, 212
Apple Pie Granola, 23
Apples
    Apple Chips with
        Cinnamon-Yogurt
        Dip, 175
    Granny Smith Green
        Smoothie, 171
Avocados
    Chocolate-Avocado
        Pudding, 198
    Chunky Guacamole, 220
    Green Goddess
        Cucumber-Avocado
        Sandwiches, 62
    Pan-Roasted Nachos, 188
    Roasted Sweet Potato
        and Hummus
        Sandwiches, 73
    soothing nausea with, 7
    Spicy Chickpea-Avocado
        Toast, 22
    Strawberry and Avocado
        Spinach Salad, 92
    Ultimate Vegan Breakfast
        Sandwiches, 35–36
    Vegan Loaded Sweet
        Potatoes, 163–164
    Watermelon Poke
        Bowls, 144

B

Bake, defined, 12
Baking dish, 10
Baking sheets, 10
Bananas
    Peanut Butter and
        Banana Overnight
        Oats, 24
    Strawberry-Banana Ice
        Cream, 195
Banh Mi Sandwiches,
    Vegan, 74–75
Barley
    Cranberry, Walnut, and
        Brussels Sprouts
        Salad, 101
Bars
    No-Bake Chocolate-
        Peanut Butter
        Bars, 177
    No-Bake Green Tea
        Energy Bars, 20–21
Basil
    Caprese Pasta Salad, 96
    Carrot-Top Pesto, 218
    Cooling Cucumber-Basil
        Soup, 40
    Lemon Basil and
        Smashed White Bean
        Sandwiches, 68
    Tomato-Basil
        Orecchiette, 116–117
Beans. *See also* Chickpeas;
    Edamame
    Baked Spaghetti Squash
        Lasagna, 119–120
    Black Bean Burrito
        Bowl, 156
    Black Bean
        Quesadillas, 187
    Chili-Lime Taco
        Salad, 105
    Freezer-Friendly Bean
        Burgers, 81–82
    Freezer-Friendly Breakfast
        Burritos, 33–34
    Lemon Basil and
        Smashed White Bean
        Sandwiches, 68
    Mushroom Taco
        Bake, 166–167
    Pan-Roasted
        Nachos, 188
    Pinto Bean and Tortilla
        Soup, 47–48
    Pinto Bean Tostadas with
        Red Cabbage and
        Cilantro Slaw, 147–148
    Pumpkin and Black Bean
        Chili, 58
    soothing nausea with, 7
    Spaghetti and Lentil
        Balls, 128–129
    stocking up on, 9
    Vegan Corn Chowder, 52
    Vegan Gumbo, 57

Vegan Loaded Sweet
  Potatoes, 163–164
Veggie and White Bean
  Pesto Melt, 79
White Bean and Tomato
  Stuffed Shells, 134–135
White Bean Sandwich
  Spread, 223
Berries. *See also* Blueberries;
  Cranberries;
  Strawberries
  Triple-Berry Flax
    Oatmeal, 30
Blend, defined, 12
Blender, 10
Blood sugar levels, 3–4
Blueberries
  Blueberry Chia
    Jam, 226
  Lemon-Blueberry Yogurt
    Bowls, 29
  Vegan No-Bake Blueberry
    Cheesecake, 205–206
Boil, defined, 12
Bok choy
  Five-Spice
    Noodles, 122–123
  Garlic and Miso Ramen
    Noodles, 114–115
Bread. *See* Croutons;
  Sandwiches; Strata;
  Tortillas
Broccoli
  Broccoli Cheddar
    Strata, 37
  Broccoli Cheese Soup with
    Croutons, 54–55
  Cheesy Broccoli Pasta
    Bake, 140–141
  Chickpea and Coconut
    Curry Wraps, 76
  Easy Edamame
    Stir-Fry, 151

Five-Spice
  Noodles, 122–123
One-Pot Broccoli Mac
  and Cheese, 121
One-Pot Pantry
  Pasta, 110–111
Sesame-Ginger Soba
  Noodle Salad, 104
Sesame Tofu and
  Broccoli, 154–155
Vegan Pad Thai, 112–113
Zucchini Pasta
  Primavera, 108
Brussels Sprouts, Cranberry,
  and Walnut Salad, 101
Buffalo Cauliflower, 184–185
Buffalo Tofu Sandwiches, 87
Bulk storage bins, 13
Burgers, Freezer-Friendly
  Bean, 81–82
Burrito Bowl, Black Bean, 156
Burritos
  Chili-Lime Tempeh
    Burritos, 80
  Freezer-Friendly Breakfast
    Burritos, 33–34
  Vegan Sushi Burritos, 78

C

Cabbage. *See also* Bok choy
  Edamame Mason Jar
    Salad, 98
  Pinto Bean Tostadas with
    Red Cabbage and
    Cilantro Slaw, 147–148
  Red Cabbage and
    Cilantro Slaw, 93
  Thai-Inspired Peanut
    Salad, 91
Caesar Salad, Vegan, 99
Cake, Chai Tea Mug, 203
Calcium, 3
Cancer, 5–6

Caprese Pasta Salad, 96
Carrots
  Carrot-Top Pesto, 218
  Chimichurri Baked Tofu
    Bowls, 165
  Creamy Carrot-Ginger
    Soup, 45–46
  Edamame Mason Jar
    Salad, 98
  Irish-Inspired Potato
    Stew, 56
  Loaded Carrot
    Dogs, 69–70
  Quick Pickled Carrots and
    Vegetables, 174
  Red Cabbage and
    Cilantro Slaw, 93
  Roasted Chickpea and
    Carrot Dinner, 152–153
  Thai-Inspired Peanut
    Salad, 91
  Vegan Sushi Burritos, 78
  Vegetable Spring
    Rolls, 182
  Whole-Grain Carrot Cake
    Muffins, 27–28
Cashews
  Vegan No-Bake Blueberry
    Cheesecake, 205–206
Cauliflower
  Buffalo
    Cauliflower, 184–185
  Chimichurri Baked Tofu
    Bowls, 165
Chai Tea Mug Cake, 203
Cheese
  Baked Potato Skins, 189
  Baked Spaghetti Squash
    Lasagna, 119–120
  Black Bean
    Quesadillas, 187
  Broccoli Cheddar
    Strata, 37

Cheese (continued)
  Broccoli Cheese Soup with
    Croutons, 54–55
  Caprese Pasta Salad, 96
  Cheesy Broccoli Pasta
    Bake, 140–141
  Eggplant Bacon
    Carbonara, 126–127
  15-Minute Cacio e
    Pepe, 109
  Greek Lasagna, 132–133
  Mushroom
    Cheesesteaks, 84
  Mushroom French Onion
    Soup, 51
  Mushroom Taco
    Bake, 166–167
  One-Pan Skillet
    Lasagna, 136
  One-Pot Broccoli Mac
    and Cheese, 121
  Pan-Roasted Nachos, 188
  Spinach and Mushroom
    Baked Egg Cups, 26
  Spinach Spaghetti Pie, 137
  Tempeh Reubens, 85–86
  Veggie and White Bean
    Pesto Melt, 79
  White Bean and Tomato
    Stuffed Shells, 134–135
Cheesecake, Vegan No-Bake
  Blueberry, 205–206
Chia seeds
  Blueberry Chia Jam, 226
  cognitive benefits, 4
  Energizing Matcha
    Smoothie, 172
  Tropical Chia Pudding
    Parfait, 25
Chickpeas
  Chickpea and Coconut
    Curry Wraps, 76

Chickpea Cookie
  Dough, 196
Classic Hummus, 222
Cranberry and Chickpea
  Salad Sandwiches, 63
Garlicky Roasted
  Chickpeas, 186
Make-Ahead Kale
  Salad, 94
Mediterranean Falafel
  Pitas, 71–72
Moroccan-Inspired
  Chickpea
  Couscous, 145–146
One-Pot Pantry
  Pasta, 110–111
Roasted Chickpea and
  Carrot Dinner, 152–153
Spicy Chickpea-Avocado
  Toast, 22
Sun-Dried Tomato and
  Farro Salad, 100
Chili, Pumpkin and Black
  Bean, 58
Chili-Lime Taco Salad, 105
Chili-Lime Tempeh
  Burritos, 80
Chili-Lime Tortilla
  Chips, 180
Chili, defined, 12
Chimichurri Baked Tofu
  Bowls, 165
Chimichurri Sauce, 217
Chocolate
  Chickpea Cookie
    Dough, 196
  Chocolate-Avocado
    Pudding, 198
  Chocolate-Covered
    Mangos, 194
  Chocolate–Peanut Butter
    Cups, 201–202
  dark, cognitive benefits, 4

No-Bake Chocolate–
  Peanut Butter
  Bars, 177
Vegan Chocolate
  Sauce, 229
Chowder, Vegan Corn, 52
Cilantro
  Chimichurri Sauce, 217
  Chunky Guacamole, 220
  Pinto Bean Tostadas
    with Red Cabbage
    and Cilantro
    Slaw, 147–148
  Red Cabbage and
    Cilantro Slaw, 93
  Spicy Blender Salsa, 219
  Vegetable Spring
    Rolls, 182
Cinnamon
  Apple Chips with
    Cinnamon-Yogurt
    Dip, 175
  Cinnamon Oat Milk
    Latte, 18
  Snickerdoodle Skillet
    Cookie, 199–200
Coconut
  Chickpea and Coconut
    Curry Wraps, 76
  Tropical Chia Pudding
    Parfait, 25
  Vegan No-Bake Blueberry
    Cheesecake, 205–206
Coffee
  Cinnamon Oat Milk
    Latte, 18
Cookie, Snickerdoodle
  Skillet, 199–200
Cookie Dough,
  Chickpea, 196
Cooking oil, 9
Cooking terms, 12

Corn
    Black Bean Burrito
        Bowl, 156
    Chili-Lime Tempeh
        Burritos, 80
    Vegan Corn Chowder, 52
Couscous, Moroccan-Inspired
    Chickpea, 145–146
Cranberries
    Cranberry, Walnut, and
        Brussels Sprouts
        Salad, 101
    Cranberry and Chickpea
        Salad Sandwiches, 63
    Make-Ahead Kale
        Salad, 94
Croutons
    Broccoli Cheese Soup with
        Croutons, 54–55
    Vegan Caesar Salad, 99
    Whole-Grain
        Croutons, 228
Cucumbers
    Cooling Cucumber-Basil
        Soup, 40
    Cucumber-Mango
        Salad, 90
    Green Goddess
        Cucumber-Avocado
        Sandwiches, 62
    Vegan Greek Salad with
        Tofu Feta, 95
    Vegetable Spring
        Rolls, 182
    Watermelon
        Gazpacho, 41
Curried Egg Salad
    Sandwiches, 65
Curried Kale Chips, 173
Curry, Lentil and
    Pumpkin, 159
Cutting board, 10

D
Dates
    Apple Pie Granola, 23
    Fruit and Nut Energy
        Bites, 176
    No-Bake Chocolate-
        Peanut Butter Bars, 177
    No-Bake Green Tea
        Energy Bars, 20–21
    Vegan No-Bake Blueberry
        Cheesecake, 205–206
Diabetes, 5
Dice, defined, 12
Dips
    Almond Ricotta, 224
    Apple Chips with
        Cinnamon-Yogurt
        Dip, 175
    Chunky Guacamole, 220
    Classic Hummus, 222
    Roasted Potatoes with
        Lemon-Chive Yogurt
        Dip, 181
    Vegan Queso Dip, 221
Dressings
    Apple Cider
        Vinaigrette, 212
    Lemon Tahini
        Dressing, 214
    Sesame Ginger
        Dressing, 213
Drinks. *See* Milk; Smoothies

E
Edamame
    Easy Edamame
        Stir-Fry, 151
    Edamame Mason Jar
        Salad, 98
    Ginger-Turmeric Rice
        Noodles, 118
    Sesame-Ginger
        Edamame, 178
    Sesame-Ginger Soba
        Noodle Salad, 104
    soothing nausea with, 7
    10-Minute Miso Soup, 42
    Thai-Inspired Peanut
        Salad, 91
    Vegan Sushi Burritos, 78
    Watermelon Poke
        Bowls, 144
Eggplant
    Crispy Eggplant BLTs, 77
    Eggplant Bacon
        Carbonara, 126–127
Eggs
    Curried Egg Salad
        Sandwiches, 65
    Eggplant Bacon
        Carbonara, 126–127
    Freezer-Friendly Breakfast
        Burritos, 33–34
    Garlic and Miso Ramen
        Noodles, 114–115
    soothing nausea with, 7
    Spinach and Mushroom
        Baked Egg Cups, 26
Energy Bars, No-Bake Green
    Tea, 20–21
Energy Bites, Fruit and
    Nut, 176
Environment, and plant-
    based diets, 6–8
Equipment and tools, 10
Exam time ingredients, 4

F
Falafel Pitas,
    Mediterranean, 71–72
Farro and Sun-Dried Tomato
    Salad, 100
Feta, Tofu, 225

Five-Spice Noodles, 122–123
Flaxseeds
    cognitive benefits, 4
    Fruit and Nut Energy
        Bites, 176
    No-Bake Green
        Tea Energy
        Bars, 20–21
    Rejuvenating Citrus
        Smoothie, 19
    Triple-Berry Flax
        Oatmeal, 30
Food-and-mood
    connection, 3–4
Food processor, 10
Food storage options, 13
Froth, defined, 12
Fruit. *See also* Berries;
    specific fruits
    cognitive benefits, 4
    frozen, for recipes, 9
    Fruit and Nut Energy
        Bites, 176

G
Garlic
    Garlic and Miso Ramen
        Noodles, 114–115
    Garlicky Roasted
        Chickpeas, 186
    Vegan Garlic-Mushroom
        Naan Pizzas, 149–150
Gazpacho, Watermelon, 41
Ginger
    Creamy Carrot-Ginger
        Soup, 45–46
    Ginger-Turmeric Rice
        Noodles, 118
    Sesame Ginger
        Dressing, 213
    Sesame-Ginger
        Edamame, 178

Sesame-Ginger Soba
    Noodle Salad, 104
soothing nausea
    with, 7
Glass jars, 13
Global warming, 6–8
Grains. *See also specific*
    grains
    stocking up on, 9
Granola
    Apple Pie Granola, 23
    Pumpkin Pie Parfait
        Jars, 204
Greek Lasagna, 132–133
Greek Salad with Tofu Feta,
    Vegan, 95
Greek Yogurt Potato Salad,
    Creamy, 97
Green Goddess
    Cucumber-Avocado
    Sandwiches, 62
Greenhouse gases, 6–8
Greens. *See also specific*
    greens
    Carrot-Top Pesto, 218
    Peanut Stew, 59
    Vegan Gumbo, 57
Green tea. *See* Matcha
Grocery lists, 11
Guacamole, Chunky, 220
Gumbo, Vegan, 57

H
Hemp seeds, 4
Herbs. *See also* Basil;
    Cilantro
    Chimichurri Sauce, 217
    Green Goddess
        Cucumber-Avocado
        Sandwiches, 62
    Rosemary and Thyme
        Red Sauce, 216

Hummus
    Classic Hummus, 222
    Roasted Sweet Potato
        and Hummus
        Sandwiches, 73
    Vegan Party
        Platter, 190–191

I
Ice Cream, Strawberry-
    Banana, 195
Ingredients
    add-ons, 9–10
    must-have, 9
Irish-Inspired Potato
    Stew, 56
Iron, 3

J
Jam, Blueberry
    Chia, 226
Jerked Tempeh with Herb
    Rice, 157–158

K
Kale
    Black Bean Burrito
        Bowl, 156
    Curried Kale Chips, 173
    Ginger-Turmeric Rice
        Noodles, 118
    Harvest Butternut
        Squash and Quinoa
        Salad, 102–103
    Make-Ahead Kale
        Salad, 94
    One-Pot Creamy Vegan
        Rigatoni, 124–125
    Peanut Stew, 59
    Pumpkin and Black
        Bean Chili, 58
Knives, 10

L

Lasagna
    Baked Spaghetti Squash
        Lasagna, 119–120
    Greek Lasagna, 132–133
    One-Pan Skillet
        Lasagna, 136

Latte, Cinnamon Oat Milk, 18

Lemon
    Lemon Basil and
        Smashed White Bean
        Sandwiches, 68
    Lemon-Blueberry Yogurt
        Bowls, 29
    Lemon Tahini
        Dressing, 214
    Roasted Potatoes with
        Lemon-Chive
        Yogurt Dip, 181

Lentils
    High-Protein Lentil
        Soup, 53
    Lentil and Pumpkin
        Curry, 159
    Lentil Sloppy Joes, 83
    Smoky Lentil and
        Portobello Mushroom
        Wraps, 66–67
    Spaghetti and Lentil
        Balls, 128–129
    stocking up on, 9

Lettuce
    Chili-Lime Taco Salad, 105
    Crispy Eggplant BLTs, 77
    Spicy Peanut-Tofu Lettuce
        Wraps, 64
    Vegan Caesar Salad, 99

M

Mangos
    Chocolate-Covered
        Mangos, 194

Cucumber-Mango
    Salad, 90
Energizing Matcha
    Smoothie, 172
Granny Smith Green
    Smoothie, 171
Rejuvenating Citrus
    Smoothie, 19
Tropical Chia Pudding
    Parfait, 25

Matcha
    about, 4, 9
    Energizing Matcha
        Smoothie, 172
    No-Bake Green Tea
        Energy Bars, 20–21

Mediterranean Falafel
    Pitas, 71–72

Milk
    Blended Golden Milk
        Latte, 170
    Cinnamon Oat Milk
        Latte, 18
    Creamy Oat Milk, 210
    Vanilla Almond Milk, 211

Miso
    about, 9
    Garlic and Miso Ramen
        Noodles, 114–115
    10-Minute Miso Soup, 42

Mixing bowls, 10

Moroccan-Inspired Chickpea
    Couscous, 145–146

Muffins, Whole-Grain Carrot
    Cake, 27–28

Muffin tins, 10

Mug Cake, Chai Tea, 203

Mushrooms
    Mushroom
        Cheesesteaks, 84
    Mushroom French Onion
        Soup, 51

Mushroom Taco
    Bake, 166–167
Smoky Lentil and
    Portobello Mushroom
    Wraps, 66–67
Spinach and Mushroom
    Baked Egg Cups, 26
10-Minute Miso Soup, 42
Vegan Garlic-Mushroom
    Naan Pizzas, 149–150

N

Nachos, Pan-Roasted, 188
Nausea, best foods for, 7
Noodles
    Five-Spice
        Noodles, 122–123
    Garlic and Miso Ramen
        Noodles, 114–115
    Ginger-Turmeric Rice
        Noodles, 118
    Sesame-Ginger Soba
        Noodle Salad, 104
    Vegan Pad Thai, 112–113

Nutritional yeast
    about, 10
    Almond Ricotta, 224
    Cheesy Vegan
        Popcorn, 179
    Tofu Feta, 225
    Vegan Caesar
        Salad, 99
    Vegan Garlic-Mushroom
        Naan Pizzas, 149–150
    Vegan Queso Dip, 221

Nuts. *See also* Almonds;
    Walnuts
    Apple Pie Granola, 23
    Fruit and Nut Energy
        Bites, 176
    Thai-Inspired Peanut
        Salad, 91

Nuts (*continued*)

    Vegan No-Bake Blueberry
      Cheesecake, 205–206

    Yogurt-Dipped
      Strawberries, 197

O

Oat milk

    Blended Golden Milk
      Latte, 170

    Cinnamon Oat Milk
      Latte, 18

Oats

    Apple Pie Granola, 23

    Creamy Oat Milk, 210

    Peanut Butter and
      Banana Overnight
      Oats, 24

    Triple-Berry Flax
      Oatmeal, 30

Olives

    Vegan Caesar
      Salad, 99

    Vegan Greek Salad with
      Tofu Feta, 95

    Vegan Party
      Platter, 190–191

Omega-3 fatty acids, 2

Onion Mushroom Soup,
    French, 51

Oranges

    Better-than-Takeout
      Orange Tofu, 160

    Rejuvenating Citrus
      Smoothie, 19

Oven mitts, 10

P

Pad Thai, Vegan, 112–113

Pancakes, Sweet
    Potato, 31–32

Pantry ingredients, 9–10

Parfaits

    Pumpkin Pie Parfait
      Jars, 204

    Tropical Chia Pudding
      Parfait, 25

Parsley

    Chimichurri Sauce, 217

    Green Goddess
      Cucumber-Avocado
      Sandwiches, 62

Party Platter, Vegan, 190–191

Pasta. *See also* Noodles

    Baked Spaghetti Squash
      Lasagna, 119–120

    Caprese Pasta Salad, 96

    Cheesy Broccoli Pasta
      Bake, 140–141

    Creamy Pumpkin-Sage
      Alfredo, 130–131

    Eggplant Bacon
      Carbonara, 126–127

    15-Minute Cacio e
      Pepe, 109

    Greek Lasagna, 132–133

    No-Chicken Tofu Noodle
      Soup, 49–50

    One-Pan Skillet
      Lasagna, 136

    One-Pot Broccoli Mac
      and Cheese, 121

    One-Pot Creamy Vegan
      Rigatoni, 124–125

    One-Pot Pantry
      Pasta, 110–111

    Spaghetti and Lentil
      Balls, 128–129

    Spinach Spaghetti Pie, 137

    stocking up on, 9

    Tomato-Basil
      Orecchiette, 116–117

    Vegan Cannelloni, 138–139

    White Bean and Tomato
      Stuffed Shells, 134–135

Peanut butter

    Chickpea Cookie
      Dough, 196

    Chocolate–Peanut Butter
      Cups, 201–202

    No-Bake Chocolate–
      Peanut Butter
      Bars, 177

    Peanut Butter and
      Banana Overnight
      Oats, 24

    Peanut Stew, 59

    Spicy Peanut Sauce, 215

    Spicy Peanut-Tofu Lettuce
      Wraps, 64

Peanut Salad,
    Thai-Inspired, 91

Peppers

    Black Bean
      Quesadillas, 187

    Edamame Mason Jar
      Salad, 98

    Freezer-Friendly Breakfast
      Burritos, 33–34

    Quick Pickled Carrots and
      Vegetables, 174

    Tempeh-Stuffed
      Peppers, 161–162

    Ultimate Vegan Breakfast
      Sandwiches, 35–36

    Vegan Corn Chowder, 52

    Vegan Greek Salad with
      Tofu Feta, 95

    Vegan Queso Dip, 221

    Watermelon
      Gazpacho, 41

Pesto

    Carrot-Top Pesto, 218

    Veggie and White Bean
      Pesto Melt, 79

Pickled Carrots and
    Vegetables, Quick, 174

Pie, Spinach Spaghetti, 137

Pineapple
    Tropical Chia Pudding
        Parfait, 25
Pizza, Vegan Garlic-
    Mushroom
    Naan, 149–150
Poke Bowls, Watermelon, 144
Popcorn, Cheesy Vegan, 179
Potatoes. *See also* Sweet
    potatoes
    Baked Potato Skins, 189
    Creamy Greek Yogurt
        Potato Salad, 97
    Irish-Inspired Potato
        Stew, 56
    Roasted Potatoes with
        Lemon-Chive Yogurt
        Dip, 181
Pot with a lid, 10
Protein, 2
Pudding, Chocolate-
    Avocado, 198
Pulse, defined, 12
Pumpkin
    Creamy Pumpkin-Sage
        Alfredo, 130–131
    Lentil and Pumpkin
        Curry, 159
    Pumpkin and Black Bean
        Chili, 58
    Pumpkin Pie Parfait
        Jars, 204
Puree, defined, 12

Q

Quesadillas, Black Bean, 187
Quinoa and Butternut
    Squash Harvest
    Salad, 102–103

R

Recipes, notes about, 13–15
Reusable storage bags, 13

Rice
    Chimichurri Baked Tofu
        Bowls, 165
    Edamame Mason Jar
        Salad, 98
    Freezer-Friendly Bean
        Burgers, 81–82
    Jerked Tempeh with Herb
        Rice, 157–158
    Spicy Peanut-Tofu Lettuce
        Wraps, 64
    Tempeh-Stuffed
        Peppers, 161–162
    Vegan Sushi Burritos, 78
    Watermelon Poke
        Bowls, 144
Ricotta, Almond, 224
Roast, defined, 12
Rosemary and Thyme
    Red Sauce, 216

S

Sage-Pumpkin Alfredo,
    Creamy, 130–131
Salads
    Caprese Pasta Salad, 96
    Chili-Lime Taco Salad, 105
    Cranberry, Walnut, and
        Brussels Sprouts
        Salad, 101
    Creamy Greek Yogurt
        Potato Salad, 97
    Cucumber-Mango
        Salad, 90
    Edamame Mason Jar
        Salad, 98
    Harvest Butternut
        Squash and Quinoa
        Salad, 102–103
    Make-Ahead Kale
        Salad, 94
    Red Cabbage and
        Cilantro Slaw, 93

Sesame-Ginger Soba
    Noodle Salad, 104
Strawberry and Avocado
    Spinach Salad, 92
Sun-Dried Tomato and
    Farro Salad, 100
Thai-Inspired Peanut
    Salad, 91
Vegan Caesar Salad, 99
Vegan Greek Salad with
    Tofu Feta, 95
Salsa, Spicy Blender, 219
Sandwiches
    Buffalo Tofu
        Sandwiches, 87
    Chickpea and Coconut
        Curry Wraps, 76
    Cranberry and Chickpea
        Salad Sandwiches, 63
    Crispy Eggplant BLTs, 77
    Curried Egg Salad
        Sandwiches, 65
    Green Goddess
        Cucumber-Avocado
        Sandwiches, 62
    Lemon Basil and
        Smashed White Bean
        Sandwiches, 68
    Lentil Sloppy Joes, 83
    Loaded Carrot
        Dogs, 69–70
    Mediterranean Falafel
        Pitas, 71–72
    Mushroom
        Cheesesteaks, 84
    Roasted Sweet Potato
        and Hummus
        Sandwiches, 73
    Smoky Lentil and
        Portobello Mushroom
        Wraps, 66–67
    Spicy Chickpea-Avocado
        Toast, 22
    Tempeh Reubens, 85–86

Sandwiches (*continued*)
    Ultimate Vegan Breakfast
        Sandwiches, 35–36
    Vegan Banh Mi
        Sandwiches, 74–75
    Veggie and White Bean
        Pesto Melt, 79
Sauces
    Carrot-Top Pesto, 218
    Chimichurri Sauce, 217
    Rosemary and Thyme Red
        Sauce, 216
    Spicy Peanut Sauce, 215
    Vegan Chocolate
        Sauce, 229
Sesame Ginger Dressing, 213
Sesame-Ginger
    Edamame, 178
Sesame-Ginger Soba Noodle
    Salad, 104
Sesame Tofu and
    Broccoli, 154–155
Shopping lists, 11
Simmer, defined, 12
Skillet, 10
Slaw, Red Cabbage and
    Cilantro, 93
Sloppy Joes, Lentil, 83
Smoothies
    Energizing Matcha
        Smoothie, 172
    Granny Smith Green
        Smoothie, 171
    Rejuvenating Citrus
        Smoothie, 19
Snickerdoodle Skillet
    Cookie, 199–200
Soups
    Broccoli Cheese Soup with
        Croutons, 54–55
    Cooling Cucumber-Basil
        Soup, 40

Creamy Carrot-Ginger
    Soup, 45–46
High-Protein Lentil
    Soup, 53
Mushroom French Onion
    Soup, 51
No-Chicken Tofu Noodle
    Soup, 49–50
Pinto Bean and Tortilla
    Soup, 47–48
10-Minute Miso Soup, 42
Vegan Corn Chowder, 52
Vegan Tomato
    Bisque, 43–44
Watermelon
    Gazpacho, 41
Spices, 9
Spinach
    Black Bean
        Quesadillas, 187
    Creamy Pumpkin-Sage
        Alfredo, 130–131
    Energizing Matcha
        Smoothie, 172
    Granny Smith Green
        Smoothie, 171
    Greek Lasagna, 132–133
    Spinach and Mushroom
        Baked Egg Cups, 26
    Spinach Spaghetti Pie, 137
    Strawberry and Avocado
        Spinach Salad, 92
    Sun-Dried Tomato and
        Farro Salad, 100
    Tempeh-Stuffed
        Peppers, 161–162
    Thai-Inspired Peanut
        Salad, 91
    Tomato-Basil
        Orecchiette, 116–117
    Ultimate Vegan Breakfast
        Sandwiches, 35–36
    Vegan Cannelloni, 138–139

Vegan Loaded Sweet
    Potatoes, 163–164
White Bean and Tomato
    Stuffed Shells, 134–135
Split peas
    Irish-Inspired Potato
        Stew, 56
    stocking up on, 9
Spreads
    Almond Ricotta, 224
    Blueberry Chia Jam, 226
    Creamy Almond
        Butter, 227
    White Bean Sandwich
        Spread, 223
Spring Rolls, Vegetable, 182
Squash. *See also* Pumpkin
    Baked Spaghetti Squash
        Lasagna, 119–120
    Harvest Butternut
        Squash and Quinoa
        Salad, 102–103
    Zucchini Pasta
        Primavera, 108
Steam, defined, 12
Steep, defined, 12
Stews
    Irish-Inspired Potato
        Stew, 56
    Peanut Stew, 59
    Vegan Gumbo, 57
Storage bags, reusable, 13
Storage bins, 13
Strata, Broccoli Cheddar, 37
Strawberries
    Strawberry and Avocado
        Spinach Salad, 92
    Strawberry-Banana Ice
        Cream, 195
    Yogurt-Dipped
        Strawberries, 197
Sugar, and mood, 3–4

Sunflower seeds
    Red Cabbage and
        Cilantro Slaw, 93
    Vegan Queso Dip, 221
Sushi Burritos, Vegan, 78
Sweet potatoes
    Creamy Carrot-Ginger
        Soup, 45–46
    Peanut Stew, 59
    Roasted Sweet Potato
        and Hummus
        Sandwiches, 73
    soothing nausea with, 7
    Sweet Potato
        Pancakes, 31–32
    Vegan Loaded Sweet
        Potatoes, 163–164

T
Taco Bake,
        Mushroom, 166–167
Taco Salad, Chili-Lime, 105
Tahini
    Classic Hummus, 222
    Lemon Tahini Dressing, 214
Tempeh
    Cheesy Broccoli Pasta
        Bake, 140–141
    Chili-Lime Tempeh
        Burritos, 80
    Greek Lasagna, 132–133
    Jerked Tempeh with Herb
        Rice, 157–158
    One-Pan Skillet
        Lasagna, 136
    Tempeh Reubens, 85–86
    Tempeh-Stuffed
        Peppers, 161–162
Thai-Inspired Peanut
        Salad, 91
Thaw, defined, 12
Thyme and Rosemary Red
        Sauce, 216

Toast, defined, 12
Toast, Spicy
        Chickpea-Avocado, 22
Tofu
    Better-than-Takeout
        Orange Tofu, 160
    Buffalo Tofu
        Sandwiches, 87
    Chimichurri Baked Tofu
        Bowls, 165
    Five-Spice
        Noodles, 122–123
    No-Chicken Tofu Noodle
        Soup, 49–50
    Sesame Tofu and
        Broccoli, 154–155
    Spicy Peanut-Tofu Lettuce
        Wraps, 64
    Tofu Feta, 225
    Tofu Nuggets, 183
    Ultimate Vegan Breakfast
        Sandwiches, 35–36
    Vegan Banh Mi
        Sandwiches, 74–75
    Vegan Caesar Salad, 99
    Vegan Greek Salad with
        Tofu Feta, 95
    Vegan Pad Thai, 112–113
    Vegan Party
        Platter, 190–191
Tomatoes
    canned, stocking up on, 9
    Caprese Pasta Salad, 96
    Cheesy Broccoli Pasta
        Bake, 140–141
    Crispy Eggplant BLTs, 77
    Greek Lasagna, 132–133
    High-Protein Lentil
        Soup, 53
    Mushroom Taco
        Bake, 166–167
    One-Pan Skillet
        Lasagna, 136

One-Pot Pantry
        Pasta, 110–111
Pinto Bean and Tortilla
        Soup, 47–48
Pumpkin and Black Bean
        Chili, 58
Rosemary and Thyme Red
        Sauce, 216
Spicy Blender Salsa, 219
Spinach Spaghetti Pie, 137
Sun-Dried Tomato and
        Farro Salad, 100
Tomato-Basil
        Orecchiette, 116–117
Vegan Cannelloni, 138–139
Vegan Greek Salad with
        Tofu Feta, 95
Vegan Tomato
        Bisque, 43–44
White Bean and Tomato
        Stuffed Shells, 134–135
Tortillas
    Black Bean
        Quesadillas, 187
    Chickpea and Coconut
        Curry Wraps, 76
    Chili-Lime Taco Salad, 105
    Chili-Lime Tempeh
        Burritos, 80
    Chili-Lime Tortilla
        Chips, 180
    Freezer-Friendly Breakfast
        Burritos, 33–34
    Mushroom Taco
        Bake, 166–167
    Pan-Roasted Nachos, 188
    Pinto Bean and Tortilla
        Soup, 47–48
    Pinto Bean Tostadas with
        Red Cabbage and
        Cilantro Slaw, 147–148
    Smoky Lentil and
        Portobello Mushroom
        Wraps, 66–67

Tostadas, Pinto Bean, with Red Cabbage and Cilantro Slaw, 147–148

Turmeric
    Blended Golden Milk Latte, 170
    Ginger-Turmeric Rice Noodles, 118

V

Vanilla Almond Milk, 211

Vegetables. *See also specific vegetables*
    cognitive benefits, 4
    frozen, for recipes, 9
    Vegan Banh Mi Sandwiches, 74–75
    Vegetable Spring Rolls, 182

Vegetarian diet
    budget benefits, 6
    environmental benefits, 6–8
    health benefits, 5–6
    pantry ingredients, 9–10
    shopping lists, 11
    specific nutrients for, 2–3
    tools and equipment, 10
    types of, 1

Vinaigrette, Apple Cider, 212

Vitamin B_{12}, 2

Vitamin D, 3

W

Walnuts
    Apple Pie Granola, 23
    cognitive benefits, 4
    Cranberry, Walnut, and Brussels Sprouts Salad, 101
    Fruit and Nut Energy Bites, 176
    No-Bake Chocolate-Peanut Butter Bars, 177
    No-Bake Green Tea Energy Bars, 20–21
    Vegan No-Bake Blueberry Cheesecake, 205–206
    Whole-Grain Carrot Cake Muffins, 27–28

Watermelon
    Watermelon Gazpacho, 41
    Watermelon Poke Bowls, 144

Whisk, defined, 12

Whole-Grain Croutons, 228

Wraps
    Chickpea and Coconut Curry Wraps, 76

Smoky Lentil and Portobello Mushroom Wraps, 66–67

Spicy Peanut-Tofu Lettuce Wraps, 64

Y

Yogurt
    Apple Chips with Cinnamon-Yogurt Dip, 175
    Cooling Cucumber-Basil Soup, 40
    Creamy Greek Yogurt Potato Salad, 97
    Granny Smith Green Smoothie, 171
    Lemon-Blueberry Yogurt Bowls, 29
    Pumpkin Pie Parfait Jars, 204
    Roasted Potatoes with Lemon-Chive Yogurt Dip, 181
    Yogurt-Dipped Strawberries, 197

Z

Zucchini Pasta Primavera, 108

Acknowledgments

Writing a cookbook has been one of my biggest dreams ever since my first day as a nutrition student. Reaching this goal would have been impossible without the love and support of my family and friends. A special thank you to my husband, Dan, for always encouraging me to follow my ambitions (and almost never complaining about all the dirty dishes). I'd also like to thank my community of fellow registered dietitians, who continually build me up and are always on standby to provide professional counsel. To my blog readers, who have given me invaluable feedback that has helped me hone my recipe development skills, thank you. Finally, I acknowledge Callisto Media for guiding me through the process of writing and publishing my first book. I am forever grateful.

About the Author

STEPHANIE McKERCHER, MS, RDN, is a nationally recognized registered dietitian nutritionist and vegetarian recipe developer living in Colorado. On her award-winning food blog, *Grateful Grazer*, Stephanie helps readers cook easy meals with lots of plants. Stephanie's work has been featured on Food Network, NBC News, Shape, Women's Health, and more. When she isn't cooking, Stephanie enjoys practicing yoga, meeting rescue dogs, and hiking with her husband in the mountains.